D1622486

THE NEW CHEMISTRY

The
NEW
Chemistry

MARTIN SHERWOOD

Basic Books, Inc., Publishers

NEW YORK

© 1974 by Martin Sherwood
Library of Congress Catalog Card Number: 72–89183
SBN: 465–05002–6
Manufactured in the United States of America
75 76 77 10 9 8 7 6 5 4 3 2

95944

Acknowledgments

The whole of this book was read, prior to publication, by Mr. Martyn Berry, of Chislehurst and Sidcup School for Boys, Professor Malcolm Frazer, of the University of East Anglia, Dr. Jeff Thompson, of the University of Oxford, and by my father-in-law, Mr. A. W. Bennett. In addition, a large part of the text was read by Mr. Robert Bruce, also of Chislehurst and Sidcup School for Boys. Miss Lynette Hamblin, of The Chemical Society of London, read parts of Chapter 8 and the whole of Chapter 9, and Dr. D. G. Jones, of ICI Ltd, read Chapter 7. For the patience and helpful comments of all these I am most grateful. I am also indebted to Alan Middleton, who prepared the illustrations, and to Miss Louise Thomas, who typed the manuscript. To the numerous people who, at one time or another, taught me chemistry, I can only say that I hope this book provides some evidence that their time was not wholly wasted. Lastly, but by no means least, my thanks go to my wife, Elizabeth, for her tolerance and understanding.

MARTIN SHERWOOD

Contents

List of Illustrations

List of Tables

THE NEW CHEMISTRY

1 ❖ Prelude

Chemistry is one of the means which man has developed to describe reality. As one of the sciences, it shares the accolade bestowed by Sir Peter Medawar, Nobel prize winning biologist, when he wrote that "Science, broadly considered, is incomparably the most successful enterprise human beings have ever engaged upon." Chemistry is a central science, not only because of its numerous and fundamental connections with other branches of science, but also because of its wide-ranging influence on the way we live.

It can be argued that only a few inventions, such as the transistor, have changed society in a major way; on the other hand, there are literally thousands of inventions which slowly alter the background scenery against which human lives are played out. Although it is often not possible to claim that these inventions have changed society, it can be said that, without them, society would have had to move in different directions. Without synthetic rubbers, the modern automobile industry would not have been able to develop as it has. Without modern fertilizers, much less food would be grown and the percentage of starving people in the world would be much higher (or, alternatively, there would be fewer people). Without modern synthetic drugs, many humans would lead shorter or less healthy lives. These are just three examples of the way in which modern chemistry contributes to the structure of modern society.

Chemistry is, of course, not just a matter of applied science. Developments in chemical research in the last few years have greatly increased human understanding of living processes. Much of this work has been the result of collaboration with

3

biologists, just as physicists and engineers have called in chemists to help them with such developments as the transistor and electronic microcircuitry.

Books about chemistry often begin with definitions. This one does not. If an adequate brief definition of chemistry could be given, there would be little need to write the rest of the book. What I have tried to do in the pages that follow is to sketch a picture of modern chemistry.

The science of chemistry can be traced back to early civilizations. The preparation of metals, such as copper, from mineral ores—practiced 6,000 years ago—is a primitive form of applied chemistry. The classical Greek view of a world made up from "atoms" has some parallels with modern atomistic chemistry. Throughout history one can chart the slow growth of chemistry, sidetracked many times by theories with which we no longer agree, then gathering momentum in about 1800 and proceeding into the twentieth century. To describe this growth justly needs the talents of the historian as well as of the scientist. Study of the history of chemistry should provide knowledge about the human mind, enabling us to see why long-abandoned theories seemed so reasonable to our ancestors.

World War II was a watershed in terms of science as an activity. Since the end of that war, all developed countries have made gigantic efforts to educate more people as scientists. Until recently, most of those trained as scientists have practiced as scientists, so the rapid growth of scientific manpower has been accompanied by an explosive growth in the quantity of scientific data at our disposal. For this reason, and because of the inherent difficulties in adopting a historical approach, this book concerns itself primarily with what has happened in chemistry since the end of World War II.

All sciences are based on theories; since many of these are long-lived, it has been necessary to introduce some theoretical ideas that originated before the war. However, although a theory may not be new, at any particular time it has a con-

temporary interpretation. In the next three chapters I have tried
to describe the basic theoretical concepts of chemistry in an
up-to-date manner. Since theory never exists in a vacuum, I
have included examples of the interaction between theory and
experiment. One of the most interesting extrapolations of
"atomic theory" is in predicting the behavior of unknown elements which man is trying to make in laboratories throughout
the world. Therefore, the next chapter contains an account of
the syntheses which have increased the number of known elements from 92 to well over 100.

A disadvantage of much modern education is that it con-
vinces people that certain areas of study are difficult, and
frightens them away. This is particularly true of the sciences.
Yet our modern knowledge of chemistry springs basically from
the fact that all men carry the scientific method within them.
More accurately, all babies do so, but by the time they reach
adulthood many of them have been persuaded to turn away
from that part of themselves which contains the germs of
science.

Look at some of the everyday substances around you—
gasoline, corn oil, water, orange juice. A course in physics is
not required to teach you that these are all liquids, yet to
describe them all as liquids is to make a scientific observation.
Similarly, most small children have observed that wood, sugar,
and sand are all solids, and have sufficient grasp of the nature
of solids and liquids to know that there is a difference in what
happens when you spill a solid rather than a liquid. The liquid
spreads out, or soaks into some other material. Spill sugar and,
although it may make a mess, it won't soak into a carpet. To
clear up spilled sugar requires a technology different from that
needed for clearing up a spilled liquid.

The child who knows these things is exploiting the germinal
scientist in him. The professional scientist, of course, goes far
beyond the child in his search for scientific knowledge and ways
of using it. But he uses the same basic tools: the human brain

and its ability to perceive logical relationships. It is foolish
for anyone to say "I'm not at all scientific," for such a person
would not live long. He would be unable to make the scientific
inferences necessary for avoiding danger from the everyday
objects that might cut, burn, or otherwise harm him. Every
time one crosses a busy street, one needs to use scientific knowledge. You may call it judgment—how far away is that car that
is coming towards you, and how fast is it coming?—but it involves quantitative measurement, one of the basic principles of
science.

It is possible to establish a set of equations for crossing the
road safely. However, we do not need these equations to tell
us that misjudgment of the speed of the oncoming vehicle and
the time it will take to walk across the road can provoke a
nasty accident. Similarly, to appreciate much of chemistry, it is
not necessary to understand descriptive equations which can
be developed; consequently, this book contains no equations.

This book will not teach anyone enough about chemistry to
enable him to go into a laboratory and make new discoveries.
Most of us probably have no real desire to push back the
frontiers of scientific knowledge, being primarily concerned
with other aspects of the world around us. But it is increasingly
important to know how chemistry can and should be used. Do
we want cheaper detergents if it means that fish cannot live
in our rivers as a result of these detergents being poured down
the sink? Without the background necessary for informed decisions, we cannot maintain the freedom that lets us devote
our lives to other endeavors.

The reader familiar with basic chemistry may wish merely to
dip into those chapters (2, 3, and 4) which set out the theoretical groundwork that underlies a chemical world view before
starting his journey through modern chemistry, which, despite
what I have said about leaving history to the historians, goes
back—in Chapter 5—more than four thousand million years,
when the planets of the solar system were forming according

to chemical laws. By following the same laws, the first living beings emerged from inanimate collections of chemical raw materials. Documentation of possible processes by which living organisms may have originated has engaged the attention of many groups of chemists since the first experiments in the field in the early 1950s. It is but one example of the fascination of chemists with biological systems. Leaving behind the primordial slimes of Chapter 5, Chapter 6 describes some of the diverse ways in which chemists have helped to unravel many of the mysteries of life in the worlds of insects and microbes as well as the world of man.

Some discoveries in biological chemistry, such as elucidation of the nature of insect sex attractants and their synthesis in the laboratory, may be reflected in new products from the chemical industry in the next few years. Chemical industry covers an enormous span, including the manufacture of valuable materials needed only in small quantities, such as pharmaceuticals, as well as the bulk production of plastics and other polymers. In terms of scale, the industry is dominated by petrochemicals. Based on the utilization of oil as a raw material rather than a source of energy, this sector of the industry has grown phenomenally in the last 30 years.

As soon as one turns to industry, another, younger science comes into play: economics. Because of the importance of the interactions between chemistry and economics, Chapter 7 has been partly devoted to describing the petrochemicals industry in such a way as to highlight these interactions. It must be stressed, however, that the economics does not reach the level of sophistication of some of the chemistry, such as the development of metal-containing catalysts for the production of polymers with clearly defined three-dimensional structures which confer on them much more useful properties than are found in the corresponding random structures.

Molecular engineering—as such conscious design of materials is called—is gradually spreading throughout industrial chemistry, and industrial chemistry is gradually spreading throughout the whole of civilized life, as Chapter 8 is intended to make clear. But that which is found everywhere will inevitably sometimes be found in the wrong place, which is one definition of pollution. It would be deceitful at present to pretend that man's knowledge of chemistry, and the uses he has made of it, have not caused social problems. Some of these are described in the first part of Chapter 9. The remainder of this chapter is given over to a brief discussion of the role of the scientist as a citizen, and of where chemistry may go in the next few years.

2 ❖ The Elements of Chemistry

All matter is made from atoms. This is an idea at least as old as the Greek philosophers Leucippus and Democritus, who flourished between 450 and 400 B.C. Perhaps the most important aspect of atomic theory through the ages is that atoms have always, until recently, been defined as indivisible, the basic units of matter. Although the atom is still firmly believed in today, our picture of it would look very strange to Leucippus and Democritus, for the high energy physics of the last 20 years has proved repeatedly that indivisibility is one property that atoms definitely lack.

The rot set in before World War I, when the electron was discovered, and continued between the wars, with the discovery of the proton and the neutron, all basic components of the atom. But, as recently as 1947, there were only a few so-called fundamental particles of which matter was believed to be composed. As the physicists spent more and more money to build ever larger machines for speeding up atomic fragments for use as bullets to shatter the heart of matter, the number of fundamental particles grew; there are now well over 30.

Fortunately, the chemist need not worry about this proliferation, for his basic building block is still the atom. The level at which he is interested in atomic structure involves only the three earliest discovered subatomic particles, the electron, proton, and neutron. Most of the time, chemists are interested only in how many electrons an atom has and how they are arranged. The electron is a very small particle—much smaller than the

9

other atomic components—with a negative electric charge (an electric current is a flow of electrons through matter). Despite its smallness, the electron is usually the only part of an atom that ever makes contact with other atoms, hence its importance in chemistry. The major part of the atom, in terms of mass, is a tightly knit bundle of protons and neutrons called the nucleus. Although neutrons and protons are each nearly 2,000 times more massive than the electron, the electrons of an atom are in communication with the outside world because they surround its nucleus. The radius of an atom as a whole is 10,000 or more times greater than that of the nucleus.

Electrons are prevented from escaping from an isolated atom by the attractive effect of protons, which carry a positive charge. Neutrons, as the name implies, are neutral, having no electric charge.

Since like charges repel, one might expect the protons in a nucleus to fly apart. To prevent this there must be a strong force holding nucleons—a term which includes both protons and neutrons—together. This is known as the nuclear force, and it is one of the few aspects of the atom in which the chemist is interested in the nucleus rather than the extranuclear electrons, for it can be used to explain why certain atoms are stable and why others undergo such processes as radioactive decay.

The Nuclear Force

Two things can be said immediately about the nuclear force: it must be stronger than the forces of repulsion between protons, and it must be a very short-range force, for when nuclei of different atoms come close together they do not adhere to form a new, enlarged nucleus. We know that this is so because the number of protons in a nucleus defines the type of atom they go to make up. Every atom of hydrogen contains a single proton in its nucleus, while every atom of iron contains 26 protons; conversely, each neutral atom of hydrogen has 1 electron, and each atom of iron, 26 electrons. Since the number of protons in an atom identifies it unambiguously, it is called the atomic number. Table 1 lists the known elements, their atomic numbers, and their atomic masses.

TABLE 1
The Elements, Their Symbols, Atomic (Proton) Numbers, and Atomic Masses

NAME OF ELEMENT	SYMBOL	ATOMIC (PROTON) NUMBER	ATOMIC MASS
hydrogen	H	1	1.01
helium	He	2	4.00
lithium	Li	3	6.94
beryllium	Be	4	9.01
boron	B	5	10.81
carbon	C	6	12.01
nitrogen	N	7	14.01
oxygen	O	8	16.00
fluorine	F	9	19.00
neon	Ne	10	20.18
sodium	Na	11	22.99
magnesium	Mg	12	24.31
aluminum	Al	13	26.98
silicon	Si	14	28.09
phosphorus	P	15	30.97
sulphur	S	16	32.06
chlorine	Cl	17	35.45
argon	Ar	18	39.95
potassium	K	19	39.10
calcium	Ca	20	40.08
scandium	Sc	21	44.96
titanium	Ti	22	47.90
vanadium	V	23	50.94
chromium	Cr	24	52.00
manganese	Mn	25	54.94
iron	Fe	26	55.85
cobalt	Co	27	58.93
nickel	Ni	28	58.71
copper	Cu	29	63.55
zinc	Zn	30	65.37
gallium	Ga	31	69.72

TABLE 1 (*Continued*)

The Elements, Their Symbols, Atomic (Proton) Numbers, and Atomic Masses

NAME OF ELEMENT	SYMBOL	ATOMIC (PROTON) NUMBER	ATOMIC MASS
germanium	Ge	32	72.59
arsenic	As	33	74.92
selenium	Se	34	78.96
bromine	Br	35	79.90
krypton	Kr	36	83.80
rubidium	Rb	37	85.47
strontium	Sr	38	87.62
yttrium	Y	39	88.91
zirconium	Zr	40	91.22
niobium	Nb	41	92.91
molybdenum	Mo	42	95.94
technetium	Tc	43	98.91
ruthenium	Ru	44	101.07
rhodium	Rh	45	102.91
palladium	Pd	46	106.40
silver	Ag	47	107.87
cadmium	Cd	48	112.40
indium	In	49	114.82
tin	Sn	50	118.69
antimony	Sb	51	121.75
tellurium	Te	52	127.60
iodine	I	53	126.90
xenon	Xe	54	131.30
caesium	Cs	55	132.91
barium	Ba	56	137.34
lanthanum	La	57	138.91
cerium	Ce	58	140.12
praseodymium	Pr	59	140.91
neodymium	Nd	60	144.24
promethium	Pm	61	—
samarium	Sm	62	150.40
europium	Eu	63	151.96
gadolinium	Gd	64	157.25
terbium	Tb	65	158.93
dysprosium	Dy	66	162.50
holmium	Ho	67	164.93
erbium	Er	68	167.26
thulium	Tm	69	168.93
ytterbium	Yb	70	173.04
lutetium	Lu	71	174.97

TABLE 1 *(Continued)*

The Elements, Their Symbols, Atomic (Proton) Numbers, and Atomic Masses

NAME OF ELEMENT	SYMBOL	ATOMIC (PROTON) NUMBER	ATOMIC MASS
hafnium	Hf	72	178.49
tantalum	Ta	73	180.95
tungsten	W	74	183.85
rhenium	Re	75	186.20
osmium	Os	76	190.20
iridium	Ir	77	192.22
platinum	Pt	78	195.09
gold	Au	79	196.97
mercury	Hg	80	200.59
thallium	Tl	81	204.37
lead	Pb	82	207.20
bismuth	Bi	83	208.98
polonium	Po	84	—
astatine	At	85	—
radon	Rn	86	—
francium	Fr	87	—
radium	Ra	88	226.03
actinium	Ac	89	—
thorium	Th	90	232.04
protactinium	Pa	91	231.04
uranium	U	92	238.03
neptunium	Np	93	237.05
plutonium	Pu	94	—
americium	Am	95	—
curium	Cm	96	—
berkelium	Bk	97	—
californium	Cf	98	—
einsteinium	Es	99	—
fermium	Fm	100	—
mendelevium	Md	101	—
nobelium	No	102	—
lawrencium	Lr	103	—

Note: Elements 104 and 105 are not included since their names are still disputed (see p. 35). Atomic masses—sometimes loosely called atomic weights —are worked out relative to the mass of the most common isotope of carbon (^{12}C); in this table, masses are shown to no more than 2 decimal places.

A particular kind of atom may contain different numbers of neutrons in its nucleus, and two atoms of the same element (i.e., with the same number of protons) with different numbers of neutrons are called isotopes. Generally, one isotope of each element predominates in nature. For example, there are 3 isotopes of hydrogen, containing, respectively, zero, 1, and 2 neutrons. These 3—also called protium, deuterium, and tritium—occur in natural hydrogen in the ratio $1:1.6 \times 10^{-3}:1 \times 10^{-10}$.[1]

Not all elements have their isotopes in such disparate ratio. Chlorine, for example, is made up of 2 isotopes which occur in an approximately 3:1 ratio in nature, while the metallic element germanium occurs in 5 isotope forms naturally, found in abundances of between 7.75 percent for the 2 rarest to 36.5 percent for the most common.

When it comes to describing what the nuclear force is, rather than what it does, we run into trouble. The answer is not known. Studies over the last 30 years have shown that protons and neutrons can convert into each other. They may do this by the exchange of a particle called a pion, which is about 250 times the size of an electron. It seems odd at first that a proton and a neutron, which are about the same size, can produce a particle without losing any of their own size, and that when that particle is absorbed by another particle, the second particle does not get any bigger. But we must remember that the world of the nucleus is extraordinarily small, and does not operate according to the laws obeyed by large masses.

Einstein's laws of relativity (which relate mass and energy

[1] Most sciences frequently use very large or very small numbers. For convenience in writing, such numbers are often expressed as being, or being multiplied by, "powers of 10." The power of 10 being used is indicated by the small number above the line, and is interpreted as "10 multiplied by itself" however many times the superscript indicates. Thus, 10^3 is three 10s multiplied together: $10 \times 10 \times 10$, or 1,000. Where the number in the superscript is negative, it means one-tenth multiplied together the number of times indicated: 10^{-3} means one-thousandth. Consequently, the number of atoms of tritium—indicated by 1×10^{-10}—is one 10 thousand-millionth of all the hydrogen atoms; in other words, out of every 10 thousand million natural hydrogen atoms, only 1 will have 2 neutrons in its nucleus.

and show their interconvertibility), and Planck's quantum theory govern interactions on the nuclear scale. The apparently impossible is achieved on this level by involving Heisenberg's uncertainty principle. Formulated in 1929, this says that, provided we are working on a sufficiently small scale, it is impossible to determine simultaneously and exactly the velocity, or a related property such as energy, of a particle and its position. There must always be an uncertainty in the measurements.

Heisenberg's principle can be expressed in another way in order to calculate the minimum permissible uncertainties in time and energy. Since the nucleus is very small, and particles like the pion move very fast (effectively at the speed of light), it can be shown that there is an uncertainty about their energy which, when converted by Einstein's equation relating energy to mass ($E = MC^2$), is almost exactly equivalent to the mass of the pion. Consequently, on this scale, conventional ideas about the indestructibility of matter or the production of something from nothing do not enter into consideration, because we can never be certain that things are as we describe them.

Whether or not pions are the nuclear glue, some interreaction certainly does occur between neutrons and protons, protons and protons, and neutrons and neutrons to keep the nucleus together—most of the time. When the nucleus gets big enough, the internuclear force and the charge repulsion force between protons are more equally balanced.

With the lighter elements, which have only a few protons, there is generally close to a 1:1 relationship between the number of protons and neutrons in the nucleus. When we look at heavier elements, we find that more neutrons have been stuffed in to counteract the growing proton-proton repulsive forces which threaten to tear the nucleus apart. For example, carbon, which contains 6 protons, also has 6 neutrons in its most abundant isotope. Iron, with 26 protons, has 30 neutrons in its most abundant isotope, while uranium's most abundant isotope has 92 protons and 146 neutrons—more than 1.5 neutrons to each proton. Despite this stuffing with neutrons, some of the heavier elements, such as uranium, are still not stable. Given a jolt by a high energy neutron, for example, they split into 2 smaller nuclei. This process is called nuclear fission.

Nuclear Structure

The account of the nucleus given so far has not indicated any internal structure. Although it has one, it is not well understood. The clearest evidence for a nuclear structure is the abnormal stability of some elements. Of the lighter elements, the binding energies—which are a measure of stability to total breakdown—of the nuclei of helium, carbon, and oxygen are all much higher than those of their neighboring elements. This is again demonstrated by recourse to Einstein. If we know the mass of a single neutron and a single proton, we can work out how much the mass of a single nucleus of carbon containing 6 of each type of nucleon should be. We find that the single nucleus of carbon actually has less than this calculated mass, but, knowing that mass and energy are interconvertible (as indicated by the Einstein equation), we can assume that the "mass defect" is a measure of the binding energy holding the nucleons together.

The helium nucleus, which is also called an alpha particle, contains 2 protons and 2 neutrons. The most common isotope of carbon, as has been mentioned, contains 6 neutrons and 6 protons, while that of oxygen contains 8 of each nucleon. Thus, we could envisage the carbon and oxygen nuclei being made up from exact numbers of helium nuclei—and such a synthetic process may occur in stars. At the other end of the scale are the heavy elements, some of which are radioactive—their nuclei decompose spontaneously. Frequently decomposition occurs by the emission of an alpha particle, because the formation of such a particle releases energy from the system.

Electrons and Their States

Since it is the part of an atom of most direct importance to the chemist, let's look more closely at the electron. The electron, being very small, is subject, like the nucleus, to laws that we do not recognize in everyday life. In addition to being a very small electrically charged particle that always hangs around a nucleus, an electron can be a wave, like a light wave. Whether electrons or, for that matter, light waves, are really waves or really particles is a philosophical rather than a scientific question. The scientist judges the electron by its behavior, which is sometimes particulate, sometimes wavelike.

Its complex nature, and Heisenberg's uncertainty principle, ensure that we never really know where an electron is. If we take a single atom of hydrogen, with only one electron, and a nucleus composed of one proton, the best we can do is divide up the space around the nucleus and estimate, for any point, the probability of finding the electron there at any particular time. Despite this, chemists generally talk about electron orbitals (a word chosen to indicate something less precise than orbits) and the distance of an electron from a nucleus. There is nothing wrong with this, so long as it is kept in mind that they are talking about probabilities, not certainties. If we say that the distance of the hydrogen atom's electron from its nucleus is 0.53×10^{-10} meter (about 2 thousand-millionths of an inch), we mean that is its average distance from the nucleus. At the instant we are talking, it might be somewhere quite different (mathematically there is a finite, although vanishingly small, probability that it is at the other end of the universe).

In order to understand electrons and their behavior, chem-

ists have developed a series of mathematical formulations known
as quantum mechanics. However, the mathematics is not really
necessary for a general appreciation, which can be obtained
from a few simple rules derived from the mathematical
formulations.

Four quantum numbers specify the state of an electron. The
basic rule is that no 2 electrons in the same atom may have
all 4 quantum numbers the same. The principal quantum number, known as n, relates to an electron's average distance from
the nucleus: n may be 1, 2, 3, 4, and so on. Since the distance
between the nucleus, with its positive charge(s), and the electron affects the electron's energy, the different quantum numbers refer to different energy levels. The average distance for
the hydrogen electron from its nucleus, as given above, was
for the lowest energy level available to it $(n = 1)$, known as
the "ground state." It is possible, in a number of ways, to
add energy to an atom so that it jumps into a higher energy
level, an "excited state."

Energy differences also exist between different values of the
second quantum number, l, which may have any value from
0 to $n - 1$. This, and the third quantum number, m, are both
related to the angular distribution in space of the electron. In
most states, the region where there is a high probability of
finding the electron is not equally distributed around the
nucleus, but shows characteristic directional preferences. The
different values of m represent different states with the same
energy, known as degenerate states, and m may be 0 or any
number not greater than $+l$ or $-l$. The final quantum
number, m_s, relates to the way in which the electron spins as
it moves about. Since it can only spin in 2 directions, there
are only 2 possible values of this quantum number.

The belief that no electrons in any atom may occupy exactly
the same state—that is, have all 4 quantum numbers the same
—is known after its discoverer, Wolfgang Pauli, as the Pauli
exclusion principle. Although it was proposed before World

War II it has never been conclusively proved. On the other hand, and perhaps more important, no one has yet disproved it, and following it enables us to explain a large number of natural phenomena.

When the chemist is interested in an atom, he wants to know the states of its electrons, since these will tell him about its chemical behavior. He is interested basically in the number and energy values of the electrons. For this reason, a short-hand has been developed for describing electron states in atoms. The last 2 quantum numbers, since they only describe states of equal energy, are not mentioned, although it is remembered how many electrons each of these states permits at a certain energy level.

The first quantum number is denoted by its number, the second by a letter. It would be convenient if these were alphabetic, but for historical reasons they are not and the letters used to denote the l quantum numbers 0, 1, 2, and 3 are s, p, d, and f. The lowest energy state we can have is that with the lowest first and second quantum numbers, denoted $1s$. Since l in this case equals 0, m must also be 0, although m_s, as is always the case, can have 2 values. Consequently, the $1s$ state in an atom has room for 2 electrons.

Hydrogen has only 1 proton (even its heavier isotopes, deuterium and tritium, still have only one proton) and, in consequence, 1 electron. Normally this is a $1s$ electron, although the atom can be excited, in which case the electron jumps to a higher energy level. Atoms in an excited state generally return to the normal state by emitting radiation; according to how big the jump is, the radiation may be in the form of visible light, or of such invisible radiation as ultraviolet.

Helium's nucleus is composed of 2 protons and 2 neutrons; to neutralize its nuclear charge 2 electrons are needed and, under normal circumstances, these are both in the $1s$ state. That is as far as this state can go. The next element, lithium, with 3 protons, can have 2 electrons in the $1s$ state, but the

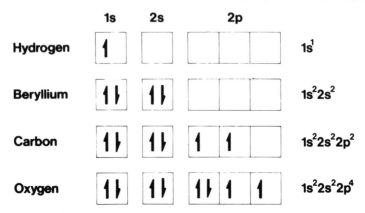

FIGURE 1. "Pigeonhole" notation for showing the distribution of electrons in an atom. Each half arrow represents one electron, each box an orbital. Consequently, each box can hold two half arrows, provided that they point in different directions (indicating opposite spins). The number and letter above each row of boxes indicates the energy level. In the cases of carbon and oxygen, the notation indicates how the electrons distribute themselves in "degenerate" states, with no more than one occupant to a box wherever possible. To the right of the pigeonholes are the shorthand electronic formulae for the atoms which are used in the text and which show graphically what the pigeonholes show visually.

third must go into another state. From the quantum rules we can see that its principal quantum number must be 2, which means that l can have the values $0(s)$ or $1(p)$. The s level is of lower energy than the p level, so lithium has the electronic structure $1s^2 2s^1$, where the superscripts after the letters indicate how many electrons are in each level. Once we pass beyond the next heavier element (beryllium, $1s^2 2s^2$), the electronic arrangements begin to get more complex.

Dr. Tom Cottrell, late principal of Stirling University in Scotland, suggested that the energy levels for electrons in atoms are rather like hotel rooms, with the electrons themselves as "guests"—each room having space for 2 such guests. Following the occupancy of the $2s$ level with its 2 electrons, we come to $2p$. Since the quantum number l in this level is equal to 1, degenerate states are possible, since m can have 3 values,

0, −1, +1. As each degenerate state can have an electron of each spin in it, the 2p level is composed of 3 rooms, and can hold 6 guests. The important point about the management of these rooms is that, as long as rooms are available, they allow each guest to have a room to himself; only when the first 3 electrons are bedded down in separate rooms do they start to double up. Chemists have developed a notation for this which is shown in Figure 1.

Although only the s states have spherical distributions of electron probability (l and m, the quantum numbers that govern angular distribution of electron probability, are both 0 for s states), it is possible to look upon each principal quantum number, n, as defining 1 layer of the skin of an onion. When all the 1s electrons are in place, as in helium, a layer is complete; similarly, when the 2s and 2p electrons are all in place, giving an atom with 10 electrons ($1s^22s^22p^6$, neon), another layer is complete. As with the nuclear structures, such completed shells are preferred states. They are particularly stable. Elements with complete skins—helium, neon, argon, krypton, and xenon—are very unreactive and were called, until recently, the inert gases. Since it was discovered in 1962 that they were not all inert but would, under certain conditions (see p. 60), form compounds, they are now called the noble gases.

If we look at the structure of argon according to the electronic shorthand, it does not look as if it completes a layer at all: its structure is $1s^22s^22p^63s^23p^6$. A quick look back at the rules for working out quantum states shows that there should be a suite of 3d rooms holding 10 electrons in all. However, by the time we reach this number of electrons, the energy levels of the different states are so muddled that the element following argon does not have one electron in the 3d state; its last electron goes into the 4s state, since this is of lower energy than the 3d state. Not until the 4s state has both its electrons in place does the 3d state begin to fill up. After that life gets even more complex, with the levels

filling in the order shown in Figure 2. Even that is a simplification, for 1, and only 1, electron goes into the 5d state before the 4f state begins to fill up. Because electrons in an
atom affect one another slightly, and because different orbitals
are differently shaped, the straightforward relationship between
principal quantum number and energy level is disturbed in
complex atoms. Hence the mixed up way in which electrons
go into the higher orbitals.

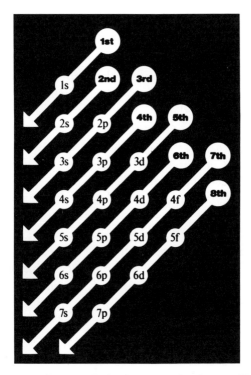

FIGURE 2. The order in which electron orbitals are filled as atoms
build up. The progression is straightforward at first, then becomes more
complex as the total number of electrons increases; the irregularities are
caused by the interactions of electrons with one another. Even this
chart is a simplification; for example, 1 electron appears in the 5d level
before any electrons go into the 4f level, but no further electrons enter
5d until 4f is filled.

The noble gases always occcur when an element has the s and p orbitals of a particular level filled, that is, not necessarily when a layer of the electron skin is complete, but before a new layer starts growing over it. For convenience, however, filling up of s and p orbitals of any level is referred to later as completing a layer.

Electron Escapology

It has already been said that an atom makes contact with the rest of the universe through its electrons. Since the electrons occur in probability shells at increasing distances from the nucleus as it increases in size, it is reasonable to assume that an atom's first interaction with other atoms is likely to involve electrons in the outermost shell. This is generally true even when the outermost electron is not the "last" electron making up the atom. For example, the metal titanium ($1s^2 2s^2 2p^6 3s^2 3p^6 3d^2 4s^2$) has two $3d$ electrons, while calcium, the element with 2 less electrons (and protons), has none. So the last 2 electrons that go to form titanium are the $3d$ electrons, as we would expect from the disorder in the energy levels $3d$ and $4s$ mentioned above. When a titanium atom loses electrons, however, the first 2 to go are the $4s$ electrons. The gaining of electrons as we "build up" the elements is not the same as when an element loses electrons. This is because, in going (hypothetically) from calcium to titanium, we are adding 2 protons and 2 electrons, thus keeping an electrical balance. When we remove 2 electrons from titanium, the nucleus is the same, so that we produce a charged titanium atom (such charged atoms are called ions) which has an overall 2-unit positive charge. This charge imbalance is sufficient to change the binding energies of the electrons so that the $4s$ electrons are the first to escape. Once the $3d$ electrons are in place, they are (statistically speaking) closer to the nucleus and tend to shield the more distant $4s$

electrons from the positive charges in the nucleus, making them less tightly bound.

Experimental evidence for this can be found by seeing how much energy is needed to remove electrons from atoms of different elements. For example, potassium (the element with 1 less proton than calcium) has a $1s^2 2s^2 2p^6 3s^2 3p^6 4s^1$ structure. The ionization energy, that is, the amount of energy needed to remove its most easily removed electron (in this case $4s$) is 4.32 electron volts (eV). If we remove a whole

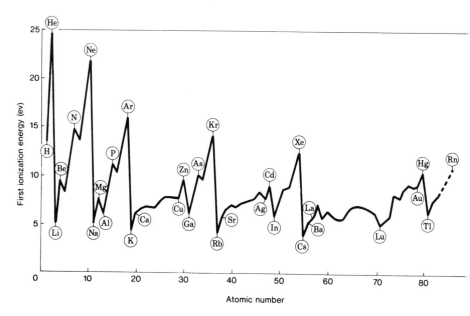

FIGURE 3.   Ionization energies of the elements. This graph indicates the relative amounts of energy required to remove 1 electron from an atom. Note that elements with complete s and p shells (helium, neon, argon, krypton, xenon) occur as a series of peaks—requiring more energy to release 1 of their electrons than do their near neighbors. Elements such as lithium and sodium, with only a single electron in their outer shells, lose this electron relatively easily, to form positively charged ions. Each dot in the graph represents an element, although only a few of the elemental symbols are shown; the others may be worked out from the atomic numbers given along the bottom.

layer of electrons, and the appropriate number of protons and neutrons, the atom we are considering ($1s^2 2s^2 2p^6 3s^1$) is sodium. According to the idea expressed above, that the negative layers of electrons shield the outermost electrons from the positive attractive force of the nucleus, it should be more difficult to remove the outermost electron of sodium ($3s$) than it was of potassium, since there is 1 less layer of shield. In fact, the ionization energy of sodium is 5.12 ev. Lithium, with 1 less layer of electrons, has an ionization energy of 5.36 ev., and hydrogen, which has only the 1 electron and no layers of negative charge, has an ionization energy of 13.53 ev. (see Figure 3). Although there is a one-to-one correspondence between positive charges in the nucleus and negative charges in the electron cloud surrounding it, there is also an averaging effect. Potassium has a positive charge of +19, so that when it has only 18 electrons, the imbalance is shared among them all; in lithium, there are only 2 electrons to share 3 positive charges when the atom is ionized.

If we move on 1 element from potassium, we get back to calcium which, as we have seen, has an electronic structure similar to potassium, but with an additional electron in the $4s$ orbital. The energy required to remove this is 6.09 ev. As we add electrons and protons to "make" new elements, we find in general that the ionization energy increases until a skin is complete, after which it suddenly drops. Of course, it is more difficult to remove the second $4s$ electron from calcium, for we are trying to remove it against a surplus of positive charge, and so require 11.8 ev. There is even greater resistance if we try to take a third electron away, for not only are we increasing the imbalance of charge even further, we are also making a hole in an otherwise complete skin, and to do this requires 51 ev. The noble gas with the same electron configuration as a calcium ion without its two outermost s electrons is argon: to remove an electron from this we are still breaking a skin, but the resistance from charge imbalance is not so great, so the voltage required is only 15.8 ev. However, this is nearly 3 times the voltage required to remove a single electron from potassium, and since it is the electrons of different atoms that interact to form bonds in chemical compounds, we can see that it is more difficult to make argon give up or share one of its electrons.

Other likely aspects of atomic behavior can also be deduced from the electronic approach. Although the outermost electron of potassium is easier to remove than that of sodium or lithium, the actual energy differences involved are small compared with the differences, for example, between removal of the outermost electrons of potassium and argon. If we accept that it is the electrons of different atoms mixing together that turns atoms of elements into chemically bonded compounds, it is logical to suspect that sodium, lithium, and potassium may behave similarly in compound formation, and differently from argon. The element with 1 proton less than argon is chlorine; it has the electronic structure $1s^2 2s^2 2p^6 3s^2 3p^5$. To remove 1 of the outermost electrons needs 13 ev.—nearly as much as argon, and certainly much more than sodium, potassium, or lithium. Consequently, we might expect the bond-forming behavior of chlorine to be unlike that of sodium and its relatives. We might also suspect that, since 1 more electron would give chlorine another layer of skin, addition of an electron, although upsetting the charge balance, might be easier than with some other element where a new skin is not completed. This is the case. The "electron affinity" of chlorine, and other elements that have atomic number 1 less than a noble gas, is greater than for other elements. This group of elements (flourine, chlorine, bromine, iodine) are collectively called halogens, and they all have similar properties.

By looking at the electronic structure of elements, it is possible to suggest certain regularities in behavior. This was not possible before the modern understanding of atomic composition. Doing it the hard way—by comparing atomic masses and similarities between atomic properties of different elements—just over a century ago, the Russian chemist Dmitri Mendeleef produced the periodic law of the elements. This was a great leap forward for chemistry, for it showed that it was not a mass of disconnected facts, but could be systematized.

The modern periodic table, with its roots in Mendeleef's brilliant work, also contains details of the electronic structure, which explains why the elements fall into groups. The periodic table shown in Figure 4 gives these in simplified form.

This table contains 105 elements, many more than Mendeleef's original chart, although, unlike predecessors who had sought to systematize the elements, he left gaps in his table for undiscovered elements which he believed must exist. Not only have the elements he predicted been found, but elements he did not predict are also in the present table. These include the ones beyond uranium—the transuranic elements, which have all been made since 1940.

Most of the manufacture of new elements has taken place in the United States, and most of it has been associated with one man: Glenn Seaborg, winner of the 1951 Nobel prize for chemistry. The next section relates what he and his colleagues have achieved in broadening scientific knowledge, as well as in broadening the very basis of matter by making new kinds of it.

Man-Made Elements

The experiments which made elemental synthesis possible took place nearly 40 years ago, when Irene Joliot-Curie, daughter of Marie and Pierre Curie, the discoverers of radium, and her husband Frederic Joliot discovered that atoms of aluminum could be converted to phosphorus by exposure to radiation from the naturally radioactive element polonium. This transmutation of the elements was taken up by Italian scientist

FIGURE 4. PERIODIC TABLE OF THE ELEMENTS

Shell	s^1	s^2	$d^m s^x$ ($n = 1$ to 10; $x = 0, 1,$ or 2)										s^2p^1	s^2p^2	s^2p^3	s^2p^4	s^2p^5	s^2p^6
1s						1 H												2 He
2s 2p	3 Li	4 Be											5 B	6 C	7 N	8 O	9 F	10 Ne
3s 3p	11 Na	12 Mg											13 Al	14 Si	15 P	16 S	17 Cl	18 Ar
4s 3d 4p	19 K	20 Ca	21 Sc	22 Ti	23 V	24 Cr	25 Mn	26 Fe	27 Co	28 Ni	29 Cu	30 Zn	31 Ga	32 Ge	33 As	34 Se	35 Br	36 Kr
5s 4d 5p	37 Rb	38 Sr	39 Y	40 Zr	41 Nb	42 Mo	43 Tc	44 Ru	45 Rh	46 Pd	47 Ag	48 Cd	49 In	50 Sn	51 Sb	52 Te	53 I	54 Xe
6s (4f) 5d 6p	55 Cs	56 Ba	57 * La	72 Hf	73 Ta	74 W	75 Re	76 Os	77 Ir	78 Pt	79 Au	80 Hg	81 Tl	82 Pb	83 Bi	84 Po	85 At	86 Rn
7s (5f) 6d	87 Fr	88 Ra	89 ** Ac	104	105													

$l^p d^n s^2$ ($p = 1$ to 14, $n = 0$ or 1 (2 or Th))

* Lanthanide Series 4f

58 Ce	59 Pr	60 Nd	61 Pm	62 Sm	63 Eu	64 Gd	65 Tb	66 Dy	67 Ho	68 Er	69 Tm	70 Yb	71 Lu

** Actinide Series 5f

90 Th	91 Pa	92 U	93 Np	94 Pu	95 Am	96 Cm	97 Bk	98 Cf	99 Es	100 Fm	101 Md	102 No	103 Lw

FIGURE 4. PERIODIC TABLE OF THE ELEMENTS. This modern version of the table indicates the outer electron configuration of the elements. Because of the anomalous way in which electron shells are filled among the higher elements, 2 rows—the lanthanides and actinides—are shown at the bottom of the table. Elements appearing vertically in columns have similar properties. Thus, lithium, sodium, and potassium all ionize relatively easily to form singly charged positive ions. Although similar, elements in vertical columns are not identical in their behavior: silicon, for example, does not show the same compound-forming properties as carbon, on which life depends. The vertical columns are like families—members have some similarities, but are also different from one another in various ways.

Enrico Fermi, who bombarded many common elements with neutrons obtained from irradiated beryllium. It is possible that in this way Fermi may have synthesized elements 93 and 94, the two elements beyond uranium, which, until recently, was believed to be the heaviest naturally occurring element.

The idea of using neutrons to transmute elements was good, since the neutron has no charge. To bombard an atom with protons, one has to give the protons sufficient energy to overcome the repulsive force of the positive charge in the nucleus. The neutron, on the other hand, can join the nucleus quite readily. But adding a neutron to a nucleus does not transmute the element, for it is the number of protons and electrons that determine the type of element. What happens in neutron bombardment is that an isotope of the original atom is produced. However, this isotope may be unstable and undergo beta decay, in which a neutron converts to a proton, emitting an electron in the process. If this happens, the atom will have the same number of neutrons as it possessed originally, but one more proton; it is thus an atom of a different element.

If Fermi made elements 93 and 94 in his experiments, he did not notice them because something remarkable happened which demanded all his attention. When a neutron hit a uranium atom, instead of sticking to its nucleus, it made the nucleus break into 2 fragments, with the emission of several more neutrons. In this fission process lies the possibility of a chain reaction—1 neutron breaking up 1 uranium atom, and thus producing several neutrons to break up several more uranium atoms, and so on. In such a manner were the Japanese towns of Hiroshima and Nagasaki destroyed in 1945 with the first two "atomic" bombs, part of the basis for which was worked out by Fermi after he had left Italy and moved to Chicago.

Fermi had been studying radiative capture of particles by nuclei, and discovered their fission. In America Edwin M. McMillan, studying the fission of nuclei, discovered the radiative capture which produced the first man-made element to be identified as such. In 1940, while examining the fission of the uranium-239 isotope,[2] he discovered element 93, later named neptunium.

Uranium-239, synthesized first in 1936, undergoes beta decay to produce neptunium-239. Neptunium-239 also undergoes beta decay, and it was presumed that this produced element 94. However, McMillan did not detect this element. Later in 1940, Glenn Seaborg, McMillan, and several other collaborators attacked uranium with deuterons, nuclei of the heavy hydrogen deuterium, which contain 1 proton and 1 neutron. In this way they made another isotope of neptunium which decayed to recognizable atoms of element 94, which they named plutonium. Plutonium has subsequently become the most important of the transuranium elements, since it can be used as fuel in nuclear reactors, and can be made from an isotope of uranium which is itself unsatisfactory as a fuel in so-called "breeder" reactors (discussed further in Chapters 8 and 9).

Seaborg, whose name has been associated with the discovery of nearly all the transuranium elements now known, has identified these 3 prerequisites for transuranic synthesis: the knowledge and experience of irradiating elements gained by the Joliots, the discovery in 1932 of the neutron, and the invention by American physicist E. O. Lawrence of the cyclotron.

The cyclotron is a machine which speeds up charged nuclear particles so that they have sufficient energy to smash into a nucleus despite their charge. Lawrence developed the cyclotron in the early 1930s; his most famous model, the 60-inch machine at Berkeley, California, was completed in 1939, and did not go out of use until the summer of 1962. During this time it produced the high energy particles which helped to synthesize 6 of the transuranic elements.

[2] Isotopes of an element can be identified with a number—the sum of protons and neutrons in their nucleus. Since uranium atoms always contain 92 protons, by definition, uranium-239 is the isotope which contains 147 neutrons. Where an element is referred to by its chemical symbol, the mass number can be indicated as a superscript preceding the symbol, thus ^{239}U.

After the first pair of transuranic elements, there was a gap of several years before 2 more were synthesized. In the meantime, Seaborg had published some thoughts about their likely chemistry. As the elements are built up, certain regularities occur, governed by the number of electrons on the "outside" of the atom; this explains the similarities between sodium and potassium, both of which have an outermost 1s electron.

With element 57, lanthanum, the first, second, and third electron levels are completely filled; additionally, the 4, 5, and 6s levels, the 4 and 5p levels, and the 4d level are also filled, and there is one electron in the 5d level. One might expect that the next element, number 58, would have two 5d electrons, but such is not the case. At this point, the 4f level begins to fill, and it is not until element 72, hafnium, when the 4f level has its full complement of 14 electrons, that electrons begin to go into 5d level again. Since the elements with between 57 and 72 electrons all have the same outermost electron structure, there are greater similarities among these elements than between them and earlier elements in the periodic table. This group is known collectively as the lanthanides. Seaborg proposed that a similar family might occur after actinium, element 89. Actinium has one electron in the 6d level, and it seemed likely that in subsequent elements the 5f level would start to fill.

This proposal explained some of the anomalous properties of the natural elements beyond actinium: thorium, protactinium, and uranium. The idea was rapidly accepted, and the elements in which the 5f level is partly filled are called the actinides. The actinides should finish with lawrencium, element 103; element 104, which has two electrons in the 6d level, should show similarities to hafnium (element 72).

In the final years of World War II, elements 95 and 96, later called americium and curium, were synthesized for the first time. Although plutonium had been produced in visible quantities in 1942, none of the other transuranium elements were synthesized in visible form at this time. Identification of the new elements was made solely on the basis of their radioactive decomposition. One of the fingerprints of an element, if it breaks down by alpha decay, that is, emission of a helium nucleus, is the energy with which the alpha particle is emitted. This is characteristic for each element. More important, it is possible to predict approximately what it will be for an unknown element. Similarly, the halflife, the time taken for half the atoms of a radioactive element to break down, is also predictable. The transuranic elements 95 and 96 were first positively identified on the basis of these properties.

There was another time lag before 2 more elements appeared. Berkelium (97) and californium (98) were discovered in 1949 and 1950. Highly radioactive, their synthesis—from elements 95 and 96—required the development of highly sophisticated remote control handling techniques.

At about this time the hydrogen bomb was being developed and tested and, in November 1952, there was a thermonuclear test explosion in the Pacific. The radioactive fallout from this contained some new, heavy isotopes of plutonium; it seemed probable that they had been formed by the decay of even heavier elements. Coral from an atoll near the test site was transported to Berkeley, California, and elements 99 and 100 extracted from it. Although this was the original discovery of these 2 elements, by the time the information was declassified so that it could be made public, they had been synthesized by neutron irradiation of other transuranic elements. These 2 elements were called einsteinium and fermium. After their discovery, elemental synthesis hit an impasse for the next 3 years.

Albert Ghiorso and Glenn Seaborg describe the night in 1955 when it started to advance again:

An atmosphere of gloom permeated the laboratory. In the attempt to produce and identify element 101 we had carried out a number of very careful experiments, and all had failed. Now a last experiment was being tried, on the basis of what seemed only a farfetched possibility. At best the minuscule sample of material we had prepared might contain one or two atoms of the elusive 101st element. There was some reason to believe that an atom of element 101 might decay in an hour or two into an atom of element 100, which in turn might break up spontaneously by the fission process. If this barely possible combination of events took place, the creation of element 101 would be signaled in an ionization chamber by a comparatively large pulse of ionization produced by a fission fragment of its decay product, element 100.

We watched with eyes fixed on a pulse recorder connected to the ionization chamber. An hour went by. The night dragged on toward dawn. The waiting seemed interminable. Then it happened: The recorder pen shot up to mid-scale and dropped back, leaving a neat red line which represented a large ionization pulse—10 times larger than would be produced by an alpha particle. No such pulse had been recorded from natural background radiation in test runs conducted for many days prior to the experiment. It looked highly probable that the pulse was indeed a signal of the hoped-for fission. The vigil continued. An hour or so later the pen recorded a second pulse like the first. We were now confident that we had witnessed the decay of two atoms of element 101—and had added a new member to the roster of chemical elements.

Thus the latest of the transuranium elements required the ultimate in sensitivity for its detection. It was identified on the basis of only a couple of atoms, produced by transmutation in an amount of target material itself so small that it was unweighable. In the case of earlier members of the strange family of elements we had worked with minute samples, but nothing so small as this.[3]

While work had been progressing on the synthesis of new elements, it had not stopped on the older transuranics. There

[3] Albert Ghiorso and Glenn Seaborg, "The Synthetic Elements—II," in *New Chemistry* (New York: Simon and Schuster, 1957), pp. 126–127.

were continual additions to the known isotopes, and more of each element was made so that the chemistry could be studied. X-ray diffraction patterns, which indicate crystal structure, and magnetic properties were measured. Interest was not restricted to Berkeley. All over the world laboratories were springing up to study—and attempt to make—elements. In the summer of 1957, it looked as if a new element had been discovered somewhere else.

A group of scientists at the Nobel Institute for Physics in Stockholm claimed that by bombarding curium with a carbon nucleus they had synthesized element 102, which they named nobelium. Unfortunately, scientists at Berkeley and at the most important Soviet laboratory in the field, at Dubna, were unable to repeat the work. In April 1958, the Berkeley scientists bombarded a different isotope of curium with a different isotope of carbon and unquestionably produced element 102. Although it is customary for the laboratory which synthesizes a new element to name it, the Berkeley group allowed the name nobelium to stand.

A new facility had been used in the synthesis of this element at Berkeley—the heavy ion linear accelerator, HILAC. It had become apparent during the earlier syntheses of new elements that there was a limit to how much progress could be made by sticking small bits into the nucleus, so it was decided to try bigger bits. HILAC, completed in 1957, accelerates the nuclei of light elements until they have sufficient energy to smash into heavier nuclei. It is able to accelerate elements as heavy as argon (element 40).

This strategy of bombardment with low-mass nuclei also permitted the synthesis of element 103, lawrencium, in 1961. Made by bombarding californium with boron ions, lawrencium should complete the family of actinides, and the next element —104—is important for testing Seaborg's theory about how the electrons will fill their shells after the actinides. Unfortunately, it seemed that transuranic synthesis was coming to an end with element 103. The halflives of the elements were getting shorter as they got larger, and it seemed as if a limit had nearly been appoached. However, during the largely unsuccessful search for element 104 the theory of nuclear structure took a new and exciting turn, which has led to the belief that it may be possible to synthesize some elements with atomic numbers as high as 168.

Arguments about whether or not element 104 has been synthesized have continued for several years. Georgi Flerov and his co-workers at Dubna in the USSR, where they have a large cyclotron, claimed in 1964 to have synthesized it by bombardment of a plutonium isotope with neon nuclei. Flerov's group called the element kurchatovium, in honor of Soviet atomic scientist Igor Kurchatov. At Berkeley it was found impossible to duplicate Flerov's work; however, it was claimed that an isotope of element 104 could be synthesized by bombarding californium-249 with carbon ions. Believing theirs to be the first true synthesis of element 104, the Berkeley group called it rutherfordium, after British scientist Lord Rutherford. However, the Americans, led by Albert Ghiorso—whose name has been associated with the synthesis of several transuranic elements—have agreed to drop their claim to the right to name element 104 if the Russians can prove that they did synthesize it first.

A similar argument concerned synthesis of element 105, but this seems to have been resolved more quickly in favor of the Californians. In May 1970, Ghiorso claimed that his group in California had identified element 105, and presented strong evidence that an earlier Russian claim was not substantiated. Element 105 was produced by the Americans with the aid of HILAC, using a heavy isotope of nitrogen to bombard californium-249, the same transuranic isotope used to synthesize element 104. It has been named hahnium, after German physicist Otto Hahn. When he announced the synthesis of hahnium, Ghiorso claimed that elements 106 and 107 might be just around the corner, but since then it seems possible that we may have leapt halfway down the next street, to element 112.

The Island of Stability

About 20 years ago, groups at the Universities of Chicago and Heidelberg carried out extensive theoretical work on the shell model of nuclear structure. This led to the "magic numbers" theory. These magic numbers, which are independent for protons and neutrons, are believed to be similar to the completed electron shells around the nucleus. Thus, there are a number of quantum states, each of which can hold only a certain number of protons or neutrons; when a shell is filled, there is a benefit to the nucleus of extra stability. When a nucleus is "doubly magic," that is, has closed shells of both neutrons and protons, it has an especially enhanced stability. The magic numbers are 2, 8, 20, 28, 50, and 82 for both neutrons and protons. There is a magic neutron number of 126 and a magic proton number of 114. The next highest postulated magic neutron number is 184, and there may be higher proton and neutron magic numbers at 164 and 196, respectively.

If we look at the "doubly magic" nuclei, we see that the lowest corresponds to helium, the stability of which has already been mentioned. Similarly, 8 + 8 nucleons gives the most stable isotope of oxygen. Another very stable nucleus is that of lead, the most abundant isotope of which is lead-208, with the magic proton number 82 and the magic neutron number 126. Since a single magic number—either proton or neutron—adds stability to a nucleus, it is not surprising that elements close to proton magic numbers tend to have more isotopes than those away from the magic numbers.

The phrase "magic numbers" is a cover for our inability to explain phenomena for which no natural explanation can be found. Scientists are at present trying to remove the "magic" from the magic numbers by relating stability to nuclear states. It is known that a nucleus can exist in a large number of quantum states, each of which represents something different, as do the quantum states of the electrons. However, only the ground or lowest energy state of a nucleus is stable.

By exciting electrons from their ground states and measuring certain properties of the relaxation process—that is, the falling back of the electron into its ground state—it is possible to learn something of the shapes of nuclei. Another way in which the nucleus can be examined is to replace an inner electron in an atom with a much heavier negatively charged particle, the muon, and observe the effects of x-ray bombardment on the atom. These experimental techniques have led to the classification of 3 types of nuclei: spherical, hard-deformed, and soft. Only nuclei with 1 type of nucleon close to a magic number are spherical. Some nonmagic nuclei, such as uranium, are so deformed that the addition of a single neutron increases deformation to the point that the nucleus breaks in 2—the fission process.

The quantum states of the nucleons are classified, like those of electrons, into orbitals. It has been suggested that these orbitals are directional, like the p, d, and f orbitals of the electrons. Since magic numbers represent filled orbitals, nonmagic nuclei, with incomplete orbitals, will be lopsided, or deformed, because of this directional bias.

Lead is a doubly magic element. It is interesting to note, in this respect, that the radioactive decay routes of the heavy elements stop at lead. During the 1960s, it gradually dawned on nuclear scientists—who at this time were depressed, since it looked as if new elemental synthesis was nearing its end—that element 114 might be especially stable. This should be particularly true of isotopes with about 184 neutrons, because of their doubly magic properties.

W. J. Swiatecki produced an allegorical picture of the stability of atomic nuclei, with existing elements as a peninsula in a sea of instability (see Figure 5). Beyond the tip of this peninsula, with water all around it, is the nuclear scientists' blessed isle, the island of stability. Landing on this is the major aim of nuclear synthesis today.

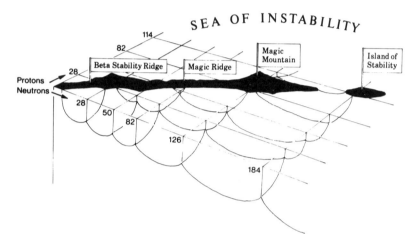

FIGURE 5. The "island of stability." A three-dimensional plot in which stability is shown vertically, while proton and neutron numbers form a plane, reveals the elements as a long peninsula jutting into a sea of instability. According to magic number theory, out beyond the shore line is an island of stability. Because elements in between would be unstable (they are submerged), they cannot be used as stepping stones from known elements to those on the island; finding a way to jump the gap is a major concern of modern nuclear physics and chemistry.

The magic numbers are not the only things that have to be taken into account. Although these indicate whether or not a nucleus should resist spontaneous fission, it is still possible for emission of an alpha particle from such a nucleus to be energetically favorable. Some theoretical calculations have suggested that the most stable element on the island may be 110, with that number of protons and the magic 184 neutrons.

The only way to test hypotheses about stability of the superheavy elements is to land on the island of stability and see what happens. The problem is how to get there. As the size of a nucleus increases, the ratio of neutrons to protons also inceases. This did not raise problems during synthesis of the first few transuranic elements, when nuclei could be attacked with neutrons to build up a single element at a time. Since they are in the sea of instability, the elements just below the projected stability range can probably not be synthesized, so stepwise progression is out. We have seen that neutron bombardment is being replaced by the strategy of attacking nuclei with ions of some of the lighter elements, but these, since they have small nuclei, have low neutron:proton ratios. A small nucleus hitting a large target nucleus may carry its proton number up to 110 or higher, but the neutron number will be too low for the element to be stable.

A possible way around this difficulty is to use an isotope of calcium, calcium-48, which is relatively neutron rich, having 28 neutrons to 20 protons. If this is used to bombard plutonium-244, it might produce element 114 with 174 neutrons (it is estimated that 4 neutrons would be emitted during the fusion process), which could be on the shore of the island of stability.

A more likely process is to use much heavier bombarding elements, such as xenon on uranium, or even uranium on uranium. This could produce very heavy unstable elements which would rapidly decay toward the stable region, much as the known radioactive elements decay to lead. It is not known at present whether this would happen, or whether some sort of nuclear transfer might take place in which one nucleus ripped sufficient nucleons from the other to bring itself to the island of stability.

There is a further method which has been tested and which seems to work, but before describing it we must postulate what the superheavy elements would be like chemically. Glenn Seaborg, who proposed the actinide series in 1944, has recently worked out how the electron orbitals of the higher elements might be filled. Element 104 is chemically important as the first transactinide—the first transuranic element in which there is a change in the outer electron shell. On the basis of its outer shell, it seems likely that it will resemble hafnium, the element with 1 shell less, but the same outer electron configuration. Working on the same principle, element 110 should resemble platinum, 111 gold, 112 mercury, 113 thallium, and 114 lead. Seaborg has gone far beyond this in his calculations, and predicted a set of superactinides beginning with element 122 and ending with element 162. However, it will be some years before his views on their behavior are put to the test.

Since some of the island of stability elements may have very long halflives, and since similar elements tend to congregate, searches are being made in, for example, platinum minerals for traces of element 110, and in lead minerals for element 114. Although no positive results have been achieved, in September 1971 uranium was deposed as the heaviest naturally occurring element when Seaborg announced that a plutonium isotope had been identified in samples of the mineral bastnasite.

The likely similarity of properties with known elements also suggests ways in which traces of the synthetic superheavy elements could be purified. Any heavy nuclear reaction will not produce a single product, and the best way to separate a particular super element would be to absorb it in the nonsuper element to which it is related by electron configuration. This may now have been done.

If a nucleus is bombarded with a very high energy proton, a large part of the proton's energy may be transferred to that nucleus, without a nuclear reaction taking place. It is possible that the now highly energetic nucleus will crash into another nucleus, overcome the repulsive forces of its protons, and fuse with it. A group of scientists at the Rutherford High Energy Laboratory in England, together with colleagues from British universities, bombarded targets of tungsten (element 74) with high energy protons, and claimed, in February 1971, to have found evidence of the fusion of tungsten nuclei into element 112. The tungsten targets, after irradiation, were treated with various metals, such as platinum, gold, lead, and mercury, and, in the mercury fraction, radioactivity was found which could not be attributed to any known radioactive element. The emission of alpha particles occurred with about the energy calculated on theoretical grounds for element 112. There was also evidence of spontaneous fission, a phenomenon which only rarely occurs with elements below uranium in atomic number. No doubt it will be some time before this claim to have reached the island of stability is thoroughly tested and accepted, but it looks as if elemental synthesis may have begun a new lease on life.

3 ⬡ A Compound Science

The chemist is interested in far more than just elements. His primary concern is with compounds, and there are many more of these than there are elements. In the preceding chapter the atomic structure of elements was described, together with some aspects of the behavior of electrons in orbitals. It was noted how the outermost skin of electrons is an atom's major source of contact with its surroundings. Through such contacts, individual atoms join together in a number of ways—collectively called chemical bonds—to form fairly permanent combinations which are called molecules.

Where atoms of just one element combine, the result is a homoatomic molecule. Heteroatomic molecules—chemically bonded combinations of different elements—are what was meant by the word "compounds" above. However, in looking at chemical bonds to determine their nature, it is often convenient to start with molecules of single elements, for many elements exist in a combined form rather than as individual atoms.

The first question is: Why should atoms join together at all? If we ask this of some of the techniques which were used to explain the differences between atoms of different elements, we might assume that 2 atoms join together because the resultant molecule is more stable than the 2 separate atoms. Stability, as was implicit in the discussion of atoms, is related to energy. If a compound is formed, it is because the process is energetically favored—the same reason a ball runs down a hill from top to bottom. Energy is given away in the process, and energy loss, in general, means stability gain.

To understand chemical bonding, chemists nowadays start with the simplest possible atomic combination, the formation of a hydrogen molecule from 2 hydrogen atoms. They even go a stage further than this implies, for instead of taking 2 ordinary hydrogen atoms, they take 1 atom (H) and 1 ion, that is, a hydrogen atom that has had its electron removed and consequently has a positive electric charge (H^+).[1]

When this forms a molecule-ion, the system consists of 2 hydrogen nuclei (protons) sharing a single electron. Such a simple system is chosen because it is easy to sort out the different energies resulting from interactions between the components, and to work out whether the molecule-ion is more stable than the separate components.

In the hydrogen atom, there is attractive force between the negatively charged electron and the positively charged proton. Since the other component of the molecule-ion is a solitary proton, there is no repulsive or attractive force when it is widely separated from the hydrogen atom. But what happens as it approaches this atom? The electron of the atom will be attracted toward it, while the proton will be repelled. The electron is thus attracted by 2 protons which, simultaneously, repel one another. We cannot work out intuitively what will happen; only by using the mathematical relationships between the repulsion and attraction and seeing which, on balance, leads to the lower energy state can we say whether or not H and H^+ will form a chemical bond. Alternatively, of course, we can see whether the molecule H_2^+ can be found in the world around us (it has been found under special conditions in a laboratory, although not in everyday life) and study its stability. Either way, we find that H_2^+ is something real. When the single electron is shared by 2 nuclei, the resultant system has less energy than the separated hydrogen atom and proton.

---

[1] For readers unfamiliar with chemical shorthand, a note on the representation of molecules by formulae appears at the end of this chapter.

If we add another electron, so that there are 2 protons and 2 electrons, we find that this system, when bound together, has less energy than 2 separated hydrogen atoms. The sharing of electrons between more than 1 nucleus seems to be favored by the electrons themselves.

The energy difference in such cases can be measured: for two hydrogen atoms forming a hydrogen molecule (H_2), the energy is about 7.6×10^{-19} joule. This is vanishingly small, but then so is 1 molecule of hydrogen. If we take a quantity of hydrogen on the same scale as we are—that is, a visible quantity—we find that the energy of formation of 1 gram of hydrogen molecules from constituent atoms is about the same as the energy we get from eating half an ounce (approximately 14 grams) of sugar.

Thus far, we can say that certain atoms will "bond" together because it is energetically favorable for them to do so, and we know that the bond that joins them is a sharing of electrons.

The electrons, as was pointed out, occupy atomic orbitals— volumes of probability about the nucleus. Since electrons in bonds are shared, it seems reasonable that they will follow similar paths, but spread out to take in both nuclei, thus forming molecular orbitals. The shapes of these orbitals can be calculated; so can the distances between the nuclei—called the bond length—for it is part of the essence of the bond that the 2 nuclei held together by shared electrons remain nearly the same distance from each other as long as the molecule exists.

Bond lengths can be calculated from mathematically produced curves like the one in Figure 6. This shows a "potential well" for the hydrogen molecule. Along the horizontal axis, we measure the distance between the 2 nuclei. As they are brought closer together, the electron sharing effect begins to operate, and the line dips down the vertical energy scale. After a while, the nuclei get so close that, if they were pushed any closer together, the repulsion of the 2 positively charged nuclei would

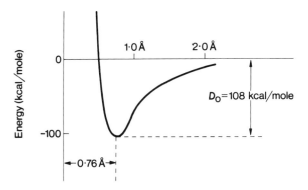

FIGURE 6. "Potential well" profile for 2 hydrogen atoms as they approach each other. As they come together, the well gets deeper, indicating that proximity is favored. However, internuclear repulsion eventually overcomes the attractive force pulling the 2 atoms together; to make them go even closer, energy must be supplied, and the side of the well shoots up steeply. From a plot such as this, the bond strength and bond length of a hydrogen atom can be calculated, as can the energy required to stretch the bond by a specific amount.

be stronger than the "cementing" effect of the 2 electrons. Consequently, the system needs energy for this to occur, and the curve on the graph swings rapidly upward.

The very bottom of the curve shows the energy which corresponds to the bottom of the well, and, at the same time, the distance apart of the 2 nuclei, which is the optimum bond length. If we want to stretch the hydrogen molecule, we can see how much energy is required; for example, to stretch it by 0.1 angstrom (10^{-11} meter) requires 0.9 kilojoule per mole[2]— about one twenty-sixth the energy of the bond itself. Such small amounts of energy are readily found in nature in the form of visible and invisible radiations, so that molecules interact with such radiations. This is 1 of the bases of spectroscopy, by which the structure of unknown molecules can be elucidated (see Chapter 4).

[2] A mole is the number of grams of a substance equal to its atomic or molecular mass—it contains more than 6×10^{23} individual atoms or molecules.

Where the Electrons Go

Molecular orbitals are bound by rules similar to those governing atomic orbitals. Nature does not like more than 2 to a bed: each molecular orbital may contain only 2 electrons, and these must have opposite spins. Hydrogen presents no problem, since it has only 2 electrons, and both go into the same orbital. In the atoms, the electrons were in *s* orbitals; in the molecule we go Greek and the orbital is called *sigma* (σ).

The element beyond hydrogen in atomic mass is helium, which has 2 electrons. What happens if 2 helium atoms try to bond with one another? To simplify the case, let us take a helium atom and a helium ion—that is, a helium atom with 1 electron removed. The total number of electrons is 3, all of which occupy *s* orbitals in the separated atom and ion. Two of these can team up and go into the sigma molecular orbital to form a straightforward bond, as in hydrogen. This leaves out the third electron. Solutions to the complex mathematical equations that describe the behavior of the electrons show that this third electron will have nothing to do with bonding; on the contrary, it spends its time trying to tug one nucleus away from the other.

The third electron alters the energy pattern in an upward direction; it is against or antibonding. But there are 2 electrons contributing to bonding, and only 1 to antibonding. As may seem reasonable, the extra energy required to get 1 electron out of its atomic orbital into an antibonding orbital is about the same as the energy released when an electron goes from its atomic orbital into a bonding orbital. So the antibonding electron in He_2^+ only weakens the bond. In the case of 2 helium atoms with their full complement of electrons (4), there are 2 bonding electrons and 2 antibonding electrons, with the result that there is no bond. Nothing about the formation of a bond is energetically advantageous, so it is not formed.

From the principle of orbital occupancy, we can see that the maximum number of electrons in a single bonding orbital is 2—and this is taken to be the number in a single chemical bond. Consequently, we can say that the hydrogen molecule has a single bond (or, as it is sometimes expressed, a bond order of 1), while both the hydrogen molecule-ion (H_2^+) and the helium molecule-ion (He_2^+) have half bonds (although for different reasons; the first because it has only a single electron available, and the second because half the bond strength is sapped by the third, antibonding electron). This halfbondedness is confirmed by the bond energies: for H_2^+, about 60 percent that of H_2, and for He_2^+, just over 50 percent of H_2.

A slightly more sophisticated procedure makes it possible to assess the bonding of more complex atoms using the same principles. Nitrogen has an atomic number of 7, thus a neutral nitrogen atom has 7 electrons which might possibly enter chemical bonds. Three of these electrons are in $2p$ orbitals. The $2p$ state is degenerate, and has directional orbitals (see p. 20) envisaged as being at right angles to one another. To indicate this, we can use a slightly extended form of electronic shorthand and indicate the configuration as $1s^2 2s^2 2p_x^1 2p_y^1 2p_z^1$, showing 1 electron in each of the 3 possible directional orbitals.

At the first electron level, nitrogen has the same configuration as helium; therefore, we can expect no bonding effect between the $1s$ electrons of 2 nitrogen atoms, for the antibonding electrons will cancel out the bonding effect. The same will be true at the $2s$ level, where again 4 electrons will take up opposing attitudes in sets of 2. The p electrons present a more complex situation. Atomic s electrons are in spherically symmetrical orbitals and result in a symmetrical sigma orbital when they combine by overlapping. One pair of p orbitals from 2 atoms—for example, those designated p_x—can also overlap to form a sigma molecular orbital. But if the p_x electrons do this, the p_y and p_z electrons cannot (see Figure 7). When the other p orbitals interact they form directionally orientated

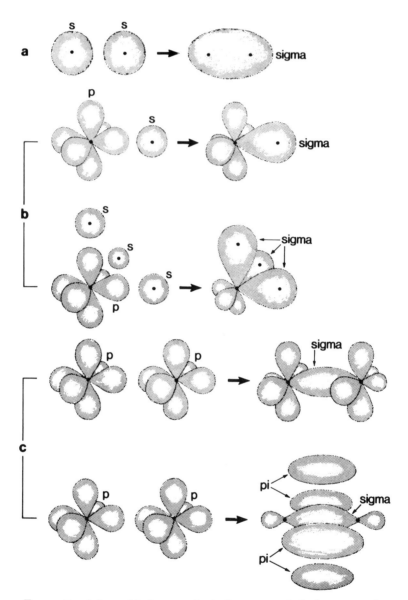

FIGURE 7. (a) s orbitals are spherically symmetrical about a nucleus. When two s orbitals on different atoms interact, a sigma bond is formed; (b) p orbitals are directional (the different directions are designated x, y, and z) and a single p orbital from 1 atom can interact with the s orbital from another atom to form a sigma bond; similarly, the 3 different directional p orbitals can each form a sigma bond with an s electron from 3 other atoms; (c) 2 p orbitals from different atoms can interact to form a sigma bond, but once this has happened, the other-directional p orbitals of the 2 atoms cannot overlap in the same way; if they are to form bonds, they must be pi bonds, which are also directional, unlike sigma bonds, and confer rigidly on the resultant molecule, since 1 nucleus can no longer twist with respect to the other nucleus without breaking a bond.

bonds. To differentiate these from sigma bonds, they are called *pi* (π) bonds.

As with sigma bonds, the rule of only 2 electrons per bond applies to each pi bond. Because they are directionally orientated in space, it is possible to have 2 pi bonds formed from p orbitals, 1 from overlap of p_y electrons and 1 from overlap of p_z electrons; hence, 6 electrons can be taken up from the p electron levels and incorporated into bonds—2 pi and 1 sigma. Thus, with nitrogen, 2 atoms will each contribute an electron to form a single sigma bond from p_x orbital overlap; similarly, they will each contribute their p_y and p_z electrons to form 2 pi bonds. The total number of electrons involved in bonding orbitals (not counting those from 1s and 2s that are counterbalanced by antibonding orbitals) is 6, with a bond strength of 3. Nitrogen forms a triply bonded molecule.

The next atom past nitrogen in the atomic table is oxygen, a vital component of the air we breathe. With 1 extra electron in its atom, how does it bond? We can envisage a 2-atom oxygen molecule bonded just like nitrogen, but with 2 extra electrons that must go into an antibonding orbital. Therefore, we can say that the oxygen molecule will have a bond strength of 2, that is, be doubly bonded, when we have subtracted the antibonding effect. We might also imagine that, since the electrons in the atoms are in the $2p_x$ orbital, we shall have an antibonding sigma orbital, but this is not the case. Because electrons interact with the whole system, they do not always follow what appear to be strictly logical progressions. Just as was the case with the ionization of some of the heavier elements, where the first electron to be removed is not the last to go in (such as titanium), so the electrons in molecules may not show the simple behavior we expect.

A pi bond in any quantum level has a slightly higher energy than a sigma bond at the same quantum level, since less energy has been released in the formation of the pi bond. Antibonding orbitals require about the same amount of energy for their

formation as bonding orbitals give up when formed. Consequently, it takes more energy to get an electron into a sigma
antibonding orbital than into the pi antibonding orbital on the
same quantum level. The antibonding electrons in the oxygen
molecule go into pi antibonding orbitals. There are 2 of these,
just as there are 2 pi bonding orbitals. Both have similar
energy and, following the principles of good management of
spare room, we assign 1 electron to 1 pi antibonding orbital,
and 1 to the other; this means that the 2 electrons are kept
apart in different regions of space, thus diminishing electron-
electron repulsion.

Unfair Shares for All

All the molecules we have studied so far have been homoatomic
—composed of atoms of the same type. These atoms all hold
their electrons with the same energy, so that when they share
electrons, they share them equally. This type of bond, called a
covalent bond, is found in its purest form in the homoatomic
molecules. However, the majority of the compounds dealt with
in everyday life are composed of molecules in which different
elements are bonded together.

As an extreme example, take the hydrogen fluoride molecule, composed of a single atom of hydrogen and a single
atom of flourine, joined by a single bond. Comparison of the
ionization energies of hydrogen and fluorine shows that fluorine
has the stronger hold on its electrons; when it shares an
electron with hydrogen, and vice versa, it will want more from
the bargain than a 50:50 split. The distribution of the bonding
electrons is skewed away from the hydrogen toward the flourine.
This means that one end of the molecule (the fluorine end)
is more negative than the other.

In the solid state or in solution, many substances exist as
ions, with a takeover of electrons by 1 species. In solid sodium

fluoride, for example, the sodium exists as positive ions (cations), and the fluoride, which has taken the sodium's outer electron, as negative ions (anions). Such bonding is called ionic. In the gaseous state, ionic compounds do not exist. (Note that an ionized compound is not the same as an ionic compound.) Because of the nature of a solid, the freedom of ions to move about is highly restricted. In a gas they are free to move, so that an ionic compound would not be bonded; the 2 components could just move apart. However, a compound such as hydrogen fluoride, in the gas phase, is said to have ionic character, the amount of which can be measured.

Let us now take a quick look at carbon and its compounds with hydrogen. Carbon is the element directly before nitrogen in the periodic table. It has a total of 6 electrons, 2 in the $1s$ state, 2 in the $2s$ state, and 1 in each of 2 separate p orbitals. Since the $2s$ state is already filled with 2 paired off electrons, while hydrogen atoms in search of a bond have a single electron each to contribute, it might seem reasonable to expect 2 hydrogen atoms to join up with a carbon atom, giving the compound CH_2, in which the p electrons combine with the hydrogen s electrons. Although CH_2 does exist, it is very reactive; the common compound formed from a single carbon atom and hydrogen atoms has 4 hydrogens attached to it (CH_4).

In atomic carbon the energy difference between the $2s$ and $2p$ levels is small. Consequently, 1 of the $2s$ electrons can easily move into the vacant p orbital, thus giving 4 unpaired electrons ready for bonding. At the same time, when 4 bonds form, they are all identical. It no longer makes sense to talk about a particular electron in an s orbital and others in p orbitals; they share their s-ness and p-ness, in the ratio $1:3$, and are consequently called sp^3 hybrid orbitals. The methane molecule, CH_4, formed by bonding with the sp^3 hybrid orbitals adopts a tetrahedral shape in which the bonds are as far away from each other—because of electron repulsion—as they can get.

A Bit of Give and Take

The sp^3 hybrids are not the only ones that can form; sp and sp^2 hybrids are also possible, depending on the electron configuration of the atoms involved. For example, boron has the electron configuration $1s^2 2s^2 2p^1$. If we try to calculate how this might react with hydrogen, we can now consider ourselves sufficiently sophisticated to avoid the pitfall of assuming that it will form BH, with its single p electron and the hydrogen's single s electron forming a sigma bond. Instead, we may imagine that one of the boron's $2s$ electrons goes into a vacant p orbital, and that the possibilities for bonding will be extended by 3 sp^2 hybrid orbitals, thus leading us to BH_3. This is not a bad guess, except that BH_3 has never been detected, being such a reactive molecule that it does not stay itself for as long as we need to prove that it is really there. If we compare the BH_3 bonds with the CH_4 bonds, there is an important difference. When all the sp^3 hybrids have bonded, the bonding orbitals at that level are all filled. With the sp^2 hybrids, there is still an unfilled p bonding orbital—completely empty and just right for a spare pair of electrons. This is just what some molecules have to offer—pairs of electrons not used up in bonding orbitals. Ammonia (NH_3), for example, has such a pair— called a lone pair—and, although BH_3 itself has never been detected, it is possible to produce the compound $H_3B.NH_3$, in which nitrogen shares its lone pair with boron. Here is a pair of shared electrons, both capable of fitting into a bonding orbital. It does not matter that they have both come from 1 atom, since the result is still a chemical bond; such donor-acceptor linked compounds are called molecular complexes.

Beryllium, like boron, has residual bonding capacity. With the basic structure $1s^2 2s^2$, beryllium shifts 1 of its $2s$ electrons to the $2p$ level, then hybridizes the pair into 2 sp orbitals, leading to compounds such as beryllium chloride ($BeCl_2$). In this beryllium compound, only one p level is filled. There are 2 vacant bonding orbitals, so 2 lone pairs can be accommodated. When beryllium chloride crystallizes to the solid form, it makes sure, because solids have their atoms packed tight together, that it gets a full share of donated electrons.

If we thought of $BeCl_2$ as an ionic solid, we could imagine beryllium giving up 2 electrons to form Be^{2+}, which has the electronic structure of helium, while each chlorine atom takes 1 electron, forming Cl^-, with the neon electronic structure. Actually, in solid beryllium chloride, each beryllium atom is bonded to 4 chlorine atoms, and each chlorine atom to 2 beryllium atoms, in the neat pattern shown in Figure 8. All the

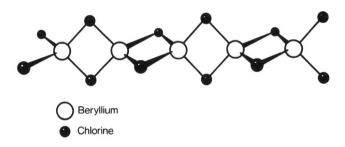

○ Beryllium
● Chlorine

FIGURE 8. The structure of solid beryllium chloride ($BeCl_2$). Non-bonding electrons on the chlorine atoms are shared by the beryllium atoms; however, in the solid, all the bonds are the same length, owing to an averaging effect between the regular beryllium chlorine bonds and the donor-acceptor bonds. In this illustration, for the sake of clarity, bonds are shown as lines joining the nuclei.

bonds are the same length, which is substantially longer than a regular covalent bond.

In fact, the beryllium atoms are helping themselves to a share of the nonbonding electrons on the chlorine, in order to fill up their vacant p orbitals. But, instead of having a regular bond and a donor-acceptor bond, the molecular orbitals average out to make all the bonds equivalent.

Coping with Electron Deficiency

This digression into beryllium chemistry should help us to understand more about boron. If, as we have said, boron hydride is so reactive that it has not yet been detected, and if there is no electron donor about to form a molecular complex, what happens to BH_3 when it is left by itself? The answer is that it forms B_2H_6. What sort of molecule is this? There is a similar looking and very common carbon-containing molecule called ethane, which is C_2H_6. You can imagine this being formed by taking 2 methane (CH_4) molecules, breaking a carbon-hydrogen bond in each, and sticking the 2 bigger broken parts (CH_3-) together, thus forming a carbon-carbon bond. But BH_3 cannot meet another BH_3 and form a boron-boron bond, for both of them suffer from a lack of spare electrons, without which there can be no making of bonds. In reality, diborane (B_2H_6) gets 2 of its hydrogens to do double duty, each of them forming bonds with each boron atom in order to make a bridge between the 2 borons. They cannot do it by becoming electron donors, like the chlorine atoms in $BeCl_2$, because there are no spare, unbonded electrons in hydrogen in BH_3. The single $1s$ electron is already in a molecular orbital. Diborane, however we look at it, suffers from a deficiency of electrons, and is an example of a class known as electron-deficient compounds.

Before we understand how such compounds can exist, we must review our notions on the chemical bond and make sure that we have not taken our assumptions too far. We defined an ordinary, covalent chemical bond as one that shares 2 electrons in a molecular orbital. This was adequate for dealing with diatomic molecules (those composed of no more than 2 atoms), since such molecules can be held together by 1 or more bonds. We then moved on to compounds with more than 2 atoms, such as beryllium chloride, with its 1 beryllium atom and 2 chlorine atoms in the gaseous state, and much longer chains in the solid state. We still assumed something that was implicit in our original discussion: that any 2 electrons forming a bond are localized around the 2 atoms that are bonded together. But if a central atom in a triatomic molecule, such as beryllium in a molecule of gaseous beryllium chloride, is sharing 2 electrons with 2 chlorine atoms to form 2 bonds, is there really no interaction between them? Of course there is, and a polyatomic molecule can be perceived as having molecular orbitals that take into account all its electrons. However, it is so difficult to work in such terms, because of the extreme complexity of quantum mathematics when dealing with the effects of different electrons on each other, that chemists generally talk only in terms of localized molecular orbitals, that is, those that obey our implicit assumptions.

However, in order to understand some molecules, it is important to bear in mind the possibility of delocalized molecular orbitals. Thus, a triatomic molecule may have orbitals that cover all 3 atoms; a 4-atom molecule may have orbitals that cover all 4 atoms. An example of the latter is the common carbonate ion, CO_3^{2-}. This has been represented conventionally in chemistry textbooks as having 1 oxygen atom doubly bonded to the central carbon atom, and the other 2 oxygen atoms, each having an extra electron (hence the double negative charge of the ion, signified by the superscript 2−), singly bonded to the central carbon atom.

Modern methods of examining carbonate ions have shown, however, that all the oxygens are bonded in exactly the same way, each having about $1\frac{1}{3}$ bonds joining them to the central carbon atom. The partial bonding is a result of a delocalized molecular orbital. Instead of being localized between 1 oxygen and 1 carbon to make a second bond, it spreads over all the atoms in the molecule to bond them partially together.

Modern techniques of physical chemistry allow very precise

measurements of the size and shape of most molecules. It is such techniques, described in Chapter 4, that have helped create the new chemistry, with its changed understanding of the chemical bonds. When these techniques were applied to B_2H_6, it was found that 4 of the hydrogens are involved in straightforward chemical bonds with the boron atoms, 2 to each boron atom. The other 2 are involved in bonds that bridge the gap between the borons. The lengths of these boron-hydrogen bonds is greater than that of the "normal" boron-hydrogen bonds. This is because each B—H—B bridge is joined by a 3-center molecular orbital, capable of holding 4 electrons, yet there are only 2 electrons in each bridge, 1 from hydrogen and 1 from 1 of the 2 borons. A single bond (2 electrons) is thus linking 3 atoms. Although the bond is weaker than the ordinary, 2-electron single bond, it is nonetheless a regular chemical bond.

One other point about the bridge is that it has an identical boron atom at each end. Each boron contributes 1 electron to each of the 2 bridges and, since the atoms at the ends are the same, their electrons have exactly the same energy. It is thus not possible to say which electron in a particular bridge comes from which boron atom; the boron nucleus merely recognizes both electrons as boron electrons. Because of the energy differences between electrons of different atoms, electron-deficient compounds held together by bridges are fairly rare, existing (as far as we know) only when holding together atoms of the same element.

This does not mean that they cannot exist in more complex forms. During the 1960s, a host of boron hydrides was discovered in which more and more boron atoms were held together by bonds containing fewer and fewer electrons. One of the largest of these, discovered in 1963, is $B_{20}H_{16}$. The bigger boron hydrides are held together by a mixture of boron-boron, boron-hydrogen, and boron-hydrogen-boron bonds, with many of the boron-boron bonds being partial bonds formed from

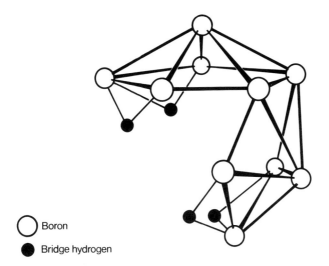

O Boron

● Bridge hydrogen

FIGURE 9. The structure of decaborane ($B_{10}H_{14}$), a highly electron-deficient molecule. Each of the boron atoms has 1 regular boron-hydrogen bond (these hydrogen atoms are not shown); in addition, there are 4 "bridge" hydrogens linking pairs of boron atoms, and each boron atom is linked to 3 or more other boron atoms. Bonds are shown as lines, for the sake of clarity.

delocalized orbitals. This gives the compounds compact structures, like that shown for decaborane ($B_{10}H_{14}$) in Figure 9. This has 10 regular B—H bonds, 4 B—H—B bridges, and 19 B—B bonds held together by a total of 16 electrons (an average of less than 1 per bond) which are in molecular orbitals that cover the whole of the boron skeleton.

While the story of boron and how it makes do with a shortage of electrons is fascinating, how important is electron-deficiency bonding in general? The answer is that every known metal is made up of electron-deficient orbital-excess atoms of the sort that are ripe for electron-deficient bonding with delocalized orbitals. Like the boron atoms in decaborane, which organize themselves into a tight structure so that their shared molecular orbital covers as small an amount of space as possible (why should an electron have to travel further than it need in its molecular "orbitaling"?), metals form tightly packed structures leading to regular crystals (an important property of metals) and mobility of electrons (another important property of metals, usually called conductivity).

Electrons Taken to Excess

The explanation of how electron-deficient compounds can exist was discovered when we found that our original assumptions about bonds, developed from diatomic molecules, were too simple. Now that we know how electron-deficient molecules work, maybe we should look again at the overall picture of bonding and see if anything else might fit in. How about, for example, a molecule with too many electrons, to make up for those with too few? Are there electron-excess compounds?

The answer is yes. The earliest known example is I_3^-, the tri-iodide ion. Iodine, which has an external electron skin similar to chlorine and fluorine, forms a diatomic molecule, I_2, in which the 2 atoms are joined by a single sigma bond, with no residual unfilled orbitals. Similarly, if an iodine atom gains an electron, it has a filled atomic orbital. Why should a mixture of I_2 and I^- form a bond to give the tri-iodide ion? The answer lies in a type of molecular orbital not mentioned before: the nonbonding orbital.

When a molecule involves more than 2 atoms, the molecular orbitals are spread out—in I_3^- to cover all 3 iodine atoms, a "3-center molecular orbital." Some electrons on the 2 outside atoms may be capable of interaction with each other, but not with the central atom. They could form a molecular orbital, but since they are separated by the central atom, the interaction is very weak, giving a nonbonding orbital which, as its name implies, does not contribute to the bonding. More important, from the point of view of the electron-excess compounds, it does not contribute to antibonding. So I_3^- has about the same bond strength as I_2. With little difference between them, we might expect to find, in a random mixture of I_2 and I^-, a number of I^- molecules.

Although a lot of scientific discoveries originate in happy accidents, there are also many cases in which we can point to discoveries not being made because they appeared impossible. Electron-excess compounds are a case in point. The tri-iodide ion remained a puzzle until molecular orbital theory explained its logical existence. Once it had been shown how electron-excess compounds can occur, a whole host of them were discovered, many quite similar to tri-iodide ion.

Perhaps the most important electron-excess compound discovered to date is hydrogen difluoride ion (HF_2^-), which is present in every solution of hydrofluoric acid. This is similar to the tri-iodide ion in a number of ways: it is formed by the mixture of 2 electronically stable species, hydrofluoric acid (HF) and fluoride ion (F^-), and it has 2 electrons in a nonbonding orbital. It differs by having its central atom (H) not identical to the other two atoms (F). Since 1960, several other hydrogen bihalide ions have been discovered (halide is a general term to describe compounds containing fluorine, chlorine, bromine or iodine), including several in which the outer 2 atoms of the triatomic molecule are different halides.

One reason for the interest in such compounds is that they are, in a way, prototypes of an important chemical bond, the hydrogen bond. Hydrogen bonds help to maintain the shape of many of the giant molecules of life. Without their stabilizing influence, these molecules would not perform their characteristic and necessary functions. Hydrogen bonds are very weak, only about one-fifth as strong as the bonds in an electron-excess compound such as hydrogen bifluoride, and about 20 times weaker than the single bond linking 2 hydrogen atoms in a hydrogen molecule.

The electron-excess, molecular orbital approach is not the only way in which to look upon the hydrogen bond. Hydrogen can also be viewed, if it is in a polar compound such as hydrogen fluoride, as an electron acceptor, able to accept a share of electrons from an electron donor atom such as oxygen. Water, one of the most common substances, is composed of just the 2 elements hydrogen and oxygen. Not surprisingly, it readily forms hydrogen bonds with itself, thus accounting for many of the properties which make it, from the chemist's viewpoint, a very unusual liquid. One such property is that many other substances dissolve in water. This is not surprising, for if they are electron donors, they will be attracted to the hydrogen atoms, and if they are electron acceptors, they will be attracted to the oxygen atoms.

The Not-so-Inert Gases

A set of compounds which contains no hydrogen, and which are not at the moment of very much importance, are the "noble gas compounds." They are noteworthy in that they provide an almost perfect case study of a discovery not being made because it is "impossible."

The noble gases were formerly called inert gases. Generations of chemists were taught that, because they had a complete set of s and p electrons, they would not form compounds. We have already seen that helium does not exist as a diatomic molecule because this means filling antibonding as well as bonding orbitals, so that everything cancels out. Imagine the surprise of Neil Bartlett, an English chemist working at the University of British Columbia, when early in 1962 he mixed together platinum hexafluoride and xenon and found that they immediately reacted to form a compound. This result was not totally unexpected. Nearly 30 years earlier, Nobel prizewinner Linus Pauling had predicted on theoretical grounds that some of the noble gases might form compounds. However, attempts to substantiate his hypothesis by experiment had failed, and such experimentation ceased in the belief that inert gas compounds were impossible.

During World War II, work on the atomic bomb, which contained uranium purified by a process that involved formation of uranium hexafluoride, led to much freer availability of fluorine, and development of expertise in its handling. The latter is a tricky business, since it is an extremely unpleasant element which can cause damage to lungs, eyes, and skin on contact.

The interest in uranium hexafluoride, which could be vaporized fairly easily—the key to its role in uranium purification—led to increased interest in the fluorides of other metals. A new way to purify a metal is always of interest because of possible commercial application, and after the war work was carried out at the Argonne National Laboratory on the preparation of fluorides of other rare metals, such as platinum, osmium, and iridium. At British Columbia, Bartlett was studying the hexafluorides of platinum, ruthenium, and rhenium. He discovered that platinum hexafluoride reacted with oxygen to form an ionic compound. Since during ionic compound formation an electron is transferred from one atom to another, it is reasonable to assume that there may be a relationship between the ease of compound formation and the ease of ionization of a molecule (ionization being the complete removal of an electron). Bartlett noted that the ionization energy of the oxygen molecule was very similar to that of the xenon atom. It was this that led to his crucial experiment.

Although he succeeded in making xenon compounds, Bartlett could not get a reaction between the hexafluoride and krypton, nor did he know what the xenon compounds were. He knew that they were compounds of xenon, but the details of how many bonds were involved and the structures of the compounds were still a mystery, although it looked as if they might be simple addition compounds, with the metal fluoride grabbing atoms of the inert gas and holding it in a bond.

Bartlett's work was soon followed up at the Argonne National Laboratory, where chemists Howard Claasen, Henry Selig, and John Malm found that the products of the reactions were not simple addition compounds. Could they be xenon fluorides? On August 2, 1962, they mixed together xenon and fluorine and heated them at 400° C for 1 hour; the result was xenon tetrafluoride (XeF_4). They later found that it was also possible to make 2 other fluorides of xenon, 1 containing 2 atoms of fluorine for each atom of xenon (XeF_2), the other containing 6 (XeF_6).

Following this exciting work, many chemists became interested in the noble gas compounds. In the last 10 years, krypton fluorides have been isolated, as well as a series of more complex xenon compounds containing oxygen, and a compound of xenon with another halogen element, xenon dichloride ($XeCl_2$). The bonding in the simple xenon fluorides is similar to that in the tri-iodide ion, and the bond energies are about the same as those found in diatomic halogen molecules, such as I_2.

Xenon dichloride has a much weaker bond, and no compounds involving other noble gases—helium, neon, argon—or other halogens—bromine, iodine—have yet been discovered. This is a function of the size of the atoms involved. The smaller the halogen, the fewer electron shells it has, and the tighter it binds electrons (and the stronger its attraction for other electrons). So it is not surprising that fluorine ($1s^2 2s^2 2p^5$), which is the halogen with the greatest attractive strength for alien electrons, forms most of the noble gas compounds. Chlorine has an additional shell of electrons shielding its nucleus from the outside world, so its nucleus has slightly less electron-pulling power than fluorine. Using the same reasoning, the noble gases which most readily form compounds are the heavier ones, with multiple electron shells shielding the nucleus, so that the outer electrons are relatively weakly held and can easily be borrowed by fluorine. The electrons in the smaller noble

gases, helium, neon, and argon, appear to be too tightly held
by their nuclei to permit sharing.

The Shapes of Molecules

Once the basic idea of a 3-center bond, such as that found
in XeF_2, is accepted, there is no reason why another neutral
molecule of fluorine should not be added to form XeF_4, and
then another added to form XeF_6. Why not go even further—
what about XeF_{28} or XeF_{102}?

Talking in general molecular orbital terms, it is possible to
forget the physical reality of molecules. What must not be
forgotten is that, as more atoms are added around a central
atom, the environment gradually becomes overcrowded. Repulsive forces between the electron clouds of adjacent atoms
come into play, altering the energy pattern until the energy
gained by bond formation is eventually outweighed by the
repulsion energies, and the result is no more bonds. Consequently, there are no molecules of XeF_{28} or of XeF_{102}

This restriction raises another interesting point. If there are
repulsive forces between electron clouds, how well can knowledge of molecular orbital theory, coupled with this concept of
repulsion, be used to calculate theoretically the shapes of
molecules? Quite well, if the molecule is simple enough. One
of the simplest with which to start is methane (CH_4), in which
4 hydrogen atoms are each joined to a carbon atom by bonds
formed from the s electron of the hydrogen atoms and sp^3
hybrids of the carbon atom. Each of these orbitals will repel
the other orbitals, and such repulsion needs energy to resist it.
So, for the most stable compound, the repulsions must be
minimized as much as possible. What is the best way to get
the orbitals as far away from each other as possible? The
mathematical answer is to place each hydrogen atom at 1
corner of a tetrahedron, with a carbon atom in the center.
This is the shape of methane: a tetrahedral molecule.

Take another compound, simple and fairly similar: ammonia
(NH_3). If we just look at this—3 bonds, 1 between each
hydrogen and the nitrogen—it would seem that the molecule
should be flat, with an angle of 120° between each bond. This
moves the *bonding* electrons as far away from each other as
possible, but nitrogen has 2 other electrons, its lone pair, to
take into account. They are just as repulsive to other electrons
as bonding electrons, so they cannot be ignored. Could the
shape be a tetrahedron again, like methane, with the lone pair
taking 1 of the hydrogen's places? This is a fair guess, but
there is another point to take into account. The lone pair
electrons are not shared with another atom; consequently, they
are more tightly bound to the nucleus than the bonding electrons, so we must place their orbital closer to the nitrogen than
the molecular orbital. This, in turn, affects the orientation of
the other 3 pairs of electrons—those involved in bonds. The
3 bonding orbitals are slightly closer together. In methane,
the angle between the C—H bonds is just over 109°, in ammonia, just over 107°.

We have now gone from carbon to nitrogen; the next step
is oxygen. Its hydride (that is, the compound it forms with
hydrogen) is water. Again we can imagine a tetrahedral water
molecule, with 2 lone pairs of electrons and 2 oxygen-hydrogen
bonds. But we now know, from our experience with ammonia,
that the lone pairs will be closer to the nucleus than the bonding pairs. Not only will they repel the bonding pairs more
strongly than the bonding pairs repel each other; the 2 lone
pairs will also strongly repel each other. The result is the
planar water molecule, with an angle between the 2 bonds of
just over 104°. The shapes of some simple molecules are shown
in Figure 10.

There is no reason why bonds formed by a carbon atom
should all form with the same other element. For example, a
carbon atom may participate in 3 carbon-hydrogen bonds and
1 carbon-fluorine bond, giving CH_3F. Will this still be tetra-

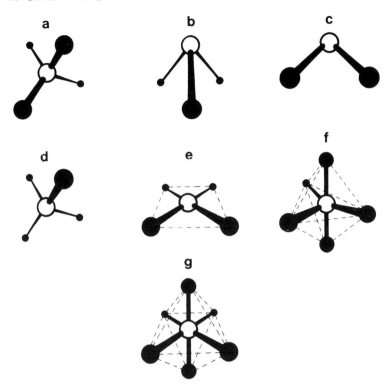

FIGURE 10. The shapes of some simple molecules. (a) methane (CH_4); (b) ammonia (NH_3); (c) water (H_2O); (d) fluoromethane (CH_3F); (e) platinum tetrachloride ion $(PtCl_4^{2-})$, a square planar molecule; (f) phosphorus pentachloride (PCl_5), a trigonal bipyramidal molecule; (g) hexaaquomanganese ion $(Mn(H_2O)_6^{2+})$, a tetragonal bipyramidal or octahedral molecule.

hedral? Basically, yes, for there are 4 bonds, each with a pair of bonding electrons that are mutually repulsive. Since we already know that fluorine has a strong affinity for alien electrons, we might expect the carbon-fluorine bond to be polarized, with the electron pair likely to be closer to the fluorine than to the carbon. For the carbon-hydrogen bonds, there will be less polarization. This means, in effect, that the carbon-fluorine bond is the reverse of a lone pair: the electron probability is

moved away from the carbon nucleus, thus reducing the electron-electron repulsion between this orbital and the 3 carbon-
hydrogen bond orbitals. However, the 3 carbon-hydrogen bond
orbitals all repel each other with equal strength. The result is
that the angles between carbon-hydrogen bonds increase
slightly, while the angle between each hydrogen and the fluorine
is slightly less than the tetrahedral angle.

This method of reasoning can be used to work out approxi-
mate shapes for many simple molecules. For example, if we
have a central atom surrounded by 5 different, but identical,
atoms, the best arrangement, allowing for electron repulsion,
is a trigonal bipyramid; for 6 surrounding atoms, the best
arrangement is a tetragonal bipyramid. Again, these shapes
may be adhered to by some molecules with lone pairs: xenon
tetrafluoride adopts a square planar shape, in which the molecule is flat with the XeF bond angles all 90°. It has 2 lone
pairs of electrons, 1 above and 1 below the plane. When these
are shown (as in Figure 10), we can see that the structure
is like a tetragonal bipyramid.

While this method of estimating molecular shapes is useful,
it does not always work, and is not suitable for large molecules containing many atoms. For this reason, all present-day
knowledge of molecular shapes comes from use of one of the
many tools that chemists and physicists have developed in the
last few decades. These methods, and some of the more complex aspects of molecular shapes, are discussed in later chapters, notably Chapter 4.

However, there is one area of chemistry which has been
closely studied in the last 20 to 30 years in which such reasoning is sufficient to predict general molecular shapes. This is the
field of coordination chemistry, which involves in particular
those elements with partially filled d electron subshells. Coordination chemistry is not restricted to these elements, for a
coordination compound is one in which there are one or more
donor-acceptor bonds, as $H_3N \cdot BH_3$ (see p. 52). However, be-

cause there are many elements with partially filled d electron subshells that will readily act as acceptor atoms (the so-called transition elements), much of coordination chemistry is concerned with them.

Although, as has already been explained, s electrons and p electrons can form sigma bonds, and p electrons may also form pi bonds, d electrons only rarely form bonds with one another. Because they are close in energy to nearby s and p states, d electrons tend to join in hybrid orbitals, such as the d^2sp^3 and the dsp^2 orbitals which form, respectively, octahedral and square planar compounds. For example, the octahedral hexacyanoferrate(II) ion is made up of an iron(II) ion (that is, an iron atom with 2 of its electrons missing) and 6 cyanide ions (CN^-). The iron atom has 6 electrons in the $3d$ subshell and 2 electrons in the $4s$ subshell. Iron(II) ion lacks the $4s$ electrons, and its 6 d electrons are spread out over 5 d orbitals. One of these has 2 electrons in it, and the other 4 hold 1 each. When iron(II) ion forms a complex with electron donor species, this arrangement alters. It is as if the 6 d electrons huddled together in 3 of the d orbitals, leaving 2 d orbitals completely empty and able to hybridize with the $4s$ and $4p$ orbitals (also empty) to form 6 empty hybrid d^2sp^3 orbitals. Each of these hybrid orbitals can be filled by a pair of electrons from a cyanide ion to form the complex hexacyanoferrate(II) ion.

Nickel, an element which shares a number of properties with iron—the ability to be magnetized, for example—has 8 $3d$ electrons and 2 $4s$ electrons. Its nickel(II) ion (no s electrons) will also form complexes with cyanide ions but, because there are 2 more electrons in the d level, only 1 d orbital is able to participate when hybridization occurs. Following from the previous example, we might expect a dsp^3 hybrid, capable of taking on 5 cyanide ions, but, although $Ni(CN)_5^{3-}$ is known, usually only 2 of the empty p orbitals join in, giving a dsp^2 (square planar) hybrid, $Ni(CN)_4^{2-}$.

How Molecules Move

An important aspect of stereochemistry, as the study of the arrangement in space of the atoms in a molecule is called, is the idea of a molecule as a dynamic rather than static object. If we take a set of molecules at a specific temperature, then the temperature (which we can measure) is an indication of the average energy content of the molecules. If the set of molecules is gaseous, it is in constant motion. Individual molecules bump into each other and into the walls of their container (it is this latter bumping that we measure when we measure gas pressure). When 2 molecules collide, they may exchange small amounts of energy, for the *average* which is signified by the temperature is made up from a collection of individual variable energy contents. We have already seen that stretching a hydrogen molecule by a small amount requires a little bit of energy, about one-thirtieth of the bond strength. Therefore, individual molecules can absorb and emit small quantities of energy by the stretching and contraction (vibration) of their bonds. The more bonds there are in a molecule, the greater the number of possible vibrations.

Another form of molecular dynamics is rotation. A hydrogen molecule, for example, can be imagined as being like a minute dumbbell, the 2 hydrogen nuclei forming the 2 ends, and the electron probability distribution representing the bar that joins them (H—H). Just as a dumbbell can be rotated about the middle of the joining bar, so a hydrogen molecule can rotate about the center of its single bond.

Both the rotation and vibrations of a molecule are restricted. All energy, as Max Planck showed at the turn of the twentieth century, is quantized. That is, it comes in small packets, and Planck's constant defines the smallest packet of energy that it is possible to have. The absorption of energy by molecules is also quantized. Particular sized packets of energies are required to effect the stretching and rotation of molecules, which means that particular types of energy are preferentially absorbed by different molecules. The differential absorption of various energy sources can be used to characterize molecules and is the basis of many of the techniques described in the next chapter.

Dumbbell style rotation is not the only way in which a molecule can rotate. In a compound joined by ordinary sigma bonds, the symmetry of the electron probability between adjacent nuclei makes it possible for them to rotate with respect to each other. In ethane, for example, 2 carbon atoms are joined together, and 3 hydrogen atoms are attached to each carbon atom. Each carbon atom is tetrahedral, as we would expect, giving a molecule shaped like that in Figure 11a. If the carbon atoms rotate about the sigma bond joining them, the 2 sets of 3 hydrogen atoms at each end of the molecule will act like little windmills. This process requires energy, because the electron clouds around the hydrogens at 1 end of the molecule will repel the electron clouds around the hydrogens at the other end of the molecule. Repulsion is minimized if the molecule adopts the "staggered" conformation, in which the hydrogens at 1 end are out of alignment with those at the other end. This allows the greatest distance between electron clouds. For rotation to be possible, the molecule must be able to pass through the "eclipsed" form, in which event it has to overcome the repulsion energy of the 2 electron clouds. Since they are well separated, this is only small—about the same amount as is needed to stretch a hydrogen molecule by 0.1 angstrom. However, it has been found with tetrabromoethane ($CHBr_2 \cdot CHBr_2$), where 2 hydrogens on each carbon have been replaced by the much larger bromine atoms, that 2 distinct forms of the molecule can be isolated at low temperatures. This is because the bulkiness of the bromines makes it difficult for them to rotate past one another. More energy is required than is available at low temperatures.

When pi bonds are present the situation becomes slightly

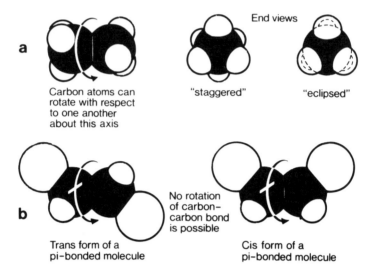

FIGURE 11.   (a) Rotation around a single bond in ethane (C_2H_6). Both atoms have other atoms arranged tetrahedrally around them but, because the 2 carbon atoms are joined by a single bond, they can rotate with respect to one another. This means that, when the molecule is looked at from 1 end, the hydrogen atoms attached to 1 carbon can adopt different positions with respect to those on the other carbon—the 2 extremes are the "eclipsed" form, in which the hydrogen atoms are aligned, and the "staggered" form, in which they are as far out of line as possible. Because of electron-electron repulsion between the hydrogen atoms attached to adjacent carbons, the "staggered" form is usually more stable than the "eclipsed" form. Where the substituent atoms are bulky, this electron-electron repulsion may hinder rotation to such an extent that different forms of the molecule can be isolated. (b) Where 2 carbon atoms are joined by a pi bond as well as a sigma bond, rotation is prevented. This means that, if the carbon atoms have different substituents, 2 distinct geometrical isomers (called *cis* and *trans*) are isolable.

more complex, for these bonds are directional in space. The 2 carbons in ethylene, which are joined by a sigma and a pi bond, can only rotate if the pi bond breaks. Although pi bonds are less energetically stable than sigma bonds, it nevertheless requires a substantial amount of energy to break a pi bond. Consequently, even at room temperature, a compound such as 1,2-dibromoethene (CHBr:CHBr) occurs in 2 forms, known as geometric isomers, which can be physically separated and which do not interconvert if kept in separate bottles on the laboratory shelf. Double bonds, or triple bonds (as found in the cyanide ion $^-C\equiv N$), are in a sense stiffeners of a molecule's backbone. This simile is particularly apt for the class of compounds known as organic compounds.

To a much greater extent than any other element, carbon is able to form bonds with itself. The result is an enormous number of carbon compounds, many of them with long chains or rings of carbon atoms linked together as a backbone. Since such compounds were first discovered in association with living things, the branch of chemistry that concerns itself with carbon chemistry has been called organic chemistry. However, this classification is breaking down as more and more interactions are found between carbon and elements with which it has not traditionally been associated.

The "stiffening" effect of pi bonds may, in certain circumstances, affect more than the 2 carbon atoms that are joined by the bond. Where more than one pi bond occurs in a molecule, with a single sigma bond separating the 2 pi bonds, it is possible for electron delocalization to occur, so that the pi electron cloud spreads over all 4 carbon atoms involved.

In addition to vibrational and rotational energy levels, which can absorb energy in a variety of ways from different sources, molecules also have electronic energy levels. Just as an electron in an atom can absorb a quantum of energy and thus move to a higher energy atomic orbital, so electrons in molecules can be promoted to higher molecular orbitals. Electrons in pi bonding orbitals can be promoted to antibonding pi orbitals, for example. In this case the molecule will still hold together, because the excess energy of the pi antibonding orbital is less than the energy deficiency of the sigma bonding orbital, which will still be filled with 2 electrons.

An electron delocalizes because delocalization alters the energy pattern favorably, thus stabilizing the molecule. It also lowers the energy level of the excited state, which means that the molecule has to absorb less energy to go from the ground to the excited state. Light is a form of energy, and the color of many objects is the result of compounds in them which contain delocalized electron systems and absorb particular wavelengths of light preferentially.

Geometrical isomerism of the type found in ethylene derivatives is not restricted to organic compounds. For example, platinum will form 4 equal bonds with chlorine atoms to give a $(PtCl_4)^{2-}$ complex, in which the electrons donated by the chlorine atoms form dsp^2 hybrids. The resultant complex is square planar, with the chlorine atoms arranged at the corners of a square surrounding the central atom. If a square planar complex is made from different constituent ligands (the atoms or groups donating electrons to the central atom), the square planar shape makes it possible to have geometric isomers which are not readily interconvertible (that is, which are sufficiently stable under ordinary conditions to be separated).

There is another aspect of the shapes of molecules that is common to organic compounds and to tetrahedral complexes of the coordination compounds. When all 4 substituents on a carbon atom are different, there is more than 1 possible way of arranging them so that they cannot be converted into one another without breaking bonds. The 2 arrangements possible with a simple compound are mirror images of each other, just as your left and right hands are mirror images (see Figure 12).

Nearly all the important molecules of life have at least 1 center of asymmetry, as such multisubstituted carbon atoms are called. Although a straightforward synthesis to produce molecules which have mirror images gives rise to a 50:50 mixture of the possible conformation, nature nearly always chooses only 1 of the 2 mirror images.

Most physical methods are unable to distinguish between

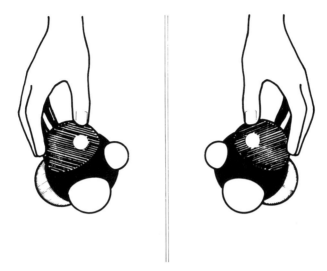

FIGURE 12. When a carbon atom (as an example of a simple compound) has 4 substituents attached, each different from the rest, more than 1 isomeric form is possible. The illustration shows 2 isomers which are mirror images of each other. Such mirror images differ in the effect they have on certain forms of light, and are consequently called optical isomers. Although 2 optical isomers behave in many of the same ways, most biological systems depend on one particular isomeric form.

a left-handed and a right-handed specimen of the same molecule. However, there are various methods based on their optical properties which can be used to differentiate them. For this reason, molecules which differ only in their handedness are called optical isomers.

A Note on Chemical Shorthand

Because many of the chemical compounds which interest scientists are complex combinations of many atoms of 2 or more elements, a shorthand system has been developed for writing down chemical structures. In its basic form, this shorthand is based on the simple combination of symbols for the elements (see Table 1) which are accepted world-wide. To represent a simple molecule, we use the symbols for the elements with subscript numbers indicating how many atoms of each element are in the molecule (where there is only 1 atom of an element, the subscript is omitted). A molecule of water, which contains 2 atoms of hydrogen and 1 of oxygen, can be written H_2O.

This system is useful for simple molecules, or for molecule-ions, such as H_2^+, in which the superscript plus sign indicates an imbalance of charge. But it only works well where it is obvious how the atoms are joined together. Since, for example, hydrogen usually forms only a single bond, it can be guessed that in H_2O each hydrogen is singly bonded to the oxygen atom. Similarly, in methane, CH_4, there are 4 hydrogen atoms all singly bonded to 1 carbon atom.

If it is important to indicate the bonds which link the atoms together, in simple cases this can be portrayed by dashes; in the case of H_2O, H—O—H shows the 2 single bonds. For methane it is necessary to use more space:

$$
\begin{array}{c}
\text{H} \\
| \\
\text{H—C—H} \\
| \\
\text{H}
\end{array}
$$

Where atoms are joined together by more than 1 bond, this system can still be used by employing double dashes for double bonds or triple dashes for triple bonds. For example, acetaldehyde is a molecule composed of 2 carbon atoms, 1 oxygen, and 4 hydrogens. The oxygen atom is doubly bonded to 1 of the carbon atoms, and this can be shown by depicting the formula as:

$$
\begin{array}{c}
\text{H} \\
| \\
\text{H—C—C=O} \\
| \ \ | \\
\text{H} \ \text{H}
\end{array}
$$

This clearly gives more information than the formula C_2H_4O. However, it is possible to combine the 2 forms to produce the formula $CH_3\underset{\overset{|}{H}}{C}{=}O$, since the CH_3 part is straightforward and does not need to be spelled out in detail. As more complex compounds are dealt with, such shorthand hybrids multiply. For example, the compound cyclopentane, made from 5 carbon atoms and 10 hydrogens, has the formula

$$
\begin{array}{c}
\mathrm{H}\diagdown\diagup\mathrm{H}\\
\mathrm{C}{-}\mathrm{C}\\
\mathrm{H}\diagup\diagdown\mathrm{H}\\
\mathrm{H}\diagdown\diagup\mathrm{H}\\
\mathrm{C}\mathrm{C}\\
\mathrm{H}\diagup\diagdown\mathrm{H}\\
\mathrm{C}\\
\mathrm{H}\diagup\diagdown\mathrm{H}
\end{array}
$$

but this is normally abbreviated to

in which neither carbon nor hydrogen atoms are indicated, but only the bonds linking the carbon atoms.

For very complex molecules, such as proteins, where three-dimensional structures are being indicated, even larger units are taken for granted, and a whole group of atoms may appear as a single point in a diagram.

Since the most important reason for illustrating many molecules is to show their three-dimensional structure, illustrations frequently veer away from straightforward chemical shorthand. Where such illustrations occur in this book, the method of illustration is explained in the caption.

4 The Mechanics of Chemistry

The importance of molecules to the chemist is that they react with each other to produce new and different molecules. In other words, the spatial relationships between atoms change; some chemical bonds break and new ones form. In a simple case, molecules of a single compound, such as the gas chlorine trifluoride (ClF_3) may break up to form a mixture of chlorine monofluoride (ClF) and fluorine (F_2) gases. Alternatively, 2 different sorts of molecules may come together to produce a single, different product (hydrogen and oxygen molecules react to form water) or a mixture of different products (methane burns in oxygen to form carbon dioxide and water).

The reactivity of molecules does not seem odd because we are used to seeing similar reactions in daily life—for example, gasoline, a liquid, goes into automobiles, and a mixture of quite different vapors emerges from the exhaust system. But are we justified in taking chemical reactivity for granted? If 2 atoms of hydrogen form a bonded molecule, with a release of energy which makes the material more stable (see Chapter 3), then we might expect that there would be no free hydrogen atoms anywhere. Similarly, when 2 hydrogen molecules and an oxygen molecule react to produce 2 molecules of water, energy is released. The 2 water molecules are more stable than the 3 elemental molecules we started with.

An immediate answer to the question of why all the hydrogen and oxygen available has not stabilized itself by conversion to water is proximity. Outer space contains numerous isolated clouds of hydrogen gas; the earth's atmosphere is 20 percent oxygen gas. An extraterrestrial hydrogen cloud, millions of miles from the earth, obviously cannot react with atmospheric oxygen. A chemical bond is very short, and it is reasonable to suppose that if such a bond is to form between 2 atoms, they must approach each other to within bond length distance. In general, we consider it necessary for 2 molecules to collide to make a reaction occur between them.

The number of collisions—and we might expect the rate of a reaction, that is, the speed with which reactants are converted into products, to be connected with the frequency of collisions of reactable molecules—will depend on the state of the reacting substances. Gas molecules, for example, move more freely than molecules in liquid, although, by comparison with solids, the motion of liquid molecules is quite free. However, gases can be kept under low pressure, with few molecules occupying a large amount of space; this will lower collision frequency. On the other hand, under high pressure, collisions should take place more often. In that case, and taking into account the extra stability introduced into the system by reaction, why is it possible to keep a mixture of oxygen and hydrogen gases together in a container at high pressure without any apparent reaction? Like a rock balanced at the top of a hill, why doesn't the reaction roll down into the energy valley and reach greater stability? Why, in the millions of years since the universe began, haven't all the energy releasing reactions between adjacent molecules taken place to produce a stable, that is, unreactive, universe?

The answer is that rocks do not always roll downhill. Often they need a push to overcome inertia: in order to release the rock's potential energy, a small amount of energy must be put into it to get it going. Chemical reactions are the same; they need a push to get them going.

Disregarding for a moment the type of push needed, do all reactions represent a downhill roll? Are there none that are like climbing uphill? A moment's thought shows that there must be some, for many reactions can be seen to work in 2 directions. We may see a set of reactants being converted into products, while elsewhere those products are being converted back into reactants. J. A. Campbell, professor of chemistry at Harvey Mudd College, California, summed this up when he wrote: "The iron sides of a blast furnace rust, while inside the furnace rust is changing into iron. . . . At one spot in the forest a tree rots in the presence of oxygen to form carbon dioxide and water, while in another spot the water and carbon dioxide just released by the rotting are reacting to form new wood and oxygen." [1]

From elementary physics, we know that a boulder perched atop a gulley has potential energy. When it starts rolling, this energy is converted into kinetic or motional energy. Because of the frictional forces between the rock and the ground over which it is rolling, this kinetic energy is converted into heat energy.

From the viewpoint of the present investigation, we are interested in the energy of molecules, which is known as free energy. The free energy of a substance can be divided into 2 parts: one is enthalpy, the other a function involving entropy. When a reaction occurs, there is usually an overall change in the free energy of the system. Before going further, let's define "system."

Scientists generally divide systems into 3 types. First is the isolated system which is never influenced from outside in any way; neither energy nor matter can be introduced into or can escape from an isolated system. The only example of an isolated system is the whole universe. Consequently, chemists are not much concerned with isolated systems, but are interested mainly in closed or open systems. In a closed system, no matter is lost to the outside, nor is any introduced, but

[1] J. A. Campbell, "Why Chemical Reactions Occur," in *Modern Chemistry*, ed. J. G. Stark (Baltimore: Penguin Books, 1970), pp. 113–140.

a closed system may exchange energy with its surroundings. A chemical reaction taking place in a sealed container is a closed system. In an open system, on the other hand, both matter and energy exchanges with the outside can take place, as when a kettle of water is boiled: energy is introduced from the outside and, if we let the kettle boil for a few minutes, water vapor is passed out of the system (the kettle). There is an exchange of both matter and energy.

Sorting Out the Energy Changes

Some of the energy change in a reaction may be visible. For example, cellulose—a major component of paper—will burn in air to form carbon dioxide and water. We can detect energy given off by this reaction in the forms of heat and light. If we measure energy changes of this kind—not necessarily flame; we might perform a heat producing reaction in which there is no sign of flame, such as mixing water and sulphuric acid, which react together and heat up the resultant solution—we are measuring the change in enthalpy.

The entropy part of a molecule's free energy is a measure of its "randomness." The change in entropy measures the change of randomness of a reacting system. If we take the burning of cellulose, it is easy to see intuitively that at the end of the reaction the system is more random—closer to chaos, if you like—than it was when we began. The molecules of carbon dioxide and water produced by the burning of a sheet of paper spread about the room in a way that the paper did not. The randomness of entropy is more general than this. Entropy increases whenever the energy of a system is spread out more at the end of a reaction than it was at the beginning. When 2 molecules of NO_2 break up into 2 molecules of NO and 1 of O_2, energy can dissipate through additional molecular movements. The overall extent of organization is less.

The free energy change in a reacting system is represented by an equation in which the entropy change multiplied by the temperature is subtracted from the enthalpy change. For a reaction to occur spontaneously, the free energy change in a system at constant temperature and pressure must be less than zero. Since the equation contains a minus sign and a variable (temperature), the spontaneity of a reaction depends to some extent on its temperature. At room temperature, calcium oxide (quicklime) spontaneously absorbs carbon dioxide gas to form calcium carbonate, the main constituent of both limestone and marble. But at temperatures of more than 800° C, the sign of the free energy change for this reaction swings from negative to positive. (Calcium carbonate is more ordered than a mixture of carbon dioxide and quicklime, so the entropy in forming calcium carbonate is negative. Since this negative value is being subtracted from the enthalpy change, it becomes positive and, being multiplied by temperature, an increasing positive factor as temperature increases. Consequently, the swing of the free energy change from negative to positive now makes the reverse reaction spontaneous. Calcium oxide is made commercially by roasting carbonate rock.)

From the size of the free energy change of a system under any given conditions, we can calculate the extent of the reaction, a measure of its completeness. If 2 compounds which react together rapidly to form a single third compound are mixed together, after a while, if the temperature and pressure are kept constant, we shall probably find that we have a mixture of all 3 substances, starting materials and product, which remains constant in its proportions. When the reaction begins, the starting materials are the only types of molecule present. Since 2 molecules must collide in order to join together, the rate at which they react should slow down as product is formed, since there will be fewer free molecules of starting material. On the other hand, there is an increasing number of molecules of product which may be bumped into by other molecules and knocked apart. As more product forms, the rate of this backward reaction will increase until it equals the rate of the forward reaction. When they are both equal, no further change occurs; a state of equilibrium has been reached.

By employing a mathematical thermodynamic treatment, it can be shown that a mixture of starting materials and products in a closed system can be more "random" than a mixture in which all the starting materials had been used up in forming products. Of course, if the product is removed from the system —if an open system is used—this equilibrium will not be established. One method used by chemists to maximize the products from a reaction is to remove them as they are formed. Although the remaining molecules of starting materials will try to catch up with the equilibrium that is thus put out of balance, their overall number, and consequently the number of collisions and the rate of the reactions, are decreasing.

Thermodynamics, which is the word used to describe the study of and formulation of laws about energy changes, also provides an equation which relates equilibrium to the free energy change of a reaction. Where this change is zero, for a simple reaction in which one molecule converts to another, the equilibrium is 50:50. An equilibrium mixture from such a reaction always contains half starting materials and half products. As the change becomes increasingly negative, the products of a reaction are favored more at equilibrium until, with quite small free energy changes, the amount of starting material present at equilibrium is immeasurably small. Such reactions are called quantitative because, insofar as we can measure, all the starting material has been turned into products.

Energy to Make Things Go

We now know how to tell whether a reaction will occur spontaneously, and to what extent. If we consult thermodynamic tables, from which we can find the free energies, enthalpies, and entropies of many materials, we see that, for a flask of hydrogen and oxygen at room temperature and atmospheric pressure, the equilibrium favors spontaneous change of nearly all of it into water (assuming that the proportions of hydrogen and oxygen are 2:1 as they are in the product). What we do not know is how fast the reaction will occur. This book has not burned away since you read that it was made primarily of cellulose, for which the free energy change of oxidation (burning) is negative. Like a flask of hydrogen and oxygen in a laboratory, the book has not had the necessary push to get the reaction going.

Not only molecules are dynamic, in constant motion; a reaction is also dynamic, being a process which follows a specific pathway and takes a definite amount of time. Complex molecules may follow more than 1 pathway to produce different sets of products, but for the moment we will keep to a simple reaction model. The fact that the time taken for an individual molecule to react is usually too small to be measured does not mean that reactions occur instantaneously; a chemist in a laboratory will be dealing with uncountable millions of molecules, so that the time taken for all, or even a noticeable amount, of the molecules to react can be quite long. The study of the time taken for reactions to occur in noticeable amounts is called reaction kinetics, while the examination of the pathways taken is the chemistry of reaction mechanisms.

A key concept in reaction mechanisms is the transition state or activated complex. Earlier it was stated that it was necessary for 2 molecules to collide for a reaction to take place, but necessary does not mean sufficient. For example, since molecules occupy space and have definite three-dimensional configurations, it is possible for them to collide so that the parts between which new bonds can form are still too far apart. The geometry of the collision must be right, or the 2 molecules will just bounce off each other. Assuming that the collision geometry is right, what happens then? In diagraming the act we can just erase any existing bonds and draw in the new ones, but in reality there must be a breaking and making of bonds over a period of time. The activated complex is the molecular state in which the alteration of structure is actually taking place. These complexes are rarely isolated, for they are usually gone too quickly to be noticed.

The compound methyl chloride (CH_3Cl) reacts in solution with a hydroxide ion (OH^-) to give methyl alcohol (CH_3OH) and a chloride ion (Cl^-). In effect, a carbon-chlorine bond is broken and a carbon-oxygen bond formed. It is possible to envisage a transition state in this reaction in which both the oxygen of the hydroxide and the chlorine are partially attached to the carbon atom (in orbital terms, there is an overlap of electron clouds of carbon with the electron clouds of the oxygen and chlorine). This is unstable, because the carbon now has an "extra" bond. Nevertheless, the complex is transiently formed and then breaks up, either to give methyl alcohol and chloride ion, or to regenerate starting materials. What happens here depends to some extent on other collisions. If other molecules bump into the reacting complex and thereby drain energy from it, they are helping a negative enthalpy change—which in this case is the formation of the alcohol. If energy is not drained off, the complex may split up into the original materials, for the complex itself has more energy than they do. The complex is unstable because it has extra energy; its formation has required this energy being put into it to overcome the decrease in entropy that usually occurs when a transition state is formed.

Energy transfer occurs by collisions between molecules, just as kicking a football transfers energy from foot to ball. The energy of any collection of molecules as a whole is an average of the energies of all the individual molecules within that collection. Some of the individuals will have more energy than most, some will have less. A few will probably have enough energy to form an activated complex. The proportion of such molecules can be calculated; they are the ones that already have the push in them to get over the energy barrier and roll downhill to form products. The height of the barrier is called the activation energy.

When a pair of molecules forms the complex and rolls downhill to form products, energy is released. If the enthalpy change of the reaction is large, a correspondingly large amount of energy is released. This may be taken up by unreacted molecules, thus supplying them with the energy required to surmount the activation barrier. A piece of paper does not catch fire spontaneously in air. If you supply energy to a small part of it by focusing the sun's rays onto it through a powerful magnifying glass, once the paper has caught fire it will continue to burn because the initial reaction produces enough energy to get adjacent molecules over the activation energy barrier. Drop a match into that flask of oxygen and hydrogen and the same thing will happen, but more quickly. It explodes.

Different reactions have high or low activation energies, depending on the reaction pathway. The chemist has available to him a number of ways in which he can supply energy to a collection of molecules to help them over the activation energy barrier—in other words, to get the reaction going at a speed which suits him. The most obvious is to heat the mixture.

Another alternative is to raise molecules to an energy level higher than the activation barrier. This can sometimes be done with light; a molecule may absorb light of a specific wavelength and, as a result, have one of its electrons promoted from a bonding to an antibonding orbital (excitation). Overall, this molecule may now be raised above the level of the activation barrier for the reaction. Assuming it makes a satisfactory collision with the molecule with which it is to react, it will probably form the intermediate complex. Light may also be used to induce those reactions in which a single molecule reacts by breaking up, collision with a "photon" of light energy being sufficient to break some bonds.

Light is required for the reaction to work between chlorine gas (Cl_2) and methane—which, among other substances, forms methyl chloride. This is because the reaction mechanism involves the collision between a chlorine atom and a methane molecule, and light supplies the energy to split chlorine molecules into single atoms.

Reassessing "Simple" Chemistry

To show that even the "simplest" chemistry cannot pass unchallenged, we shall mention here a favorite reaction of all chemistry textbook writers: the reaction between hydrogen and iodine molecules to form hydrogen iodide. For years it was taught that this reaction involves a 4-atom complex: a molecule of hydrogen (2 singly bonded atoms) and a molecule of iodine (2 singly bonded atoms) collide and form a square, joined together by "half bonds." This reaction intermediate was then supposed to break up into 2 molecules of hydrogen iodide. However, in early 1967, J. H. Sullivan published the results of a reexamination of this reaction, which showed that the first step may be the breakup of the iodine molecule into iodine atoms, and that 2 separated iodine atoms then react with a hydrogen molecule.

Only a few years earlier than Sullivan's discovery, Norman Davidson, working at the California Institute of Technology with a technique called flash photolysis, had shown that another reaction involving iodine was not as simple as imagined. In flash photolysis, a technique developed in 1949 by Nobel prizewinners R. G. W. Norrish and Sir George Porter, a reaction is subjected to a very intense flash of light of very short duration.

When iodine is flash photolyzed, the molecules break down
into atoms, and a spectrometer is used to follow the rate at
which free iodine atoms recombine to form iodine molecules.
It was found that the rate of recombination was higher
when the reaction occurred in solution than when the reaction
was performed in the gas phase. The reason put forward for
this was that the solution contained abundant other molecules to drain off energy when 2 iodine atoms collide, so that
the bond between them is formed and they do not fly apart
again. In the gas phase, such "3 body" collisions are less likely,
hence the rate of recombination is lower. Closer examination
of the reaction revealed that this was too simple an explanation, for as the concentration of iodine molecules increased,
the rate of recombination also increased (since there would be
fewer free iodine atoms to recombine, we would expect it to
decrease). Davidson showed that what was happening was
the formation of I_3 as an intermediate. A free iodine atom
collides with an iodine molecule and forms a 3 atom iodine
molecule. When I_3 collides with another iodine atom, 2 molecules of I_2 are formed. So what we might have suspected
to be a very simple reaction mechanism—the bumping together
of 2 atoms—is actually a process with 2 steps. The 2 steps
make it easier to dissipate the energy released by bond
formation, and thus make reaction more likely than recoil of
the reactants.

As activation energy also depends on reaction pathway, it is
possible to effect some difficult reactions (those with high
activation energies) by providing an alternative pathway which
has a lower activation energy. By changing the reaction pathway, we do not change the energy relationships between the
starting materials and the products. The only energy change is
in the height of the barrier—the amount of inertia that prevents the whole system rolling downhill to equilibrium. Consequently, the equilibrium is not changed by altering the reaction pathway.

Of great importance to living as well as to industrial processes are substances called catalysts. Traditionally these are defined as substances which alter the rate of a chemical reaction, but which remain unchanged themselves at the end of the reaction. From this definition, it seems likely that catalysts work by changing the reaction pathway, smoothing out the bump of activation energy. In addition, some also help in ensuring that when a collision between reactants occurs, the collision geometry is right for reaction.

Since catalysts do not affect equilibrium, are they of any use in effecting reactions for which equilibrium is unfavorable? They can be, for while a catalyst only alters the activation energy, a molecule reaching the activated state can run downhill from that peak into either the products side or the reactants side. Statistically, equilibrium will make it roll one way or another according to the change in free energy of the reaction. But we must remember that free energy only measures the likelihood of a reaction occurring spontaneously. A particular free energy value is only good for a particular temperature—we have already seen that the chalk into quicklime and carbon dioxide reaction depends on the temperature. The free energy equation also depends on there being no change in temperature or pressure. In the end, because no reaction is an isolated system, it is usually possible for the chemist who really wants to make a particular compound to juggle energy inputs and matter outputs in such a way that he gets it.

While the good chemist is always conscious of the limitations placed upon him by thermodynamics, he is usually more interested in making particular products, regardless of cost in terms of money or energy (this is not true in industry, which generally does not bother with reactions which have a substantially positive free energy change), and in finding out what the compounds he has made are, and how they form. Except with simple reactions, he is likely to produce a mixture of products which needs to be separated and identified.

New Instruments for Chemical Tunes

Take a chemist who wants to make an entirely new compound, perhaps because he believes it will be useful as a new pharmaceutical. He first decides on the structure the final molecule should have, and then on how it is likely to be made (this may involve many consecutive reactions), mostly from researching published work that may have a bearing on the different pieces of molecule he is putting together. Once he has his scheme, he can start work in the laboratory. But how does he know if things are coming out right? Is his first reaction producing the desired product, or a different product, or a mixture? How fast is it producing whatever products are being formed?

These are questions which can be answered by an increasing range of instruments. A century ago, it was impossible to work out the structure of any but the most simple molecules. Fifty years ago, the structures of more complex molecules could be worked out in greater detail, but only by lengthy procedures which often consumed substantial quantities of material in the process. A chemist who has worked to make a small amount of some new substance does not want to see it used up in analytical tests to determine its structure. Fortunately, the rise of instrumental chemistry now allows most chemists to determine structures, frequently in minutes and days (although sometimes still in months), with small quantities of materials. What has happened to make today's chemical laboratories so different in their methods and techniques from laboratories before World War II?

The major breakthroughs have been in spectroscopy, which may be divided into several distinct types. All the instrumental methods rely on the interaction between matter and some portion of the electromagnetic spectrum. The electro-

TABLE 2
The Electromagnetic Spectrum

	X-RAYS NEUTRONS ELECTRONS	ULTRAVIOLET VISIBLE	INFRARED	MICROWAVE	RADIOWAVE
Wavelength	1 Å (10⁻¹⁰ m) 1000 Å (10⁻⁷ m)	1 μm (10⁻⁶ m) 10 μm (10⁻⁵ m)	100 μm (10⁻⁴ m) 1 mm (10⁻³ m)	1 cm (10⁻² m) 1 m	10 m 100 m
Frequency (Hz; cycles per second)	3×10^{18}	3×10^{14}	3×10^{12}	3×10^{10} 3×10^{8}	3×10^{6}
Energy quantum (kcal per mole)	286,000	286	2.86	2.86×10^{-3}	2.86×10^{-6}

magnetic spectrum is merely a blanket phrase covering all those waves that travel at the speed of light and do not need a medium for their propagation; that is, they can travel through a vacuum. Table 2 shows the main subdivisions of the electromagnetic spectrum, from x-rays at the high energy end to radio waves at the low energy end. All these forms of electromagnetic radiation are used in chemical analysis today, but for the moment we shall stay near the middle, in the ultraviolet and visible part of the spectrum.

It has already been mentioned that certain molecules absorb ultraviolet or visible radiations because these contain the amount of energy required to bump a pi electron from a bonding into an antibonding orbital. Bonding electrons may also be jerked into nonbonding orbitals by similar amounts of energy and, in certain cases, a lone pair electron can move to a higher energy state by absorbing ultraviolet or visible radiation. Generally, the ultraviolet spectrum of a compound is measured over a narrow range that will only show up absorptions from p and d orbitals, and pi orbitals. (It should be borne in mind that, even in organic compounds, pi bonding is not restricted to carbon-carbon bonds; double bonds between carbon and oxygen and carbon and nitrogen, in which 1 bond is sigma, 1 pi, frequently occur.)

An ultraviolet spectrum can be measured in a number of ways. The most general is to pass ultraviolet radiation through a sample of the chemical being studied, and determine how much of the radiation is absorbed. By using scanning spectrometers it is possible to vary the wavelength over a range, and thus detect which wavelengths are most strongly absorbed. This would be the method of choice for examining a compound of unknown structure. By comparing the wavelengths of maximum absorption with reference data, it is possible to suggest particular groupings of atoms which seem likely to occur.

Although the spectroscopies, with some exceptions, are not

new, their rapid development since the end of World War II has been dependent on 2 factors: advances in instrument manufacture, and increasing availability of reference data correlating particular aspects of molecular structure with particular absorptions. Determining the ultraviolet spectrum of an unknown compound would be useless if the absorptions at different wavelengths could not be identified by reference to data previously collected by examining the spectra of a wide range of known compounds.

Ultraviolet spectroscopy can be extended to more energetic wavelengths which energize sigma bonds, but this technique is not widely used since the experiments must be performed under vacuum conditions, to prevent the interaction of air molecules with the radiation. In consequence, unless a compound contains p and d or pi orbitals, its ultraviolet spectrum will tell us nothing. The same is not true of infrared spectra.

In 1953, Professor Bryce Crawford, Jr., of the University of Minnesota, wrote: "Infrared spectroscopy has grown like a mushroom in the past 10 years. Before the war it was employed by only a few chemists and physicists, using home-built or custom-built infrared spectrometers. Now the instrument is a standard commercial item supplied by a competitive industry to chemical and medical researchers all over the country [U.S.]. More than 1300 commercial infrared spectrometers, each representing an investment of two to six Cadillacs, are earning their way in scientific laboratories and industrial plants." [1] The mushroom has continued growing; you would now have to trade in a handful of infrared spectrometers before getting a Cadillac in exchange. But then, there are far more to trade in. Most chemical laboratories have several, generally ranging from a simple routine model, which an undergraduate student can learn to use in half an hour, to complex machines designed for

[1] "Chemical analysis by infrared," Bryce Crawford, Jr., *Scientific American* (October 1953), p. 42.

advanced research into infrared spectroscopy itself. The latter are gradually pushing back the wavelength frontiers to the limits of the infrared region of the spectrum, making the technique useful for a wider range of chemical problems. For example, many routine infrared machines have a wavelength range from $0.25 - 1.5 \times 10^{-5}$ meter, which is useful for the study of organic compounds. However, many metal-ligand bonds interact with longer wavelength radiations (ca. 2.5×10^{-5} meter, and this range is only gradually becoming available on routine laboratory instruments.

In what way does a molecule interact with this part of the electromagnetic spectrum, which cannot be sufficiently powerful to push an electron from one energy level up to the next higher? Molecules do undergo other transitions of lower energies; these have already been described as stretching—generally called vibration spectra—and rotation of bonds. Since the development of infrared spectroscopy in the 1930s, an enormous number of spectra of known compounds has been catalogued and, from this, it has been possible to isolate particular groupings with characteristic absorptions. For example, the ketone or aldehyde group, C=O (carbonyl), usually absorbs strongly radiation of between about 0.57 and 0.59×10^{-5} meter wavelength. No exact absorption wavelength can be given, because the remainder of the molecule interacts with its carbonyl function, and such interactions shift the carbonyl absorption up or down the scale by a small amount. However, by comparing a spectrum of an unknown organic compound with a table of absorptions, it is possible to gather numerous clues about its molecular structure.

A chemist studying an organic compound of unknown structure will find a scanning infrared spectrometer most useful, quickly showing him the major absorption frequencies over a wide range. For following a particular reaction, both infrared and ultraviolet spectroscopy at a single wavelength can be used. If, for example, we are studying the kinetics of a reaction (that is, the rate at which it occurs and the factors on which it depends), and we know that one of the products has a strong infrared or ultraviolet absorption at a particular wavelength which is not present in any of the starting materials, it may be possible to perform the reaction in a vessel linked to a spectrometer set at that specific wavelength, and thus follow the build-up of product by the increase in intensity of absorption. Intensity of absorption can be related to concentration by using simple equations, thus allowing the actual amount of product formed to be calculated.

If a chemist is performing an unknown reaction, he can follow the disappearance of starting materials by the disappearance of a characteristic frequency. Such techniques are useful for checking qualitative progress. For example, suppose that a ketone is being converted to some other compound which contains no carbonyl group. If the reaction has not been done before, the chemist will have no idea how long it will take or even where the equilibrium lies. But if once every half hour he removes a tiny portion of his reaction mixture—only the smallest drop is required—from the reaction flask and quickly runs an infrared spectrum on it, he will be able to see whether the carbonyl peak is disappearing satisfactorily. If a noticeable decrease takes place at first and then stops, he can guess that equilibrium has been reached and there is no point in continuing the reaction. He can now set about separating his products from the residual starting materials. Among these separation processes, he will probably use at least 1 that was not available 30 years ago. But separation must wait until we have finished with the spectroscopies. The next ones we consider owe a lot to World War II, for it helped them to get going.

Molecular Radio

The interaction of radiofrequencies with molecules was noticed in the 1930s, but it was the extensive development of radar during World War II that provided the expertise required to make spectroscopy in this part of the spectrum feasible. The earliest to be developed was microwave spectroscopy.

Microwave spectroscopy, which utilizes wavelengths between 1 mm and 10 cm, measures the rotational spectra of molecules, and is restricted to fairly simple molecules. As mentioned earlier, we can imagine a diatomic molecule as a dumbbell in which the 2 ends rotate about the center. Altering the speed of rotation requires energy in quantized units which is often from the long infrared or microwave regions. Microwave spectra provide information on bond lengths and, in more complex molecules such as sulphur dioxide, bond angles. Although this technique is not applicable to problems involving the extremely complex molecules of interest to many chemists, it is of use to the physical chemist in making precise measurements on simple molecules and in providing some information not available from other sources.

The compounds formed between small organic chemical groups and transition metals are not open to complete structural elucidation by infrared or ultraviolet spectroscopy; however, as an example, microwave spectroscopy provided the clues necessary in 1958 to deduce the structure of nickelcyclopentadienyl nitrosyl (C_5H_5NiNO). It is also possible to demonstrate minor peculiarities in molecules. Benzene (C_6H_6) has a flat ring structure; using microwaves, it was possible to show in the early 1960s that in certain substituted benzenes, such as benzonitrile (C_6H_5CN), the ring is deformed by the group attached to it.

Hindered rotation of groups past one another in propyl fluoride was also detected in the 1960s; microwave spectroscopy showed 2 distinct forms similar to the different forms of tetrabromoethane, mentioned at the end of Chapter 3. Finally, microwave spectra can be used to pinpoint unusual isotopes in a molecule. The most common form of carbon is carbon-12, which has 6 neutrons and 6 protons in its nucleus. Another isotope, carbon-13, has an extra neutron. Obviously, this makes the atom slightly heavier, and affects the energy needed to rotate a molecule containing it. In addition, the energies will differ slightly according to the location of the heavy carbon atom in the molecule. Thus, microwave spectroscopy can be used to identify molecules of methylacetylene with a ^{13}C atom in the methyl group ($^{13}CH_3C\equiv CH$) as different from those in which the ^{13}C is the middle carbon atom in the molecule ($CH_3{}^{13}C\equiv CH$).

More important to the chemist trying to work out structures of complex compounds are forms of spectroscopy which combine the behavior of molecules in magnetic fields with their interaction with radiowaves or microwaves. Some of these techniques were made possible by the immense technical development of radio and microwave generation methods during work on radar systems in World War II, but the actual effects involved were not discovered until after the war. In 1946, building on the basis of prewar work on nuclear magnetism by Nobel prizewinning physicists Otto Stern and I. I. Rabi, American physicist Edward Purcell and Swiss-American Felix Bloch discovered the nuclear magnetic resonance (nmr) effect. They were awarded the Nobel physics prize jointly for their discovery in 1952; like a number of other physicists' discoveries, this proved of more benefit to chemists as a practical tool.

Basically, any element which has an unpaired proton in its nucleus will behave like a small bar magnet. In a magnetic field, the nucleus can take up either of 2 orientations: one aligned with the magnetic field, the other opposed to the magnetic field. The second state has the higher energy and, by passing microwave or radiowave frequencies through molecules containing such nuclei, it is possible to flip the aligned nuclei into the higher energy state. Not many common nuclei have unpaired protons (a nucleus with an odd number of protons is not the same; from a nuclear spin point of view, a proton can pair with a neutron). Fortunately for the organic chemists, one of the elements most common in the compounds with which they deal does have an unpaired nuclear spin. That is hydrogen.

Proton magnetic resonance—nuclear magnetic resonance concerned solely with hydrogen—can provide the chemist with much information about the environment of hydrogen atoms in a molecule, for the surroundings—how electron clouds are spread around in nearby orbitals—slightly affect the interaction between the applied magnetic forces and any particular hydrogen atom. As a result, differently placed hydrogen atoms in a molecule have slightly different flipping energies. From the "perturbations"—energy changes caused by "shielding" or "deshielding" of a particular nucleus—it is possible, for example, to tell the difference between a —CH_3 group and a =CH_2 group. Since the spectrum also gives an idea of the concentration of particular species, it is possible to solve points of fine structure that are ambiguous in infrared studies.

A few other nuclei have the required unbalanced spin for nuclear magnetic resonance; fluorine is one example. It is also possible to use unusual isotopes of nuclei that commonly do not have unpaired spin. The heavy carbon isotope ^{13}C is currently in wide use for advanced nuclear magnetic resonance studies.

In addition to unpaired nuclei, unpaired electrons can also flip in a magnetic field to give electron spin resonance (esr) spectra. Unfortunately, most chemical compounds do not have unpaired electrons. However, if a molecule with paired electrons breaks up, so that a 2-electron bond is broken evenly, 1 electron goes to each part of the molecule, and both fragments, called "free radicals," will then have unpaired electrons. This is not the only way bonds break. Both electrons may go to 1 fragment, making it negatively charged and leaving the other fragment positively charged. However, unpaired electrons are found sufficiently often to make esr a useful addition to the chemist's armory of instruments.

Electron spin resonance is fashionable for studies on the mechanisms of reactions and their kinetics (where free radicals are involved). It can also show some interesting structural features of molecules that might not be expected. For example, both methane (CH_4) and tetrafluoromethane (CF_4) are tetrahedral molecules, involving carbon sp^3 hybrid orbitals. When 1 bond in each is broken to give the radicals $\cdot CH_3$ and $\cdot CF_3$ (the dot indicates the single electron), different structures result: $\cdot CH_3$ forms a planar molecule, the sort one would get from sp^2 hybridization, while $\cdot CF_3$ stays tetrahedral. Although it might be possible to anticipate this result from theoretical considerations, esr shows it to be the case.

Make Way for a Gamma-Ray

The most recent addition to the spectroscopic work force is another example of experimental physics being appropriated by the chemists. During the late 1950s, Rudolf Mössbauer was studying aspects of the behavior of γ-rays at the Munich Institute of Technology in Germany. A few months after he finished his doctoral work, during the summer of 1958, he first observed the Mössbauer effect. If a nucleus emits γ-rays, these usually have a range of energies, because the nucleus itself recoils as the γ-ray is emitted, just as a rifle recoils when a bullet is fired. However, if the nucleus is embedded in a solid matrix to prevent recoil, all the γ-rays are emitted with a closely defined energy. If such a γ-ray collides with another nucleus of the same element, it is absorbed. This resonant absorption is highly specific; consequently, it was not until recoilless emission was developed that the Mössbauer effect was noted.

This effect has been useful in physics—it has helped confirm some of Einstein's views on relativity—and Mössbauer was awarded the 1961 Nobel prize in physics for the discovery. Now it is proving useful in chemistry. The Mössbauer effect has been observed or predicted for about 50 elements, mostly heavy ones with 26 or more protons in the nucleus. The exception is potassium, with only 19 protons.

Like the shielding effects of the molecular environment in nmr, the structure surrounding a Mössbauer absorber alters the energy absorption level slightly, and thus the energy of the γ-rays which it can absorb. The γ-rays can be produced over a range of energies by using another physical principle, the Doppler effect. In practical terms this means that the γ-ray target is moved away from the γ-ray emitter at different speeds, until resonant absorption is achieved. From the speed of movement it is possible to calculate the extent of the Doppler effect, and the change in the γ-ray's energy between emission and absorption.

About half of the studies of Mössbauer absorption have involved compounds of iron (the element with 26 protons). For example, using Mössbauer spectra, it was possible in 1966 to work out the kinetics and mechanisms of the breakdown of iron oxalate compounds, a problem which had puzzled chemists since the turn of the century. Because of the very finely determined energies of emission of the γ-rays, Mössbauer spectroscopy is the most precise form of spectroscopy yet discovered, and its use will no doubt grow dramatically in the next few years. In addition to the mechanistic/kinetic type of study mentioned above, Mössbauer spectra also provide information about the structure and bonding of molecules. They have been used to determine the isomerism of tin and iron coordination compounds, and the type of bonding in different interhalogens. Part of this latter work, carried out at the Israel Nuclear Research Center, showed that $I_2Cl_4Br_2$ is a proper compound and not a mixture of 2 molecules of I_2Cl_6 and 1 of I_2Br_6. It also indicated which atoms were serving as bridges in electron-deficient bonds.

Knocking Off Electrons

The use of magnetic characteristics of molecules is not restricted to nuclear magnetic and electron spin resonance spectroscopies. If a molecule is bombarded with an energetic electron, it is possible to knock off 1 of the molecule's own electrons, making the molecule positively charged. If such a positively charged molecule is placed in a magnetic field it can be made to travel in an arc, the exact shape of which depends on the mass:charge ratio. By using electrons with about 7 times the energy required to knock an electron from a molecule, it is possible to produce a number of charged fragments—some of the excess energy goes into breaking chemical bonds—with different masses. These can be detected in a number of ways and, for a particular molecule, will give a characteristic pattern of fragments.

Known as mass spectrometry, this technique is widely used for determining structures of complex organic molecules. Since the molecule has to be vaporized, it is not widely applicable to inorganic compounds or to very large molecules which are not easily vaporized. This is a temporal judgment, for the usefulness of the technique is leading to extensive studies of means for preparing volatile derivatives of involatile materials. Such research has been especially intense since methods have been developed for analyzing complex mass spectra by computer. Peptides, small fragments from proteins but still highly complex molecules in themselves, are now successfully being analyzed by this technique. Another technique developed during the 1960s, when computer analysis of mass spectra began, is the combined use of mass spectra and gas chromatography.

Machines to Separate Mixtures

Gas chromatography is 1 of the separational methods that has revolutionized the chemical study of complex mixtures in the last 2 decades. Coupling it with mass spectroscopy has produced a very powerful tool, useful for such purposes as analyzing minute samples of rock brought back from the Moon for traces of the chemicals of life.

Gas chromatography was invented by 2 British scientists, Archer Martin and Tony James, in 1952, the same year that Martin shared the Nobel chemistry prize with R. L. M. Synge for their discovery during World War II of paper chromatography, a similar but less versatile separational technique. Both of these techniques go back to a nineteenth century Russian chemist, Mikhail Tswett, who found that a solution of natural pigments (from grass, for example) can be separated into different, colored bands by adsorbing it on the top of a column of powdered solid, and gradually pouring through it a liquid in which the pigments are partially soluble.[3]

All chromatography works on the basis underlying this phenomenon. Different molecules have different affinities for various solids and liquids. An obvious example is the lack of affinity between oil and water: they do not mix with one another. A mixture of similar molecules may dissolve in the same liquid, and be adsorbed on the same solid. But the strength with which the different compounds are held by solid and liquid will differ slightly. This means that, once adsorbed, they can be desorbed at different rates, and will separate.

A simple example is to take a strip of white blotting paper

[3] Chemists make a distinction between the similar words absorption and adsorption. When a substance is absorbed in a solid, it permeates the whole solid. When it is adsorbed, the substance occurs only on the surface of the solid.

and place a spot of blue or black ink (fountain pen ink, not ballpoint ink) about halfway along the strip. Dip 1 end of the strip in a glass of water and let the rest of the strip hang downward. Water gradually travels along the strip. As it passes the ink mark, the spot begins to streak. By the time the water gets to the end of the paper, you may be able to see that the "blue" or "black" ink is made from a mixture of different colors. It was a highly refined form of such paper chromatography that won Martin and Synge their Nobel prize.

In gas chromatography, a column packed with a solid coated with a special, high boiling-point liquid, is used in place of the paper; instead of water, the adsorbed compounds are removed by a stream of gas. When they reach the end of the column, which may be at quite a high temperature, they are detected in a variety of ways, and the composition of the mixture can be ascertained. For example, wines and beers have been analyzed by gas chromatography to uncover the secrets of their individual flavors. Since chemists know most of the compounds likely to appear in such a mixture, individual compounds can be identified by comparing the "retention times" (how long a compound stays on a particular type of column at a particular temperature) published in the scientific literature with the retention times recorded in the experiment.

If we want to find out the ingredients of a complex mixture of hitherto unknown compounds—isolated perhaps from a newly discovered plant in the South American jungles—chromatography will separate the mixture, but cannot identify the individual compounds as they emerge. Mass spectrometry, on the other hand, can be used to indicate likely structures for pure compounds, but not for mixtures. The answer is called combined gc-ms: a gas chromatograph with a mass spectrometer fitted on its butt end. Since both techniques need only tiny quantities of material, this marriage of instruments is ideal for analyzing rare samples that cannot easily be replaced, such as samples of new plants or of moondust.

To be analyzable by gas chromatography, a compound must be volatile, as is the case with mass spectrometry. In that sense, both types of analysis are compatible. But neither is very useful for the analysis of large molecules, such as proteins. There are techniques for isolating and identifying the structures of such large biological macromolecules, some of which are described later (Chapter 6), when recent work on biological chemistry is discussed in more detail.

The X-ray Eye

The most accurate technique for structuring an unknown molecule, whatever its size, is not spectroscopic, but a diffraction method. However, like the spectroscopic methods, it relies on the interaction between matter and part of the electromagnetic spectrum. X-ray diffraction was discovered in the early years of this century by 2 British scientists, W. H. Bragg and his son, W. L. Bragg. Rather than being absorbed by matter, x-rays are diffracted, that is, bounced off. If a beam of x-rays is aimed at a crystal, it is possible to work out the crystal's structure from the pattern of diffracted x-rays as shown on a photographic plate.

Like mass spectrometry, x-ray diffraction did not come into its own as an analytical technique until the development of computer programs for interpretation of the data obtained. It has subsequently been possible to work out the precise three-dimensional structures of complex molecules such as enzymes and, from their shapes, to postulate various ideas about how they act as catalysts. Neutrons and electrons can be used in place of x-rays in diffraction experiments. The powerful neutron sources required for neutron diffraction are available only in nuclear reactors, so this technique is still limited in its applications; however, the method provides a useful adjunct to the more conventional x-ray technique. Electron diffraction is usually applied to gases, and is consequently limited to use with gaseous materials, where it comes into competition with microwave and rotational infrared spectroscopy.

From the viewpoint of the chemist attempting to determine a structure accurately, there is no doubt that x-ray diffraction gives the most complete answer. It draws a three-dimensional picture of the molecule that shows not only bond lengths and angles, but also specific stereochemistry. Unfortunately, it still takes several months for most complete x-ray analyses and, for most purposes, the chemist will satisfy himself with 1 or a combination of the spectroscopic tools at his disposal. Additionally, he will use 1 of the now generally available techniques of optical analysis, such as circular dichroism or optical rotatory dispersion, if he is studying molecules that have asymmetric centers (those that can exist in optically isomeric forms).

Watching Reactions at Work

Not only can a chemist identify the products of a reaction with the varied methods just described, he can also folllow the kinetics in many cases, and possibly establish the mechanism of the reaction from spectroscopic evidence. For example, by a simple reaction between acetone, which is an organic compound containing a carbon doubly bonded to oxygen, and also having 2 other carbon atoms directly attached to it, and hydroxylamine (NH_2OH), an oxime is formed, with the place of the doubly bonded oxygen being taken by a doubly bonded nitrogen.

$$\underset{CH_3\overset{\textstyle O}{\overset{\|}{C}}CH_3}{} + \underset{H}{\overset{H}{\diagdown}}NOH \rightarrow CH_3\overset{\textstyle NOH}{\overset{\|}{C}}CH_3 + H_2O$$

On paper this looks like a simple removal of the oxygen and replacement by nitrogen. But we must not forget that, in reality, this replacement involves breaking 2 existing bonds and forming 2 new ones. If we examine the reaction spectroscopically, we can detect both starting material and product by characteristic absorption of infrared radiation. In some cases, it is possible for the characteristic absorption of starting material to disappear completely before any sign of the absorption characteristic of the product appears. At this stage, it would seem, the mixture contains neither starting material nor product. This is the case; an intermediate compound—not a reaction intermediate, for 2 separate reactions are taking place—is formed. The first of the 2 reactions involves the breaking of 1 of the 2 bonds to oxygen and the formation of a single bond to a hydroxylamine molecule's nitrogen atom. As part of the process, the hydroxylamine molecule loses a hydrogen atom, which forms a bond with the oxygen atom, which now has a spare electron. The result looks like this:

$$\begin{array}{c} OH \\ | \\ CH_3CCH_3 \\ | \\ H-N-OH \end{array}$$

The reaction by which this is formed occurs rapidly; a slow reaction now takes place in which this molecule loses the elements of water to form the oxime product.

Spectroscopic methods are not the only ones used to study reaction mechanisms. Experience in the handling of unfamiliar isotopes of common elements has been of help in elucidating reaction mechanisms. For example, a common class of organic compounds is the esters. Esters can be hydrolyzed to form an acid and an alcohol in 2 possible ways: by the breaking of either of the 2 carbon-oxygen bonds (see Figure 13). During hydrolysis, the elements of water add on, so one could imagine H from H_2O joining the oxygen atom whose bond has just broken, and OH joining the carbon atom whose bond has just broken. But how can we determine which bond has broken?

By using water containing an uncommon isotope of oxygen,

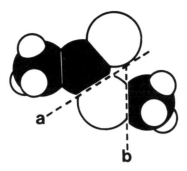

FIGURE 13. An ester molecule can be hydrolyzed by a water molecule in 2 ways: either carbon-oxygen bond (a) or carbon-oxygen bond (b) might break. The use of heavy water, which contains the uncommon oxygen isotope ^{18}O, enabled experimenters to find out which of the 2 bonds breaks under different conditions.

^{18}O (common oxygen is ^{16}O), it was possible to find out which of the 2 products—acid or alcohol—the OH portion of the water molecules latched onto, and consequently to identify the point of breakage of the carbon-oxygen bond. Since oxygen-18 is not radioactive, to find out which products contained the heavy oxygen it was necessary to fall back on spectroscopy—in this case mass spectroscopy—to complete the experiment.

This is a simple example of the use of isotopes in elucidating reaction mechanisms. Isotopes can also be used for working out the rates of very slow reactions. The amino acid alanine, found in most proteins, breaks down very slowly in aqueous solutions, releasing carbon dioxide as it does so. By keeping alanine solutions, in which part of the alanine has been "labeled" with the radioactive carbon isotope ^{14}C, for several weeks, then blowing out the apparatus with ordinary carbon dioxide, it is possible to remove any radioactive carbon dioxide formed and measure it accurately. This procedure has shown that, in many aqueous solutions, it would take about 4,000 years for half the alanine present to decompose.

Labeling experiments are based generally on the assumption

that a heavy or light isotope of an element will behave in the same way as the most common one. In some cases, because different masses are involved, this is not true, and the difference can also be exploited. This is particularly the case with hydrogen, for its isotopes, deuterium and tritium, are almost 2 and 3 times as heavy as normal hydrogen, which means that the strength of a bond between hydrogen and another element is different from that between the other element and either deuterium or tritium. If a reaction involves the breaking of a bond to hydrogen, a proof may be possible by checking the effect of substituting deuterium or tritium into the molecule in place of the particular hydrogen atom under investigation.

Quick-Mix Chemistry

Although tracer methods can be useful in determining the rates of very slow reactions, in the last 20 to 30 years chemists have become interested in unraveling the mechanisms of very fast reactions. The advances in this field are truly amazing: it is now possible to study what happens during a few nanoseconds in a fast reaction, and a nanosecond is one thousand-milllionth of a second. As chemists don't move fast enough to remove samples from such fast reactions from their reaction vessels, place them in a spectrometer, and analyze them, how is the study done?

Until special methods were developed, it was not possible to study reactions which occurred in less than a few seconds. One of the problems was bringing the reactants into contact with one another. It was the solution to this during the 1920s that led to the first breakthrough. By keeping reactants in separate solutions, and moving these steadily down the twin arms of a Y-shaped tube, it is possible to get the reaction to start where the arms of the Y meet. By adjusting the speed of the solution down the tube and placing a measuring instrument a specific distance down the leg of the Y, the state of the mixture at, for example, one-hundredth of a second after mixing can be recorded.

If the speed of travel of the solutions is kept constant, and new solution added all the time, measurements made at the downstream point need not be done quickly, for the mixture passing the observation window always represents the reaction after a certain time. Consequently, the reaction stage can be studied at leisure; by speeding up or slowing down the flow, the point will see the reaction at an earlier or later stage. In this way, reactions which are over in a few parts of a second can be studied. By 1940 American chemist Britton Chance had reduced the actual mixing time for this technique to one-ten-thousandth of a second. The technique has been used, for example, for measuring the speed at which hemoglobin, the important respiratory pigment of blood, gives up oxygen which it has picked up on its travels through the lungs (half the oxygenated hemoglobin in a sample deoxygenates in 0.015 second).[4]

When we study the mechanism and kinetics of reactions, it should be remembered that although we talk of converting reactants to products, it is more correct to talk about reaching an equilibrium of reactants and products. Another way to study fast reactions is to allow them to reach equilibrium under a set of conditions and then change these suddenly, such as

4 For many processes, a simple rate law operates: half the amount of reactant present changes into product in a fixed period of time. The importance of this law is that it makes no difference when we start measuring, for whenever we start, and however much material we start with, we know that half of it will be gone after a fixed period of time which is called, not surprisingly, the halflife. Spontaneously radioactive elements decay in this way. If a piece of rock contains 10 grams of a radioactive element with a halflife of ten years, at the end of 10 years only 5 g of the radioactive material will remain. After 20 years (another halflife period), half the remaining amount will have gone, leaving only 2.5 g, and so on. In the hemoglobin case, given 1,000 molecules of oxygenated hemoglobin, 500 of them will shed their oxygen within 15 milliseconds—after one-tenth of a second there would be less than 15 molecules of hemoglobin with oxygen still bound to them.

by discharging an electric current through a solution, which may raise the temperature by 10° C in about one hundred-thousandth of a second. The rate at which the mixture comes to its new equilibrium point can then be measured by, for example, spectroscopic techniques. Relaxation methods, as such sudden changes are called, were introduced in 1954 by German chemist Manfred Eigen, who shared the 1967 Nobel chemistry prize for his development of these methods.

One of the earliest reactions studied by Eigen and his colleagues was the combination of hydrogen and hydroxyl ions to form water molecules. The result indicated an enormously high rate—higher, in fact, than the calculated rate of collisions for hydrogen and hydroxyl ions under the conditions used. Can reaction occur without a collision? The answer is no. The calculation was wrong, for the reaction does not involve collisions between hydroxyl (OH^-) and hydrogen (H^+) ions. These 2 ions go about in association with water molecules, and it was found that the reaction between hydrogen and hydroxyl takes place under the guise of 2 more complex aggregates coming together, $H_9O_4^+$ and $H_7O_4^-$ (1 ion surrounded by 4, the other by 3, neutral water molecules). When the collision rate of these was calculated, it gave the answer achieved experimentally by Eigen.

Quick as a Flash

Another fast reaction technique currently enjoying widespread use in the untangling of some of the secrets of photosynthesis is flash photolysis. Its discoverers, Reginald Norrish and Sir George Porter, both British chemists, shared the 1967 Nobel chemistry prize with Eigen. Flash photolysis began life in Cambridge, England, in 1949, and has since proved its value again and again. The basic principle is to initiate a photochemical reaction (one in which the necessary energy is supplied by light) with an intense, controlled flash of light which is complete in a very short time, and to follow this, after a specified interval, with a weak beam of electromagnetic radiation which measures any spectroscopic changes brought about by the earlier flash.

A large number of chemical systems have been studied in this way, ranging in complexity from recombination of iodine atoms into molecules (see p. 85) to photochemical reactions involved in such complex biological processes as photosynthesis. The development of lasers during the 1960s, and their application as a light source for the flash, has extended the technique to an examination of shorter and shorter time scales. As Porter pointed out in his Nobel speech, "without special techniques, [man] is limited in his perception to times between about one-twentieth of a second [the response time of the eye] and about 2×10^9 seconds [his lifetime]." [5] Working in the picosecond (10^{-12} second) region, chemists are now observing events that are over in one ten-thousand-millionth of the eye's response time.

Although many chemical reactions occur in microtime, and need advanced techniques—lasers, oscilloscopes, spectrometers, and so on—for their study, analysis of chemical reactions still relies on the human brain. Instruments only extend our senses; they do not replace our intelligence. Intuition is still important for the chemist interested in elucidating how a reaction occurs, for unless he has an idea about what is happening, he is unable to plan the crucial experiment that will tell him whether he is right or wrong.

Nevertheless, for the remainder of this book, which is about the factual side of new chemistry, it is worth bearing in mind that few of the results described could have been achieved without the techniques described in this chapter. For that matter, many of the explanations underlying the phenomena de-

[5] George Porter, "Nobel Lectures, Chemistry 1963–1970," (New York: Elsevier, 1972), p. 241.

scribed would not seem so plausible if we did not have the theoretical background of molecular orbital theory behind us. With this knowledge of modern theory and technique, we can go on to the rest of the new chemistry. Oddly enough, we start by going back 4.5 thousand-million years.

5 ❧ Chemistry in the Beginning

The chemical principles described so far are not of theoretical interest alone, with no application to everyday life. They underly the shaping of the world we live in, from our synthetic fiber clothes right back to the cataclysmic upheavals at the dawn of terrestrial time. Although the early history of the earth can be seen in chemical terms, can we call such a vision part of the new chemistry? In a genuine sense the answer is yes. Not only is one of the most valuable techniques for studying the ages of objects—radioisotope dating—a development of postwar chemistry, but a modern knowledge of chemistry also takes in the behavior of compounds at high temperatures and pressures—conditions only recently obtainable in a laboratory, but likely to have obtained on the earth during its development. Thus, a knowledge of modern chemistry adds new evidence to the arguments of geologists about the earth's formation and history, and it may be chemical evidence which finally confirms 1 of the current geohistories as correct.

To begin with a brief piece of evidence from radioisotope studies, in which the ratios of different isotopes of a particular element are used to indicate the age of the material in which that element occurs, it seems that the earth is probably about 4.5×10^9 years old, although the oldest known rocks were formed about 0.6×10^9 years after this.

How the earth formed in the first place is not a question for chemists, but the most likely answer seems to be that it formed by the conglomeration of particles of "dust" orbiting the sun.

For convenience and because at present there is no way of finding out the real truth, it is assumed that this dust had the same elemental composition as the overall composition of matter now in space. Of course, since the matter was much younger, it is assumed that it contained much radioactive material which has since decayed. The heat produced by this radioactive decay, together with the heat produced by the gravitational condensation of the dust, gradually melted the earth. It would be wrong to think of "melted" as meaning that the earth turned completely liquid. More likely it was melted in the way that chocolate melts on a hot day—into a sticky mass that could slowly flow, deform, stretch, or break apart.

If one looks at the quantitative elemental make-up of the visible universe, and then at the abundance of those elements on earth, the contrasts are surprising. For a start, hydrogen is nearly 300,000 times as abundant in the universe at large as it is on earth. (This does not mean that there is 300,000 times as much hydrogen in the rest of the universe, but merely that, taking the average for the universe as a whole, any lump of universe with the same mass as the earth has 300,000 times as much hydrogen. When we compare elements in this way, we are talking about *relative* abundance.)

One of the first things we must assume in constructing a history of the earth is that the hydrogen on the original earth obeyed the same laws of chemistry that it does now. As the earth was much hotter then, hydrogen moved about much faster, and would not have been held by the force of gravity, for it would have exceeded the escape velocity needed to get it away from the earth. Presumably, in company with helium, neon, nitrogen, and chlorine, many molecules of hydrogen did just this and returned to the universe at large, thus accounting for the relative hydrogen-poverty of our planet now.

Helium, the second most abundant element in the universe, is rare on earth; it too must have escaped. It might be added that it is no surprise that hydrogen and helium are the most abundant elements in the universe, for it is through them that all other elements are synthesized. Formation of the elements is a complex story belonging to physics rather than chemistry, but it has been told in detail in recent years, so that from the nuclear burning of hydrogen to helium and the corresponding burning of helium it is possible to account for all elements up to iron. By juggling the insides of atoms, it is possible to explain how all the other elements have arisen. We cannot go back that far. As chemists we have already assumed that the 90 elements now found on earth were there when the earth began. Of course, we must consider that there are or were other elements that we have not so far found, or have only very recently found, such as natural plutonium (see p. 40).

Of the 92 basic elements in the periodic table, technetium is found in stars. If present on the original earth it would by now have all decayed. The other "missing" element, promethium, has not yet been found in nature. But, following the latest views on the "island of stability," we can no longer say with certainty that there are not traces of some of the as-yet unsynthesized higher elements on earth which we have not found because we did not believe until recently that they might be there.

To go back to the escaping elements and some very old chemistry: at any temperature, the average velocity of a molecule is related to its molecular weight, so that the smaller the molecule, the faster it moves. If a body is moving away from the earth fast enough—at present the minimum speed, known as escape velocity, is nearly 7 miles a second—it will never come back. Since temperature is only a measure of the average velocity of molecules, some molecules will be moving faster than average, some slower. Clearly, as the primeval earth heated up, light molecules such as hydrogen and helium began to escape. Some idea of the extent of escape can be gained from looking, as we have already done for hydrogen, at the relative abundances of the molecules in the universe at large and on the earth.

Thus, even elements as heavy as carbon and oxygen are relatively rare on earth. The relative universe:earth abundances for these are 1300:1 and 5.5:1. Oxygen is only slightly heavier than carbon; why do the abundance ratios vary so much? The answer is in the chemistry. The early earth was not a mixture of elements; it could only be that if the laws of chemistry had been repealed. It was a mixture of elements and compounds. Those elements that are reactive now were reactive then, while those, like helium, that are unreactive now, were un- reactive then. It is probable that much of the oxygen became tied up in compounds with other elements, and the resulting molecules were too heavy to escape from the earth. In fact, it seems likely that any free oxygen did escape, and that the development of the present atmosphere, containing free oxygen, came later in the earth's history, after the beginning of life. The same is probably true of nitrogen, and, fortunately for us, sufficient carbon remained behind, locked up in heavy mole- cules, to allow carbon-based life to originate when things had settled down a bit.

The Earth as a Layer Cake

Although this early history is indistinct, there came a time when the physical properties of certain elements began to play an important role. Like the smelting of iron in a blast furnace, molten iron would have begun, owing to its density, to sink to the bottom (in the case of the earth, the center), leaving a slag floating on top of it. Following the primary separation of elements on the basis of volatility came the secondary separa- tion on the basis of density. The basic smelting process would have involved the separation of iron from the slag composed mainly of silicon-oxygen compounds, with other elements dispersed through as a thin concentration of compounds (including, of course, iron compounds). However, if the iron sank to the bottom as droplets that gradually coalesced into a molten core, other metals with an affinity for iron would have been carried down with it—nickel, gold, platinum, and palladium, for example. Exactly what was carried down is still and perhaps always will be a mystery.

At present it seems that the earth is made up of several layers. In the middle is the inner core, probably solid. Surrounding it is another, liquid core of similar composition. Outside is the mantle, made of rock. Surrounding that is the thin crust, basically of a different type of rock, which forms the surface

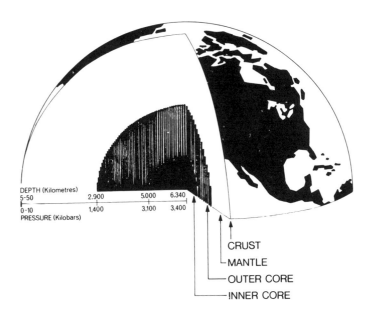

FIGURE 14. A cross section of the earth's interior, showing the layers of which it is believed to be made up.

and supports the hydrosphere (water) and atmosphere. Figure 14 shows a cross section of this pictured earth, with the sizes of each part. For many years it has been believed that the core is primarily an iron-nickel mixture containing about 90 percent iron, but there are problems associated with this view.

The inside of the earth is under very great pressure. After World War II, the Los Alamos Scientific Laboratory tried to simulate such pressures by using explosive shock waves. They found that, at inner earth pressures, the density of pure iron is 10 to 15 percent greater than the actual core density. Nickel should have an even higher density, so its presence with iron did not appear to remove the anomaly. Fortunately, someone decided that this theory should not be taken at its face value. In the early 1960s, T. Takahashi and W. A. Bassett of the University of Rochester, New York, decided to study the properties of materials at high pressures by another method— squeezing the samples between 2 diamond "anvils" and examining the results by x-ray diffraction, which is one of the structure determining techniques mentioned in Chapter 4.

Iron is a polymorphic element. At ordinary temperatures and pressures it exists in the so-called alpha-form. This has a crystal structure known as "body-centered cubic," in which iron atoms are so arranged that an imaginary cube contains 9 of them, 8 situated on the faces of the cube and 1 right in the middle (i.e., the center of the body). If iron is heated, at just over 900° C it turns to the gamma-form, which has a face-centered cubic structure. In this case, the imaginary cube contains 12 iron atoms; instead of 1 in the center, there is 1 in the middle of each face of the cube, in addition to the original 8.

Takahashi and Bassett found that at room temperature, but very high pressure (130,000 times the ordinary pressure of the atmosphere), a new form of iron appeared, which they christened epsilon. Its crystal structure proved to be close-packed and based on a hexagon. The change of structure was accompanied by a sudden change in density. At ordinary temperature and pressure iron has a density of 7.86 g/cm³. As pressure is increased, density increases to 8.46 g/cm³ just before the structure change, after which it jumps to 8.81 g/cm³.

These results, although interesting, seemed only to confirm the Los Alamos results. But when Takahashi and Bassett used an iron-nickel mixture, a different picture emerged. Although at 115,000 atmospheres a 95:5 iron-nickel mixture was denser than pure iron at the same pressure, at 300,000 atmospheres it was less dense. Extrapolation of the results to a 90 percent iron-nickel alloy at the even higher pressures and temperatures predicted for the core indicated that the density would be 10 percent less than that of pure iron, thus canceling out the anomaly indicated by the original Los Alamos work.

You might think that is the end of the story, but it is not. After all, since we cannot visit the core, we cannot verify the Takahashi–Bassett hypothesis. We have no way of guaranteeing that it is the right solution to the problem. In 1966 it was suggested that the density anomaly might be accounted for by a lighter element, such as silicon, being mixed with the iron in the core. The obvious disadvantage to this suggestion was that silicon and oxygen readily form compounds. Where would the free silicon in the core have come from? So, in 1970, it was suggested that the other element in the core was actually sulphur. This overcame the objection leveled at silicon, and also provided a neat explanation of why the earth's crust and mantle are relatively depleted of sulphur compared to other similarly volatile elements. Also in its favor was the discovery that, at 60,000 atmospheres, a particular mixture of iron and iron sulphide has the right combination of low melting point, low viscosity, and high density to make it a good candidate for sinking down through the slag. In addition, the difference in density between this mixture and pure iron could account for the density anomaly in the core.

The Great Separation

Once the iron core had formed, and the slag floating atop it cooled sufficiently, stable compounds would have formed according to chemical laws. As solids appeared in the melt, they would have obeyed physical laws and floated to the surface or sunk, according to their density. Clearly, this is a very simplified account. Under the extreme conditions prevailing, other processes, such as injection, would have played a part. In injection, molten droplets or crystals of material would have been forced under pressure into solidifying rock, and would then have been carried with that rock wherever it went. The world's largest deposit of exploitable nickel and platinum metals in Sudbury, Ontario, is believed to have arisen in this way.

In 1949, geochemist H. Neumann briefly summed up how his discipline should work: "The primary principle of geochemical classification of the elements must obviously be their tendency to form ionic, covalent or metallic bonds." [1] If one looks at the elements in the light of this dictum, a number of features of the present-day rocks are explicable.

The metallic elements can be broken down into 3 categories, roughly corresponding to the 3 types of bonding. The first class, called siderophiles, are elements that tend to associate with metallic iron—the ones that form metallic bonds, and which have already been discussed, such as nickel and platinum. Gold is strongly siderophile, but why? If we look at its electronic structure, the outermost ring of electrons contains a single electron, just like sodium and potassium, which are highly reactive metals. Why is gold so unreactive that it is found as a free metal in metallic mixes? Of course it has many more electrons than sodium and potassium, and an anomalously high first ionization energy. The ionization energy, as explained in

---

[1] *Mineralogical Magazine*, Vol. 28 (1949), p. 575.

Chapter 2, is a measure of how strongly an electron resists being removed from the element. Normally, as elements get heavier, the ionization energy falls, because the inner rings of electrons shield the outermost electrons from the nucleus and lower its binding effect. Possibly, in gold, the inner rings, the $4f$ and/or the $5d$ shells, are inefficient in shielding the outermost electron, so that the nucleus does bind it strongly. Whatever the answer, gold has a high ionization energy, which is a sign of a siderophile.

The other 2 classes of metallic elements are chalcophiles and lithophiles, which, respectively, favor covalent and ionic forms of bonding. Chalcophiles predominantly form sulphides, and the lithophiles form silicates. There are borderline cases: manganese, for example, is found in both sulphide and silicate minerals. In general, metals can be classed as 1 of the 2 types on the basis of ionization energy, which depends on 3 important factors: screening efficiency (already mentioned), ionic charge, and ionic size.

What effect does ionic size have on the formation of the chalcophile minerals? The most abundant rocks in the earth's crust are basalt and granite, one of the principal components of which is K-feldspar, a potassium aluminium silicate. Potassium is a relatively abundant element, more abundant than the other monovalent elements that appear directly beneath it in the periodic table: rubidium and caesium. There are no mineral deposits containing only rubidium, but all K-feldspar contains traces of this element. On the other hand, the rare element caesium is found in a mineral called pollucite, and not as a contaminant of K-feldspar. All 3 cations are singly charged, so, as crystals of K-feldspar were formed from a melt containing other elements, it seems logical that some other singly charged cation might jostle a potassium ion out of place every so often. In fact, an element from another part of the periodic table, tantalum, is a contaminant of K-feldspar because its most stable cation is singly charged.

Of course, an intruder can only move in if the outgoing potassium cation leaves sufficient room for it. The ionic radii of the elements we are talking about are (in angstroms) potassium, 1.33; rubidium, 1.44; caesium, 1.67; and tantalum, 1.45. Caesium is much bigger than the others, and will not fit into the K-feldspar crystal lattice, which is why it has to form a mineral on its own.

Similar arguments can be applied to other families of elements. K-feldspar, in common with all aluminum-containing minerals, contains traces of gadolinium, for the gadolinium cation, like aluminum, is triply charged, and its ionic radius is within 20 percent of that of aluminum (a 15 to 20 percent difference in size seems to be as much as a crystal lattice can tolerate). Feldspars also contain silicon. Below silicon in the periodic table is germanium, which forms a cation of the same charge and has a 15 percent larger ionic radius. Not surprisingly, silicon-containing minerals always contain traces of germanium.

In all our arguments so far we have taken a single property at a time, and kept others (such as ionic charge) constant, in an attempt to build simple models that will help us understand the immensely complex chemical system of the early earth. But we must always bear in mind that, when we change from one element to another, other properties may change and make our model invalid. For example, in the ionic radius/charge model, sodium feldspars should always be contaminated with copper, the ionic radius of which is only 5 percent smaller. This does not happen, because there is more covalent character in a copper-oxygen bond than in a sodium-oxygen bond. Recent attempts have been made in the lab to synthesize minerals that do not occur naturally, but they do not always work. For example, it has not been possible to synthesize the copper analogue of the common sodium aluminum silicate, albite (Na-feldspar).

We also must not forget that, although at some time on earth the formation of a particular mineral was favored, conditions may have changed—perhaps on a local rather than a global scale—and altered the mineral structures, just as an increase in pressure alters the crystal structure of iron.

Sodium analcite, for example, is a mineral composed of oxides of sodium, aluminum, silicon, and hydrogen (i.e., water). If heated very strongly, sodium analcite turns into albite. On the other hand, if synthetic Rb-feldspar is heated, it turns into Rb-analcite. This is because analcite has a more open crystal structure than the feldspars; in Na-analcite, the water and sodium ions are used to fill space in the crystal structure. Because of their size, they are not very effective fillers, and under the influence of heat the structure collapses to the more compact feldspar structure. Conversely, rubidium has very little shoulder room in the feldspar structure. Given the heat necessary for the change, it opts for the more open analcite structure. The larger caesium cation, as we have already mentioned, will not fit into the feldspar structure at all, but its analcite structure, the mineral pollucite, is very stable.

Gradually, through a closer look at the structure of cations and their properties, and the results of mineral synthesis, we are building up a picture of how the earth formed. It may not be detailed, but it is sufficient to reinforce our confidence in the laws of chemistry and to show that they have helped to form the ground on which we stand.

Water and Air

Some 99.6 percent of the earth's mass lies buried in the core and mantle, beyond our reach. The crust, from which all our exploitable minerals come, contains only 0.375 percent of the mass. Even less is contributed by the remainder, the hydrosphere and the atmosphere, with the latter accounting for only 0.0001 percent of the mass. Yet it is largely these 2 tiny portions that gave life to the planet and kept it going. In a way, the reverse is true of the atmosphere, for life has made it what it now is. In early times, it is probably quite different and, by our standards, very unpleasant. As Von R. Eshleman of Stanford University wrote: "It is now clear that the presence of life has been, and continues to be, a controlling influence on the composition of the earth's atmosphere. Conversely, the apparent absence of life on Venus and Mars may explain much about the nature of their atmospheres." [2]

What are the atmospheres of our neighboring planets, and how do they relate to our own? Space probes in recent years have made it possible to determine accurately the composition of extraterrestrial atmospheres. On both Mars and Venus, the main component of the atmosphere is carbon dioxide (0.03 percent of the earth's atmosphere); nitrogen makes up no more than a maximum of 20 percent, free oxygen is absent, and very little water vapor is detectable. Is this what the earth was like before life? According to Eshleman, if life ceased, the atmosphere could become like those of Mars and Venus, with oxygen and nitrogen gradually being removed from it and tied up in new materials.

Neon is a very rare element on earth (in the atmosphere it makes up only 0.0018 percent), but in the sun and stars it is only slightly rarer than oxygen. If free water had been in the atmosphere when neon was lost, it too would have been lost. Consequently, it has been suggested that all the water now present in oceans and atmosphere (80,000 cubic miles of sea are evaporated each year into the atmosphere and returned to the earth as rain) must have been tied up in rocks, such as hydrous silicates, and only gradually appeared as surface water during the first 10^9 years of earth's history.

From this water came atmospheric oxygen, formed by photo-

<hr>

[2] Von R. Eshleman, "The Atmospheres of Mars and Venus," *Scientific American* Vol. 220, no 3 (March 1969) : 78–88.

chemical decomposition in the upper atmosphere (probably with loss of the hydrogen into space) and later by biological action. Oxygen now accounts for nearly 21 percent of the atmosphere.

There are at present 2 main theories on the composition of the early atmosphere. According to Nobel prizewinner Harold Urey, the primeval atmosphere was composed of methane, ammonia, and water vapor, while W. W. Rubey thinks it was made up of carbon dioxide and nitrogen. In the latter case, one could propose that Mars and Venus may have had a similar atmosphere and that the nitrogen has gradually been removed to form solid compounds. But we can go a step further back.

If the primeval earth had had a Urey-type atmosphere and life had not developed, it is possible to envisage the gradual conversion of water vapor to oxygen and hydrogen, with irrevocable loss of hydrogen. As the oxygen increased, it could react with the methane to form carbon dioxide and water, and with the ammonia to form nitrogen and more water. This is a neat way of resolving 2 apparently contradictory theories. However, we must not forget that a wrench was thrown in the works. Us.

The Beginnings of Life

How life originated is a question that man has tried to answer for thousands of years. Early attempts—from the ancient Greeks onward—provide a fascinating insight into the way in which men's minds have worked, but contain precious little that we would call science.

The modern approach to the origin of life problem dates back to the 1920s. It was in 1924 that young Soviet biochemist Aleksandr Oparin published a short pamphlet in Russian suggesting that life could have arisen from inanimate matter over a very long period, by purely natural processes. On the face of it this appears to be a plausible hypothesis, and it might seem strange that it had not been put forward earlier. The reason for this lies in the last half of the nineteenth century. The idea of spontaneous generation had been considered by naturalist Charles Darwin, but only as a conjecture. Many others considered it in the same way—as a vague possibility —but the extensive work of Louis Pasteur in defeating all existing experimental claims for spontaneous generation convinced most people that it just could not happen. This was despite the basic negative in Pasteur's approach. All he had done was show that specific claims of instances of spontaneous generation were due to faulty experimental techniques, and in 1878 he wrote: "La generation spontanee, je la cherche sans la decouvrir depuis vingt ans. Non, je ne la juge pas impossible." ("I have looked for spontaneous generation for 20 years, and I have not found it. No, I do not judge it impossible.") [3]

Until Oparin, Pasteur's 20 years of failing to find spontaneous generation deterred others from looking for it. He not only drew attention once more to the problem, but suggested new ways of testing the hypothesis of spontaneous generation. Oparin is still active in pursuing this problem, on which he is undoubtedly one of the world's leading authorities.

Four years after Oparin published his initial remarks, English biochemist J. B. S. Haldane, unaware of the publication, wrote an essay on the spontaneous generation of life that closely shadowed Oparin's in its concepts. Apart from a few isolated experiments, however, this new interest in the origin of life did not reach an experimental stage until after World War II. It has since grown enormously, and a coherent body of information is emerging that enables us to draw a likely scheme for the origin of life. We can never prove that such a scheme

[3] J. Marquand, *Life: Its Nature, Origins and Distribution* (New York: W. W. Norton, 1968). My translation.

is correct, although if we discover life on other planets in earlier stages of evolution than our own, it may help to increase our certainty about the correctness of current views.

The major steps in our contemporary view on the development to life are threefold. First, it is necessary to have the small molecules on which life is based—amino acids, fats, sugars, nucleotides, and so on. Second, schemes must be devised to show how these could have polymerized to produce the giant molecules common to all life forms—proteins, carbohydrates, and nucleic acids. Third, how did these macromolecules come together to form systems that could perform the functions which we recognize as characteristic of life?

To answer this question in depth, it is necessary to decide first what life is. A purely chemical account can avoid this issue to some extent. Given a chemical "scenario" which leads to an organized self-reproducing system, one can say that life as we know it will follow. If one faces the issue directly, it is difficult to produce a definition of life that is neither too simple nor too complex. Even striking a happy medium between the 2 extremes produces a difficult definition.

For example, noted British crystallographer and science historian J. D. Bernal defined life as "a partial, continuous, progressive, multiform and conditionally interactive, self-realisation of the potentialities of atomic electron states." [4] A longer, but perhaps easier, definition of the function called life is offered by American chemist Melvin Calvin: "That function in a first approximation seems to be the directed use of energy to create order from a disordered, or less ordered, environment: in biological terms, growth and differentiation . . . further, function seems to be to generate and transmit the 'program' for growth and differentiation to another system, that is, reproduction. Finally, function includes changes in the 'program' in

[4] J. D. Bernal, *The Origin of Life* (New York: Universe Books, 1967), p. xv.

response to a changing environment; the correlative biological terms would be mutation and selection." [5]

Even if we fulfill the definitions of life in the terms of these distinguished scientists, we shall not end up with dogs and cats. What we shall end up with is a life potential that has somehow led, through biological evolution, to the dogs, the cats, and us. What happened in between is the "missing link," and to identify that is a task for future science. At present work is still not complete on the earlier stages.

First Organic Molecules

The first major experimental breakthrough in the chemical approach to the origin of life came in 1953, when Stanley Miller, then at the University of Chicago, published an account in the weekly magazine *Science* of an experiment in which he had produced amino acids and other simple "biological" molecules under "prebiotic" conditions.

Prebiotic conditions are those believed to have prevailed on earth prior to the emergence of life. Miller, a pupil of Harold Urey, whose views on the early earth's atmosphere have already been mentioned, took as his prebiotic conditions a reducing (oxygen-free) atmosphere composed of methane, ammonia, and water vapor. In order to produce more complex compounds from this mixture, it was necessary to have an energy source. Miller circulated his mixture of vapors through a chamber in which there was an electric spark discharge. The compounds formed in this discharge were then swept on by the circulating gases into a water reservoir, where they could be tapped off, separated, and identified by chromatographic methods.

[5] Melvin Calvin, *Chemical Evolution* (New York: Oxford University Press, 1969), pp. 106–107.

Miller's experiments were not the first in the field. In 1938 German scientists, using short wavelength ultraviolet radiation as the energy source, had converted carbon dioxide and water to formaldehyde and glyoxal, and it had been known since the 1860s, following the work of Russian chemist A. M. Butlerov, that formaldehyde could be polymerized to sugars. In 1950, Melvin Calvin's research group at Berkeley, California, had irradiated carbon dioxide and water in the presence of ferrous ions with the radiation from 40 meV helium ions (this was intended to simulate the type of radioactivity that might have been present in the earth's crust in prebiotic times). Formic acid and formaldehyde were formed.

Despite these early experiments, it was Miller's work that excited other chemists and gave the impetus to what is now a world-wide experimental study of prebiotic-type syntheses. The reason for the excitement was that Miller produced amino acids, the basic building blocks of proteins. Even more interesting was that the preponderance of amino acids formed were of the alpha type found in natural proteins, rather than isomeric types, such as beta-alanine, which occur only rarely in nature.

Miller's experiments also produced a host of other compounds: simple organic acids, such as formic, acetic, and propionic; urea; and, at that time considered strange as a "biological" chemical, hydrogen cyanide (HCN). A deadly poison to current life forms, hydrogen cyanide has now achieved a pre-eminent place among the list of simple molecules that were probably involved in the emergence of biological materials. It has turned up in nearly all experiments and, during the 1960s, significant experiments showed how crucial its role may have been. In company with more than 2 dozen other molecules in the last half decade, it has also been detected in outer space.

Following Miller's first experiments, Calvin and his colleagues repeated the work with the reducing atmosphere, but used electron bombardment as their energy source, again simulating radioactivity from the young earth's crust. They produced an

even larger range of products, including adenine, one of the
4 base compounds found in the nucleic acids, which play a key
role in transmitting genetic information from one generation
to another.

During the 1950s and 1960s an immense range of experiments was carried out. Each needed an energy source, and all
the possible sources of energy that might have been present
were used. Crustal radioactivity simulation has already been
mentioned; it has been estimated that the radioactivity from the
potassium isotope ^{40}K must have been much higher in primeval
times than it is now. Similarly, in a reducing atmosphere there
would have been no ozone shield in the upper air to keep out
ultraviolet radiation, and the earth's surface would have received much more of this, which is of sufficient energy to cause
a variety of reactions. Lightning storms could, like Miller's
electrical discharges, have been potent sources of energy, as
could the heat produced by volcanoes—both effects believed to
have been more frequent and extensive on the early earth
than now. Last, but not least, is the possibility of energy having
been derived from meteors colliding with the earth.

First suggested by A. R. Hochstim in the early 1960s, the
idea that meteoritic impacts could provide energy for chemosynthesis came from the American space program. When the
first *Mercury* space capsule reentered the earth's atmosphere
in February 1962, radio contact was lost with astronaut John
Glenn, which caused great alarm on the ground. The space
capsule was, however, safe, and radio contact was soon re-
established. It was not long before space scientists realized that
the space capsule hurtling through the atmosphere had heated
up the surrounding air by friction; this had consequently
ionized the atmospheric gases, and it was this ionized layer
around the capsule which had prevented transmission of radio
waves.

Hochstim thought of what might happen if this enormous
energy were to come from a meteorite entering the primeval

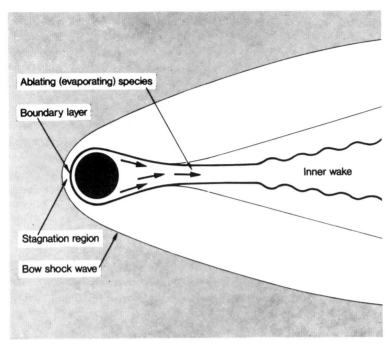

FIGURE 15. Hypersonic flow around a sphere, such as a meteor, entering the earth's atmosphere, showing the regions in which chemosynthesis would occur.

atmosphere. If a spherical body tears through the earth's atmosphere as a result of gravitational pull, a number of different regions of surrounding air can be identified, as shown in Figure 15. For a meteorite of 1 meter radius traveling at 5 kilometers per second (about 11,000 miles per hour), Hochstim calculated that the temperature in the stagnation region in front of the meteorite would be 7,000 °K,[6] and the pressure 200 times atmospheric. He also estimated that the stagnation region would hold 3 kilograms (6.6 lb) of material.

[6] Scientists frequently measure temperatures on the absolute or Kelvin scale. One degree on this scale is the same as 1 degree on the Centigrade or Celsius scale, but the freezing point of water occurs at 273.15 °K, rather than zero.

For a larger meteorite, the figures increase staggeringly: With a radius of 500 meters, and a velocity of 11 kilometers per second, the compressed wave of the stagnation region holds 400,000 tons of material, with another 200,000 in the inner wake. The stagnation region has a temperature of 16,500 °K and a pressure 1,500 times that of the atmosphere. Such conditions would produce highly reactive atomic particles. If the reaction was suddenly "quenched" by rapid cooling and return to normal pressure, the reactive particles might form a wide variety of compounds. Many meteors impacting on the primeval earth must have been quenched in just this way by impact with the sea.

Although large meteorites do not fall to earth very often— 1 every 10,000 to 20,000 years—they probably did so at a greater rate in the earth's early days. It has been estimated that a large meteor (500 meters in radius) passing through the earth's atmosphere now would produce 100 million kilograms of nitrogen monoxide (NO) and a million kilograms of carbon dioxide (CO_2). It seems likely that such large-scale chemosynthesis in the primeval atmosphere may have accounted significantly for the formation of the original organic molecules.

One of the major factors in considering likely energy inputs for primordial chemosynthesis is their deleterious effects on organic molecules. Early workers on synthetic systems found that the longer they left their apparatus running, the more biological molecules formed initially broke down as a result of the energy source acting destructively on them. Clearly, sources of energy such as meteors or lightning storms are sporadic; the energy is only available in short bursts, so the destructive effects would be minimized. But for a stock of molecules to build up, a protective mechanism must have been necessary.

The need for such protection led to the view that molecules may have concentrated in the sea to form a dilute molecular soup in which they were less likely to be exposed to the deleterious effects of radiation. Various additional suggestions have been made. For example, molecules could have been adsorbed onto moist sand or clay at seashores, where they would not only have been protected, but also concentrated. Similarly, isolated pools or lakes could have served as reservoirs for the slowly growing mass of organic molecules. If these lakes were subject to evaporation, they too could gradually have concentrated the organic matter.

How the Little Molecules Grew

Both these points must be considered in the second stage of the origin of life, the formation of polymers. Most important biological polymers are formed by condensation reactions in which water is removed from the molecules as they link together. In very dilute solutions, the reverse is likely to happen. Small bits of polymer will tend to be hydrolyzed to their basic ingredients. In consequence, doubt has been thrown on the idea that polymers could have formed in the oceans, and one argument is that there must have been a concentration mechanism to bring molecules sufficiently close together in sufficient numbers to allow polymerization to take place. Other mechanisms have been proposed that might have helped polymerization in an unfavorably aqueous environment; most of these involve the poisonous little molecule, HCN.

Of the many experiments that followed Miller's initial synthesis, nearly all, despite wide variations in conditions, produced HCN as 1 of the products. Philip Abelson, codiscoverer with Edwin McMillan of the first transuranium element, had attempted to form "biological" molecules in a nonreducing atmosphere, since he did not accept Urey's ideas on the primeval atmosphere's composition. He showed that organic synthesis did not take place, but even in these unfavorable experiments, HCN turned up.

In 1960 J. Oro polymerized concentrated mixtures of HCN and ammonia and found the important biochemical adenine in the mixture. Later it was found that at high temperature this mixture could produce a number of amino acids, such as glycine, alanine, aspartic acid, and serine. (The reaction did not actually form these compounds as such, but formed reactive intermediates which, on contact with water, hydrolyzed to the amino acids—and noone doubts the presence of abundant water on the early earth.)

Miller's first projected mechanism for the formation of amino acids involved HCN as an intermediate, although as a substance that added to another molecule, rather than polymerizing with itself. But, as Calvin wrote: "The appearance of many of the nitrogen-containing compounds in the earlier primitive atmosphere experiments is now emerging as being due to the presence of HCN." [7]

Calvin has also shown how HCN may have formed. In a mixture of methane and ammonia, an equilibrium is set up in which these 2 compounds can react to form HCN and hydrogen. At normal temperatures, the starting materials are favored thermodynamically—the reaction needs a lot of energy to produce HCN. As the temperature rises, the thermodynamic disadvantage is removed until, at just over 1,000 °K, it disappears. Such temperatures are readily imaginable on the early earth and if, as seems likely, the hydrogen formed escaped to outer space, more HCN would have been produced as the reaction struggled to reach equilibrium.

Even if one does not accept the presence of reduced carbon in the early atmosphere, formation of HCN is not precluded. A mixture of hydrogen, nitrogen, and carbon monoxide will react to produce HCN and water. Unlike the previous reaction, the equilibrium of this can be used to favor product formation

[7] Calvin, *Chemical Evolution*, p. 134.

if it is assumed that water was frozen out of the system—a possibility in polar regions.

It has been known for 150 years that HCN, in aqueous solution, will form polymers. What has not been known until recently is the molecular form of these polymers. The polymer formed, with energy supplied thermally or photochemically, is always a dark, at times completely black, material. The first few stages of this polymerization have now been worked out extensively. In 1970, Monsanto chemists Clifford Matthews and Robert Moser showed how the HCN polymerizes to its tetramer (4 molecules) cis-enaminonitrile. Under the influence of ultraviolet light this isomerizes and rearranges to an imidazole (the imidazole ring forms part of the side-chain of the amino acid histidine, which is essential to the catalytic activity of a number of enzymes). This imidazole can add a further molecule of HCN to form adenine. Alternatively, it can be hydrolyzed, then add another molecule of HCN to form guanine. Both adenine and guanine are essential base constituents of nucleic acids (Figure 16).

A decade before this, Japanese chemist S. Akabori had proposed a mechanism for the formation of protein from HCN. According to his scheme, after polymerization of 3 molecules of HCN to form a trimer, hydrolysis, followed by loss of carbon dioxide, would give the amino acid derivative glycinonitrile (glycine is the simplest of the amino acids; imagine a methane molecule in which 1 hydrogen has been replaced by an *amino* group and a second hydrogen by a carboxylic *acid* group; in glycinonitrile, the carboxylic acid group is replaced by the nitrile group, –CN).

Glycinonitrile, according to Akabori, could polymerize to polyglycinimide, which could hydrolyze to polyglycine. If the polyglycine were then to react with aldehydes (also formed in prebiotic synthesis experiments), it would form a variegated polymer of different amino acids.

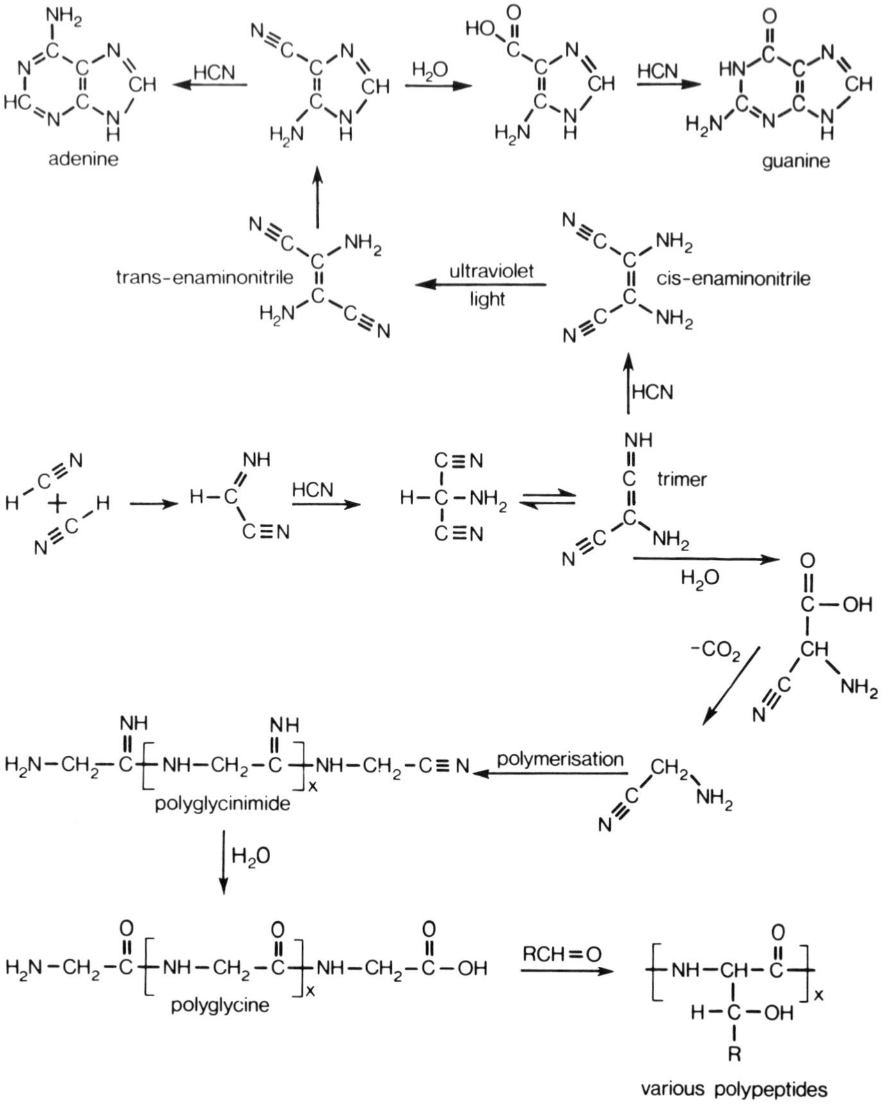

FIGURE 16. Proposed scheme for the synthesis of "biological" molecules from hydrogen cyanide (HCN).

Matthews and Moser showed in 1967 that peptides could be obtained by water treatment of the polymer formed by concentrated mixtures of HCN and ammonia. However, they attributed to ammonia only the role of a catalyst, and produced a scheme to show that HCN by itself could produce a polymer which would turn into a protein when treated with water. From their reactions they identified 14 of the common amino acids. The other half a dozen normally present in proteins, with sidechains that cannot be formed from these few components, could have arisen from reaction with other simple molecules likely to be available on the primeval earth, such as acetylene and hydrogen sulphide.

Getting Water Out of the System

While work on the polymerization of HCN is leading to a possible origin for protein, it is not the only procedure being investigated. This is fortunate, for it is a scheme that skirts certain problems. In the Miller-type experiments, amino acids as well as HCN were found, and Matthews and Moser have suggested that these were obtained from the breakdown of HCN-polymers. At some time in the evolution toward life, certain proteins—notably those with catalytic properties, the proto-enzymes—must have become favored molecules. It would no longer have been possible to rely on the proteins formed by chance from HCN and then reacted with other materials to give the different side-chains. It is necessary for us to find a mechanism that can polymerize amino acids into proteins in a regulated way.

One of the methods that has been investigated by Calvin and his coworkers again involves the ubiquitous HCN molecule, but in a different role. From HCN and ammonia, the compound cyanamide can be formed. Although the formula for this is generally written H_2N—CN (a *cyan*ide group attached to an *amide* group), each nitrogen is actually bonded equally strongly to the carbon atom (delocalized molecular orbitals) so that the central structure is more like —N=C=N—. Cyanamide can polymerize to dicyandiamide or, alternatively, can react with another HCN molecule to form dicyanamide, in which the amide has two cyanide groups attached to it. All these molecules contain the —N=C=N— structure.

Calvin noted that this structure also occurs in a class of compounds called carbodiimides, which have been used for some years on a laboratory scale in the chemical synthesis of peptides from amino acids. These compounds remove the water formed during the type of condensation polymerization that is involved. The actual parent compound, carbodiimide, is none other than the H—N=C=N—H form of cyanamide. When the elements of water add to this, they form the simple compound urea, another of the substances found among the products of the early Miller-type synthesis.

In 1966, Calvin and his colleagues dripped a solution of the simple amino acid glycine into a slightly acid solution of dicyandiamide. Analysis of the mixture disclosed the peptide tetraglycine (formed by the condensation of 4 glycine molecules), and its lower molecular weight analogues made, respectively, from 3 and 2 glycine molecules.

It is not only the condensation of amino acid molecules that can be assisted by carbodiimides. Carboxylic acids, in the presence of alcohols, are converted to esters, and it is worth pointing out that fats which, although not macromolecules, are still an important class of biological molecules, are esters of carboxylic acids and the small molecule glycerol. Similarly, phosphoric acid or its derivatives can be condensed to pyrophosphates which may, in turn, serve as dehydrating agents, and are now the principal class of agents used in living substances for this purpose.

This is not the only way in which pyrophosphates may have arisen. In 1964 Miller showed that if the mineral calcium hydroxyapatite (in which phosphate is the major anion) was treated with potassium cyanate (an inorganic substance which contains a modified cyanide grouping), pyrophosphate was released on heating. However, this is a controversial area and demonstrates some of the uneasiness that can arise when scientists borrow information from disciplines other than their own; in this case, chemists are borrowing from mineralogists. Often, a more experienced person in the field borrowed from may raise objections. Here is the late J. D. Bernal, mineralogist and crystallographer, on the subject of phosphate:

> Phosphorus is not a very abundant element on the crust of the Earth and its liberation from the rocks, on the one hand, and its fixation in organisms, on the other, determine the total rate of life activity on this globe.
>
> Much may depend on the various forms in which the phosphate ions were first liberated from the basic mineral, apatite, $Ca_5(PO_4)_3F$, and even on the detailed texture of this mineral, because it would appear that the activity of an apatite as it yields up the phosphates, is itself a function of the imperfection of its individual crystals. The various dislocations which may occur in apatite crystals may be actually the way in which the phosphate radicals appear in pairs as metaphosphates and thus enter for the first time into biological combinations, because the orthophosphates are at once very little soluble and very stable compounds.[8]

Metaphosphoric acid, HPO_3, can formally be converted to ordinary or orthophosphoric acid by addition of 1 molecule of water. Similarly, in the formal sense, 1 molecule of water shared between 2 molecules of metaphosphoric acid will give pyrophosphoric acid. In fact, metaphosphoric acid is more complex than it appears, since it polymerizes with itself to form chains and rings of metaphosphoric acid molecules. On prolonged

---

[8] Bernal, *The Origin of Life*, p. 50.

contact with water, the viscous polymeric liquid gradually hy-drolyzes to orthophosphoric acid. Chemists seem now to have centered their interest on the organic phosphate esters as de-hydrating agents. It has been suggested that the use of phos-phate esters is unrealistic, since they would be unlikely to have formed on the primitive earth. This is an unanswerable criticism, and it does seem that, rather than using such compounds, the role of metaphosphates as possible dehydrating agents might be investigated, since a likely mechanism for their formation does exist. This does not appear to have been done.

Pyrophosphoric acid—which might well be an intermediate in the hydrolysis of meta- to orthophosphoric acid—can also be formed by other mechanisms that are plausible for the early earth. In the presence of organic activator molecules, phos-phoric acid can be converted to pyrophosphoric acid by the action of ultraviolet light. Similarly, in a system containing ferrous ions and hydrogen peroxide, which is produced by irradiation of water, pyrophosphate is also formed from orthophosphate.

Development of the ideas of using the carbodiimide linkage either to condense, for example, amino acids into peptides in dilute solution, or to produce the type of phosphates that will in turn perform this function, has overcome, to some extent, criticism of the "primeval broth" idea. By such mechanisms it is possible that condensation polymerization could have taken place against the concentration gradient leading toward hydrolysis.

In this brief account, simplification has produced what may appear to be a puzzle. Why should active molecules such as carbodiimide react with water released during a condensation polymerization, but not react with the water—and a much greater amount of it—in which they are dissolved? The answer is that they do not react with water produced by condensation polymerization. They add the elements of water during the condensation, a little at a time. Although they will react with water, they react preferentially with the carboxylic acid end of an amino acid, to form a substituted amino acid. The new compound formed is reactive toward the amino end of another amino acid and, in linking with this, it expels the carbodiimide which, in these 2 stages, has gained the elements of water. There is no actual reaction with water molecules, but a multistage reaction which gives the overall appearance of reaction with water.

Putting on the Heat

Having given the arguments critical of the "primeval broth" hypothesis and shown a way around them, it would be unfair to just stop. We are not trying to produce a single picture of the origin of life. At the stage of big molecule formation there were likely to have been multiple origins rather than merely an origin, just as it is likely that the original chemosyntheses of starting materials used more than 1 energy source.

Condensation polymerizations can be performed by supplying thermal energy, by driving off water as steam to leave a polymer behind. One of the alternatives proposed to the oceanic origin of life is that it might have occurred in isolated pools, where alternate heating and cooling could concentrate the organic ingredients so that they would polymerize. Subsequent cooling and rainfall, reconstituting the pool, would then have allowed them to interact with one another.

A leading proponent of this theory is Dr. Sidney Fox, Director of the Institute of Molecular Evolution at the University of Miami. Fox's interest in the origin of life problem goes back a number of years, and covers the formation of the original small molecules as well as the polymers. In the early 1960s, together with Dr. Kaoru Harada, he synthesized a large number

of amino acids of the type used in protein building by passing
a mixed vapor of water, ammonia, and methane at high temperatures through a tube packed with particles of silica or
quartz, thus showing how high temperature might have provided energy for chemosynthesis, and also indicating the possible involvement of the mineral surfaces as catalysts.

For more than a decade Fox and his coworkers have been
studying the properties of proteinoids, materials resembling
proteins which they have synthesized under the intermittent
hot/cold conditions which they believe formed the seedbeds
of life. In the late 1950s, Fox found that if a mixture of amino
acids were heated to 150° C and then plunged into water, insoluble proteinoids were formed which had the same type of
chemical linkage as real proteins.

To achieve these results, Fox had to use very high concentrations of aspartic and glutamic acids or lysine. In a typical
experiment, a mixture composed of 33 percent aspartic acid,
17 percent glutamic acid, and 50 percent mixture of equal parts
of 17 other amino acids, was heated together at 100° for 150
hours. Alternatively, such a mixture could be heated at less
than 100° in polyphosphoric acid solution to give proteinoids.

Fox and his colleagues now claim to be able to produce
proteinoids from mixtures of amino acids in which the aspartic
or glutamic acids or lysine are at no higher concentration than
the other amino acids. This is an important step forward, since
a criticism of Fox's early work was that it was unlikely that
there would be such large excesses of these 3 particular amino
acids.

Molecular weights of the proteinoids are between about 3,000
and 11,000. The molecular weight of glycine is about 75, that
of tryptophan (the heaviest amino acid) just over 200, with
many of the others falling in the range of 125 to 175. Fox's
proteinoids probably contain somewhere between 20 and 75
amino acid residues, which is small by the standards of present-
day proteins.

Self-Selecting Structures

One of the most interesting results is the selectivity of the proteinoids. Superficially, one might imagine that heating a random mixture of 18 amino acids would produce random proteinoids. But in the typical early experiment mentioned above, although 33 percent of the starting material was aspartic acid, this amino acid accounted for 51 percent of the proteinoid material. Other amino acids which were all present in about 3 percent concentration in the original mixture were incorporated into proteinoid in amounts varying from nearly 6 percent for phenylalanine to barely half a percent for threonine.

This selectivity is important, as is the discovery that if one starts with all the amino acids present as the same optical isomer, the type found in nature, for example, the proteinoids are optically active, although unreacted amino acids are found in the reaction product as racemates of both isomers. An interesting sideline of this later work is that the proteinoids have nutritive value, and are presently being investigated from this viewpoint, presumably as a potential food additive to improve natural protein quality.

The proteins synthesized by living organisms today have specific structures, and it is becoming increasingly clear that their functions—as enzymes, connective tissue, and so on—depend closely on their structures.

Early in the search for clues to the chemical origin of life, it was believed that amino acids would have polymerized randomly to a great variety of proteins, only a tiny fraction of which would have been of any use. This implies a great element of luck in the formation of a significant protein configuration, and also suggests that all nonviable proteins would have been destroyed by natural processes, either by weathering or by being eaten. However, recent years have shown that nothing in chemistry is as random as it could be, and it may be, as Bernal said, that life is a function of the electronic configuration of atoms. A logical pattern might be built up from the atoms themselves, with no element of luck involved.

Fox's proteinoids are an important part of the evidence for this. On polymerizing, a random mixture of amino acids tends to reduce its own randomness. This is not so surprising, for when we talk about a random mixture of amino acids poly-merising, we tend to conceptualize "amino acids." In reality, of course, each amino acid is a molecule with definite molecular characteristics and a specific shape, or number of preferred shapes. The chemistry of polymerization is thus three-dimensional. One must take into account not only the basic polymer chain which forms from the amino acid backbone, but the effects of the different side-chains. For example, if an amino acid has a bulky side-chain, like tryptophan, is it more difficult for its backbone to fit into the right place next to the chain for condensation to take place? Or, since long-chain carbon molecules with no other substituents but hydrogen have an affinity for one another, will an amino acid like leucine be selected preferentially by the growing end of a protein chain in which the preceding addition to the chain was a similar amino acid—leucine, isoleucine, or valine—over one of a quite different character, such as aspartic acid?

Once the chain begins to lengthen, it takes up a three-dimensional configuration of its own that may bring disparate parts of the molecule together. Therefore we must not exclude the possibility that the character of an amino acid at an early position in the chain may affect the choice of additions much further away than would appear possible if we looked on the molecule as a long chain spread out in a nearly straight line. Much of this is conjectural, but testable. One of Calvin's colleagues, Gary Steinman, has done some work on the problem. He attached glycine to a polymeric (nonprotein) material and reacted this with amino acids to form dipeptides. In each experiment, equivalent amounts of the amino acids were used, but the yields from the reactions differed widely. Steinman then compared the yields of his dipeptides with the frequencies of dipeptide occurrence in all natural proteins for which the amino acid sequence was known. Although the figures differed, the rank order in each case was the same: the dipeptides that had formed in the poorest yields were also those found least often in known protein structures.

When did nucleic acids take over the control of protein sequences? Proteins are manufactured in animals and plants according to instructions laid down in the nucleic acid code. But when was this code formed? Did the interaction take place after the origin of useful proteins, so that at least some of today's proteins are descendants of protoprotein that arose according to strict chemical laws, and not the strict instructions of the genetic code?

Another major question relates to the optical isomerism of amino acids. All the primeval broth experiments, following Miller, produced predominantly the alpha amino acids found in nature, but they were produced as racemates—equal amounts of both optical isomers. Yet all life today is based on only a single type of isomer.

Just as a growing polymer may affect its own continued growth, randomness can also give way to selectivity of isomeric forms. In 1954 E. Havinga showed how such selectivity may arise in a series of compounds called quaternary amines. These occur in 2 isomeric forms which rapidly interconvert with one another in solution. When he crystallized solutions of the amines slowly, Havinga found that all the solid which precipitated did so in only 1 of the 2 possible isomeric forms. Whichever isomer happened to form the first crystal nucleus, because of its three-dimensional structure, encouraged all the other molecules to adopt its isomeric form as they deposited on it. A growing protein can influence its further growth in a similar

way. Fox's proteinoids from a single isomeric type gave proteins of the same isomeric type, although the reaction product
contained unreacted acids in both forms.

An "optically pure" amino acid polymer will take up a helical
configuration, like a spring, with hydrogen bonds forming between any 1 turn of the spiral and the next turns above and
below, thus helping to stabilize the structure. The only difference between homopolymers of the different optical isomers is
that the helix turns in different directions. In the naturally
occurring protein it is called the alpha helix. If an optically
impure polymer is formed, it will tend to twist 1 way and then
another, according to the configuration of the last few monomers
added to the chain. It will not produce a structure stabilized
by hydrogen bonding, and is therefore more tedious to synthesize. We tend to think that everything tends toward increasing chaos, but here we can see that simple chemical considerations may lead to increasing order as a more natural process.

Similar considerations are found in studies on the origin of
the nucleic acids. The structure of proteins is, in a sense, simple:
amino acids have a common backbone which polymerizes, and
this backbone is not a complex structure. The nucleic acids are
different, for they are made up of 3 components: the nucleic
acid bases, 5 in number, the sugar ribose, or its analogue
2-deoxyribose, and a phosphate group. If one takes a hydrogen
from orthophosphoric acid and a hydroxyl group from a particular point in the ribose or deoxyribose molecule and links
the 2 residues, then removes the elements of water from 1 of
the bases and another part of the ribose molecule, the result
is a nucleotide, the basic building block of the nucleic acids.
The polymer itself is built up from such tripartite groups, by
loss of the elements of yet another water molecule from the
phosphate part of 1 unit and the sugar part of the next.

Toward Life's Master Molecules

Before considering the polymerization of the nucleic acids and looking for directedness,[9] it is important to backtrack a little, for there are problems in the formation of the tripartite monomer unit. Why, for example, are the molecules of water lost in such a way that the phosphate always links onto the sugar in 1 place, and the base in another place, but it is always the same place that either of these 2 components is linked to the central sugar?

The 5 bases commonly found in nucleic acids are called cytosine, thymine, uracil, adenine, and guanine. The last 2 can be produced by polymerization of HCN, as already mentioned. In the early 1960s, Oro and his colleagues not only synthesized adenine from ammonium cyanide, but also obtained 2-deoxyribose from formaldehyde and acetaldehyde in aqueous salt solutions. Subsequently Cyril Ponnamperuna synthesized both ribose and deoxyribose by irradiating dilute formaldehyde solutions with ultraviolet or γ-rays.

There has been much concentration on adenine and guanine, the most complex of the 5 bases used in nucleic acid synthesis. The other 3 have been rather neglected and do not seem to have appeared as products in many prebiotic synthesis experiments. Uracil has been synthesized from urea and maleic acid, both simple compounds that have appeared as the products of prebiotic synthesis experiments, in the presence of polyphosphoric acid. In 1968 cytosine was synthesized from cyanoacetylene and cyanate. Thymine, the remaining nucleic acid base, could similarly be prepared from urea and the 2-methyl homologue of maleic acid.

In 1964 G. Schramm reacted low concentrations of adenine

---

[9] Directedness is the property which makes the structure of the large molecules inherent in the building blocks, although not obviously so.

and ribose in a nonaqueous solvent, and obtained a 20 percent yield of adenosine, the compound in which adenine and ribose are coupled (as in nature). Ribose has 6 hydroxyl groups on it which could react with adenine, so a 20 percent yield of the "natural" material implies chemical selectivity. On treating nucleosides (the compounds made from the sugar and nucleic acid base) with polyphosphates, Schramm obtained polynucleotides (smaller polymers than the natural nucleic acids, but having the same structure). Since the conditions used by Schramm are similar to those chosen by Fox for his work with amino acids, the intermittent heating/cooling in isolated areas can account for the rise of nucleic acids as well as of proteins.

One of the great triumphs of modern science has been the discovery of the fundamental nature of the nucleic acids, particularly the discovery—described in more detail in Chapter 6—by Francis Crick and James Watson of the double helix, the ordered conformation by which 2 complementary chains of nucleic acid form helices that are stabilized in an intertwined double helix by hydrogen bonds between bases on both helices. In deoxyribonucleic acids (those in which the sugar moiety is 2-deoxyribose), adenine hydrogen bonds to thymine and cytosine to guanine; in ribonucleic acids, uracil substitutes for thymine.

In searching for the ways in which order might have developed from disorder during the preevolution of life, it was only reasonable that attempts should be made to see what effect 1 strand of a double helix has on the synthesis of its complement. It was found that in the presence of polyadenylic acid, a homopolymeric nucleic acid in which the base is adenine, the polymerization of uridine monophosphate (uridine is the condensation product of uracil and a ribose sugar) occurred at a greater rate than in the absence of the adenylic polymer. Similarly, Calvin found that if one linked together hexathymidines to the dodecamers (2 6-chain units forming 1 12-chain unit), using carbodiimides as condensing agents, the rate of reaction was increased tenfold when polyadenylic acid was present. Clearly, the existing polymer, by hydrogen bonding to its complementary fragments, brings their reactive ends more accurately into proximity for reaction than if there is nothing to hold them in place.

In the present biological system, not only do nucleic acids replicate their counterparts to transfer genetic information among parts of an organism, they also control the synthesis of proteins. Part of this mechanism involves a series of small nucleic acid molecules, the transfer-RNAs. All the t-RNAs examined so far have the same order at the end to which the amino acid attaches. The final base is always adenine (A), and it is preceded by two cytosines (C).

At some time, proteins and nucleic acids, both presumably formed independently, began to interact, and gradually evolved toward the precise mechanisms that prevail today. At the University of California at Berkeley, Calvin's group is carrying out a long-term study to see if nature has evolved the most efficient combination in this —C—C—A ending. Is this a chance evolution, or another example of the working of straightforward, if ungrasped, chemical principles? The procedure for this investigation is similar to Steinman's procedure for establishing protein-structure preferences. A small nucleic acid fragment is attached to an inert nonbiological polymer, and the rates at which amino acids link to the terminal base sugar are measured. The work is still at the stage of assessing the very last base in line, but results are promising. In a given time the amount of the amino acid phenylalanine which links to an adenylic end-group is more than twice as much as links to a cytidylic end-residue.

The idea of molecular directedness has brought about a great change in thinking about the origin of life problem in the 20 years during which experimental studies have been under way. From setting out to prove that random chemistry could, on a large time scale, produce the requisites for ordered life to form, we have actually found order at a much earlier stage. This means that hypotheses can involve a shorter time scale, which is proving to be necessary as older and older fossil remnants shorten the speculated period between formation of the earth and the first true living organisms.

As Calvin wrote: "The high efficiency in all of these stages of the polymer formation, the replication system and the coupling of the replication system will depend upon ordered chemistry. This chemistry is different from what we are accustomed to thinking of when we put reactive reagents together in a flask, all of them randomly distributed as individual molecules." [10]

Even with the order inherent in the molecules, they still need a container that is smaller than, for example, a rock pool. At some time discrete systems had to form, protected from the environment as a whole by a skin—the beginnings of present-day cells.

In the Bag

Polymers of a biological type could have been synthesized on the primeval earth from the supply of simple organic compounds formed by the interaction between energy and the constituents of the early atmosphere. Once the synthesis took place, it created another difficulty which had to be solved before life could originate. The polymers gradually used up the supply of simple building blocks; if they developed simple catalytic properties, such as that shown by polyadenylic acid in the polymerization of polythymidine, they could have removed them much faster than new material was formed. Gradually the supply of readily available "food" for polymer construction would have been depleted. Some development was needed to protect polymers against breakdown and encourage the concentration

---

[10] Calvin, *Chemical Evolution*, pp. 180–182.

of raw materials from the surrounding solution. The answer was the development of an enclosed organic unit, a protocell.

All living organisms today have cells; the simplest organisms are single-celled creatures. The contents of the cell are bounded by a membrane which can take in useful matter from the environment and eject waste products. Just because single-celled organisms now exist, it does not mean that these are also the oldest living organisms. The minute bacteria of today are highly sophisticated, and there is reason to believe that they have evolved a long way from the original life forms, just as multicelled organisms have done.

It has been suggested, to get away from too simple an analogy which may mislead us, that we consider the possibility that the first living systems were not enclosed by cell-like membranes but, perhaps, by the physical boundaries of a rock pool; that a metabolizing system may have extended over an area of an acre. Although this may be true, cells did arise and, in order to survive, life forms needed cells. What, for example, would happen to a living pool if it were dried up by volcanic heat?

Consequently, much research effort has gone into simple cell-like systems and to showing how boundary membranes could arise under primitive earth conditions. A relevant aspect of Fox's work on thermal proteinoids is that, when his polymerized mixtures are poured into water, they separate into discrete units (microspheres) which appear, superficially, like cells. They are similar in size, shape, and tendency to agglomerate to some coccoid bacteria. They can also grow and proliferate by producing buds which eventually break off to form new microspheres. This little understood aspect of their behavior is being closely investigated at the moment.

For many years, Soviet scientist Oparin has experimented with another type of microsphere, the coacervate droplet. These discrete droplets automatically form in solutions of different polymers, such as gum arabic (a carbohydrate polymer) and gelatin (a protein). This work has been attacked because it uses present-day biological polymers, but, despite this criticism, coacervate droplets are useful models for showing how a membrane may aid in the survival of its contents.

For example, Oparin has produced coacervate droplets which incorporate an enzyme capable of polymerizing adenine to polyadenylic acid. Into the solution in which such droplets were suspended was placed a source of adenine, adenosine diphosphate. The coacervate droplets grew visibly as polyadenylic acid formed inside them and was unable to diffuse back out of the droplets' boundaries. A by-product, inorganic phosphate ions, appeared in the surrounding medium. A simple catalytic system protected by a membrane was thus able to extract material from solution, use it, and throw away the waste products.

Fox has shown similar simple metabolism in specially prepared proteinoid microspheres. This might be assumed to weaken the argument in favor of Oparin's coacervate droplets having played a role in chemical evolution. However, experiments in which mononucleotides were polymerized to polynucleic acids in the presence of polypeptide (small protein) have shown that coacervate droplets can arise naturally—just as naturally as Fox's microspheres. Again it is important not to place too much faith in any single answer to the origin of life problem. In the time that life has existed, there has been plenty of opportunity for the clues to its origins to be destroyed, so we can never be sure that there was a single origin.

There are other ways in which protocells might have arisen. For 30 years Bernal advocated consideration of mineral surfaces as areas where organic molecules might have concentrated by adsorption. Seashores would be a good example. Seafoam on the surface of the oceans has a higher concentration of organic material than the water below. Therefore, one might assume that at the seashores, where molecules would be more abundant through the presence of foam and minerals, protocells might have formed. Imagine a small patch of water insoluble, nearly straight-chain polymer floating on the sea, like a patch of oil. It will move with the water surface, following its contour. If the water is whipped up by the wind, foaming as it crashes on to the beach, the polymer patch will be converted into spheres. Some of these will have air inside (as Figure 17 shows), but others will have water inside them, and whatever that water contains in solution or suspension. Here again is the possibility of a protocell, although in this case the contents are dictated by chance.

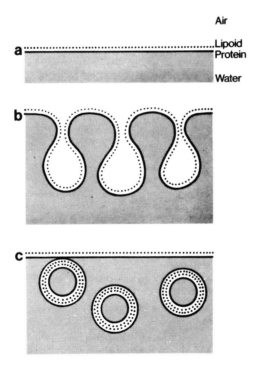

FIGURE 17. Polymeric organic molecules, floating on a water surface in primeval times, could have formed droplets by the action of wind and waves. Some of these droplets would have been air-filled (bubbles), others would have been filled with the water and any dissolved materials; if the skin of polymer protected the contents by forming such droplets, the result may have been a prototype of the modern biological cell.

Assemble in an Orderly Fashion

There is another aspect of macromolecules that fights against chance: self-assembly. It can be illustrated by a modern-day example. Tobacco mosaic virus (TMV), which causes disease in tomato plants, is made up of nucleic acid and a protective protein sheath. These can be dissociated. When the components are mixed together again, they reassemble automatically, yet when separate they are only a pair of macromolecules. As Calvin says, "The construction of what is marginally, if not unequivocally, a living organism, is self-contained within the structures of the polymers of which it is made." [11]

More and more, as natural polymeric systems are studied, it is realized that their overall structure is only a reflection of their fundamental structure. We have not yet reached the stage of predicting overall properties from the "electron states," to use Bernal's terminology, but we are getting there.

Since the study of self-assembly is still in its infancy, research is mainly directed toward studying the incidence of self-assemblies of living systems of today. This is a very valuable study—it was, for example, disassembling TMV that made it possible to show that the infective part of the virus was the nucleic acid, and that the protein part did not contribute to the virulence—but it has meant that studies on possible self-assembly of prebiotically synthesized polymers are not yet underway.

Some of the experiments with modern materials do offer guidelines as to how primitive assemblies may have taken place, and such assemblies must have played an important part in concentrating molecules. As enzyme called transacetylase, for example, is composed of 32 identical protein units. The enzyme can be split into individual protein molecules, and a mixture of these will again combine into colonies of 32. It is only

11 Ibid., p. 218.

owing to the sophistication of modern separation techniques that we know that transacetylase is an enzyme at all. In living systems, enzymes often occur in linked groups, forming a metabolic pathway in which a single molecule is modified a number of times, each modification being mediated by a single enzyme. This is rather like the game in which a word is converted into another in a specified number of steps by changing only 1 letter at a time, with each intermediate also forming a word (e.g., POST → PAST → LAST → LASH → LATH). Transacetylase is part of such a system of 3 enzymes; at one time it was believed that these 3 were a single enzyme. They were even given a single name, pyruvic acid oxidase. If the 3 enzymes are split up, they will recombine into the multiple system, as fully active as it was before it was taken apart.

The reasons for this self-assembly are not known in detail, although they can be guessed at. Just as polyadenylic acid assembles to form a double helix with a polymer of 1 of its complementing bases, thus establishing a system stabilized by hydrogen bonding and the good physical fitting together of the components, so these more complex ordered systems must fit together according to similar rules.

If this is applied to primitive synthesis, how accurate must such fitting together be? Although the formation of proteins is not a completely random process, as Fox's experiments showed, different proteins must have formed. What would their affinities have been? Modern research on this aspect indicates that the requisites for a good fit may be very stringent—not a positive contribution to origin of life studies.

Molecules of the same protein from different species, in which the differences are likely to be quite small, have been shown to be able to tell each other apart. Hemocyanin, which in molluscs and arthropods plays the part played in man by hemoglobin, consists of assemblies of between 100 and 1,000 identical units. In Chicago in 1966, H. Fernandez-Moran prepared pure samples of the hemocyanins from 2 species of snail and a crab. Each was found to have its own specific shape. When Fernandez-Moran split the 2 snail hemocyanins into their single protein subunits and mixed the 2, he found that they recombined selectively.

Once more J. D. Bernal has cut into the problem with an insight from his own field of study. Segregation and concentration of molecules is not a problem, he claims; witness the segregated nature of minerals in the crust, with like and like joined together in the same minerals. This is perhaps an oversimplification of the issue, but it does bring home the fact that, at this stage of studies in the field, one cannot expect an easy answer to how life originated. The problems of sorting out self-assembly on a less organized scale remain, but there seems no doubt that they will be solved with time and patience; it must be remembered that on the young earth there was lots of time in which they could be solved, although not as much as was once thought.

When and How Long?

According to current views, the earth condensed from a dust-cloud between 4.5 and 4.8 aeons (an aeon is 10^9 years) ago. There are remnants of protozoa (single-celled organisms) which are just over 3 aeons old, while remains of multicelled organisms dating back 2 to 25 aeons have been found. There is some doubt about the authenticity of such early fossils. During the early 1960s, great excitement was caused by studies on materials found in a particular class of meteorites called carbonaceous chondrites, which contain higher percentages of carbon than other meteorites. Analysis of these showed the presence of a number of biological materials, such as porphyrins. It was further claimed that the chondrites contained structures resembling living organisms. The structures were mineral in nature, but it was argued that they could be the mineralized fossils of living organisms. Detective work by a number of scientists, notably George Mueller, now a professor at Miami's Institute of Molecular Evolution, showed that such structures may arise in minerals in a number of ways that do not involve the intermediacy of living organisms. It has also been shown that all the organic molecules found in the meteorites can arise abiologically, as in the primitive earth syntheses.

Having applied such rigorous testing to the carbonaceous chondrites, one must be equally severe with "mineralized fossils" found on earth. The whole of the earth is contaminated with biological materials, so the presence of biological molecules cannot be used as evidence for early life forms. Most of the evidence must come from formations in rocks that appear to have organic structure. One piece of evidence for early life forms is a fossil found in rocks known as Gunflint Chert, which occur in Michigan, and are probably about 1.7 to 1.9 aeons old. Microfossils discovered in this Chert in 1965 were found to look like a modern organism with the almost unpronounceable name of Kakabekia umbellata. This rather rare organism was found at the base of Harlech Castle in Wales, and had the odd characteristic of requiring an environment of 30 percent ammonia for growth. This, by the way, is why it was found at the base of a medieval castle, where the urine of generations had produced a urea-enriched environment just right for the growth of an ammonia-needing organism. But the real significance of this discovery is that if the Chert microfossil was, during its lifetime millions of years ago, an organism like Kakabekia, it strengthens the claim that the atmosphere of the primitive earth was loaded with ammonia.

Kakabekia, or its prototype, is a youngster compared with the presumed fossil remains in Fig Tree Chert from South Africa. Dated at 3.1 aeons old, this contains objects which appear to be bacterial fossils and which, from the structure of sections of the rock, must have been there when the rock was formed. It has to be admitted, however, that these structures might be merely physicochemical curiosities, and not biological remains.

There are immense difficulties in tracing back organisms, for the organic materials of which they are composed are in many cases unstable. During the 1950s Philip Abelson analyzed fossil organisms up to 300 million years old for traces of organic material, and found minute quantities of amino acids in fossil bones. It was possible to show that some amino acids were far more prevalent than others, owing to differences in stability. Much of this work could not have been done without the aid of paper chromatography, used in the separation and identification of the vanishingly small quantities of material involved.

Although we can assume that amino acids from fossil bone were produced by life processes, the presence of amino acids in ancient rocks cannot be used for dating the origin of life, for we have seen how readily amino acids can form abiologically. There are, however, molecules which, it is believed, can be used as biological markers. These are mostly hydrocarbons, which are exceptionally stable molecules, and are sought in conditions where they will have been protected from the deleterious effects of atmospheric oxygen. Hydrocarbons contain only carbon and hydrogen and can be produced, for example, by the removal of carbon dioxide from the fatty acids found in biological lipids.

Despite the great variety of metabolic processes in living organisms, there are certain features common to biological materials that one would not expect to find in abiologically formed materials of a similar nature. For example, 2 important pathways for the biosynthesis of complex molecules are the acetate and the isoprenoid pathways. Fatty acids are built up from 2-carbon acetate units, thus giving predominance to even-numbered carbon chains for fatty acids and odd-numbered chains for the hydrocarbons derived by decarboxylation. Abiological synthesis of hydrocarbons would not be expected to give such a high ratio of odd:even chains as would be found in material that had been biologically formed.

The 5-carbon isoprene unit is used by a variety of plants in forming such polymers as natural rubber. Its major characteristic is that the backbone of the polymer chain forms from 4 of these carbons, the fifth emerging as a side-chain at definite repeating intervals. Adding up all the possible hydrocarbons that can be formed from as few as 19 carbon atoms and 40 hydrogens, taking into account all possible types of branching of the chain, there are found to be about 100,000 isomers. Consequently, even a small predominance of 1 particular isomer for which a biosynthetic pathway is deducible can be used as evidence for the presence of life at the time the molecule was formed.

Ancient sediments, dated by isotopic techniques, have been analyzed for organic content by the combined gas chromatography-mass spectrometry technique described in Chapter 4. Results so far have been promising in showing that biological markers do leave an indelible mark on history. Most of the studies to date have been done with sediments which are known to have formed much later than the origin of life, but this is a necessary study, since it enables critical evaluation of the methods used—a prerequisite for drawing conclusions from the older sediments.

In a number of such sediments, relatively high concentrations of the branched hydrocarbons phytane and pristane have been found. The phytyl group occurs as a side-chain attached to the central porphyrin ring of the important plant pigment chlorophyll a. The porphyrin ring has been found in a number of ancient crude oils, but since Fox showed in 1968 that porphyrins can form abiologically by thermal synthesis, this complex molecule cannot be accepted as a biological marker. On the other hand, phytane and its degradation product pristane are both isoprenoid molecules, and can be assigned a biological origin on at least statistical grounds.

The farther back one goes, the more diffuse the pattern of found compounds becomes, but the Fig Tree Chert still has an appreciable quantity of isoprenoids in its hydrocarbon fraction. Taken together with the tentative microscopical evidence of bacterial fossils, it seems that some form of monocellular life must have existed on the earth at least 3.1 aeons ago. Another possible test for ancient life is the ratio of the ^{13}C and ^{12}C isotopes in carbon-containing rocks. The ratio of these two isotopes is altered during photosynthesis—a life process. In 1972, scientists from the University of California at Los Angeles and NASA's Exobiology Division found a discontinuity in the $^{13}C:^{12}C$ ratio in rocks formed about 3.3 aeons ago, which suggests that this may be the date of life's origin on earth.

The main aim of organic geochemistry, as the subject is called, must now be to push the frontiers back even further, to try to find organic materials that show a gradation in biological content which can be linked to their age. In this way it may be possible to plot a time scale for the transition from preformed organic molecules to molecules synthesized biologically. This is a challenge so large that it could keep chemists occupied for the rest of this century, or even longer. In the meantime, it is a study that will be greatly helped, and stimulated, by the study of extraterrestrial rock samples.

In the rocks from planets and satellites elsewhere in the solar system, all of which can be dated by isotopic means, we may be able to distinguish the patterns of abiological synthesis— which, although not as highly organized a process as biological synthesis, is clearly not totally random—and even detect some first drafts for life that never got off the drawing board. For example, not only have abiologically synthesized amino acids been discovered in meteorites, but also, in late 1972, Soviet scientists Alexander Vinogradov and Gennady Vdovykin reported the isolation of DNA-like polymers from the Mighei meteorite, which landed in the Ukraine in the late nineteenth century.

6 ⬡ The Chemistry of Life and Death

Somehow, from the primordial slime, came man. Between the simple chemical postulates about how life might have originated and the masses of men and animals that now inhabit our planet is a great span that lies outside the realm of the chemist. Yet, if there is a dominant theme in the new chemistry regarding basic research, it is the continuing and detailed analysis of the chemical make-up of man and the other life forms.

If I had to pick a single event as the significant "starter" for this chemical-biological activity, it would be the elucidation of the structure of insulin by Frederick Sanger and a few colleagues in Cambridge, England, during the 1950s. The task took Sanger nearly 10 years. He began with the then nearly brand new technique of paper chromatography, without which his task would have been impossible. The real importance of the insulin analysis was that Sanger, by his patient and continued use of this technique, showed scientists that a whole new order of problems could be tackled. Life was still difficult to understand, but chemists could help put pieces together.

Insulin had been known since the 1920s, when George Banting and Charles Best, working in Toronto, Canada, showed that if a dog's pancreas is removed the dog develops the symptoms of a disease known to man since Greek times, diabetes mellitus. Banting and Best also showed that an extract from pancreas alleviated diabetic symptoms; the active ingredient of this extract was the hormone insulin.[1] On the basis of this discovery

---

[1] Hormones are compounds produced by living organisms which profoundly affect their activities, although present in only tiny amounts.

was built an industry, preparing insulin from animals for the relief of humans suffering from diabetes. Yet nobody really knew what insulin was.

It was not difficult to find out that insulin is a protein, but this was not a great advance on previous knowledge. Proteins, as was explained earlier, are large molecules made up from about 20 naturally occurring amino acids. In the simplest proteins, amino acids are joined together in a single long chain. However, many proteins are made from more than 1 chain, the different chains being held together by sulphur-sulphur bonds (disulphide bridges), formed from the side-chain sulphur atoms of the amino acid cysteine. To "know" the structure of a protein, it is not sufficient to know how many of each type of amino acid is present in a single molecule; it is also necessary to know the order in which amino acids occur on any chain, how many chains there are, and at what points they are joined to one another.

In the early postwar period, it was not difficult to establish how big a protein molecule was, and how many of each type of amino acid were in it; reliable methods for molecular weight determination existed, and chromatography could identify the individual amino acids and the ratios in which they occurred. But take a small fraction of a protein molecule (called a peptide), made up of a chain of 4 amino acids. If simple analysis shows that the 4 are all different, with only 1 of each in the peptide, there are 4 possible alternatives for first position in the chain, 3 alternatives for second, 2 for third, and 1 for last, giving, in all, 24 possible peptides. Insulin contains 17 different amino acids and a total of 51 amino acid residues; how can one begin to determine their sequence?

Sanger started at the end—or rather, ends. Each amino acid molecule carries in its structure an amino group and a carboxylic group, both attached to the same carbon atom; peptide linkages form when the amino group from one and the carboxylic group from another come together in an amide bond.

This means that, in a peptide or protein chain, all the amino and acid groups are taken up in bonds except for a free amino group at one end of the chain and a free carboxyl group at the other. Sanger found a chemical which reacts with protein chains by tagging on a yellow-colored dinitrophenyl group to any free amino group. After it is tagged, the molecule can be broken down (hydrolyzed) to free amino acids, and the tagged amino acid can be identified by chromatography.

Sanger identified 2 such tagged amino acids, which indicated that insulin was composed of 2 peptide chains. In 1 of the chains, the N-terminal (so-called from the *N*itrogen in the amino group) amino acid was glycine. By using mild hydrolysis, it was possible to break the marked chain into small peptides, rather than individual amino acids, and then identify the peptide fragments individually by further hydrolysis. For example, 1 fragment hydrolyzed to 2 amino acids, the labeled glycine and isoleucine; another consisted of 3 amino acids, glycine, isoleucine, and valine. Had only the tripeptide glycine-isoleucine-valine been found, it might have had 2 structures, with the isoleucine sandwiched between the glycine and valine, or with the valine sandwiched between glycine and isoleucine. Because Sanger had also found the dipeptide glycine-isoleucine, he knew that glycine-isoleucine-valine must be the correct structure.[2]

With the aid of colleagues Hans Tuppy and E. O. P. Thompson, Sanger worked out the complete structures of the 2 chains by splitting them into fragments and comparing them to see where overlaps occurred. For example, from identifying 2 peptides from 1 chain as Ser.His.Leu.Val and Leu.Val.Glu.Ala,

[2] For convenience, the names of amino acids are abbreviated when the structures of peptides are described. The abbreviations for glycine, isoleucine, and valine are Gly,Ileu,Val, and the peptide just referred to is shown, in the shorthand form, as Gly.Ileu.Val. The other amino acids commonly found in proteins (with their abbreviations) are: alanine (Ala), arginine (Arg), asparagine (Asn), aspartic acid (Asp), cysteine (Cys), glutamic acid (Glu), glutamine (Gln), histidine (His), leucine (Leu), lysine (Lys), methionine (Met), phenylalanine (Phe), proline (Pro), serine (Ser), threonine (Thr), tryptophan (Try), and tyrosine (Tyr).

it was possible to postulate that part of the chain sequence is Ser.His.Leu.Val.Glu.Ala. By 1952 Sanger had the structures of both chains, but as separate molecules. It still remained to work out how they were joined together. One chain contained 4 cysteine residues, the other 2, thus making several combinations possible. Discovering which was the natural combination was difficult, for disulphide bonds have a tendency to break and reform in a different order during experiments. Sanger finally found a way to prevent this, and identified the disulphide bridges correctly.

This was a most important step, for if the disulphide bridges are joined wrongly, the molecule shows no insulin activity. The same is true of many multichain proteins, and this raised a problem that was not solved to everyone's satisfaction until the late 1960s when, again, insulin played a part.

Building Bridges in Proteins

Proteins are one of the most important classes of molecule in living organisms. Hair, cartilage, and muscle are all made of protein. Perhaps more important, so are enzymes, the catalysts which plants and animals use to speed up reactions which might otherwise take hours, days, or even years, certainly, at an uncatalyzed rate, too long for life to continue.

The major component of any enzyme is a protein. As chemists studied enzymes to find out how they worked, they noted some important lessons about chemistry. First, even if you specify the order of amino acids in a protein, it will not necessarily behave properly; it has to be folded up in the correct way. Not only does each part of the molecule have its own stereochemistry, but the overall shape that comes from putting all the pieces together in the right way is also essential. This opened up an important question: How does nature do it? When scientists broke the disulphide bonds in multichain enzymes, they could not get them to rejoin in the right order.

This spoiled a nice but tentative theory which had been put forward by scientists working with single-chain enzymes. In the late 1950s they had found that, with enzymes such as ribonuclease, it was possible to break the disulphide bonds; when they were rejoined, all the parts went back in their proper places. The theory was that nature needs no elaborate mechanism for making disulphide bonds in special ways; as a long protein chain is synthesized, it curls up in a way that is inherent in the order of the amino acids. When the time is right to form disulphide bonds, all the sulphur atoms are positioned so that only the right bridges are built. The uncooperative nature of multichain enzymes spoiled this theory. To overcome this difficulty, another theory was needed.

It had been discovered, for example, that certain digestive enzymes, such as chymotrypsin, are stored in the body in an inactive form. Chymotrypsin digests protein that we eat. If it were kept in the body with no outside protein to feed on, it would start feeding on the body itself—an unsatisfactory and unpleasant prospect. So chymotrypsin is stored as chymotrypsinogen, which contains several more amino acids in each molecule than chymotrypsin itself, but is enzymically inactive. It is also a single-chain molecule; when an active enzyme is needed, 2 small peptides are bitten out of the chymotrypsinogen by another enzyme. This changes the three-dimensional structure, and produces a 3-chain active enzyme. When the disulphide bonds in single-chain chymotrypsinogen are broken and rejoined, they, like those in ribonuclease, all link up in the proper places.

Because there is good reason why enzymes should have precursor molecules, the chymotrypsinogen-chymotrypsin relationship was not sufficient to establish a watertight case for believing that all multichain proteins come from single-chain precursors. Interest was aroused in looking for precursors of other proteins and, because of its importance as a therapeutic material, various groups searched for an insulin precursor. Despite a number of experiments using radioactive labeling techniques which indicated that there was no "proinsulin," 2 University of Chicago scientists, Donald Steiner and Philip Oyer, decided that there probably was a single-chain insulin precursor, and published details of studies of insulin synthesis in living cells which had led them to this conclusion. Their work was read by a team, working for the Lilly Research Laboratories in Indianapolis, led by Ronald Chance. The group realized that a substance they had discovered while purifying pig insulin might be the precursor.

When it was analyzed—modern techniques are much faster than Sanger's original ones—the substance from Indianapolis was found to be a single-chain protein, the ends of which were identical to the 2 chains of insulin, with an intermediate chunk of 33 amino acid residues holding them together. Proinsulin had been found. When it was treated with trypsin, the enzyme which turns chymotrypsinogen into chymotrypsin, a large section was removed from the middle to give a 2-chain molecule almost identical with insulin; the only difference was that trypsin had bitten too hard, leaving 1 chain a single amino acid residue short.

Insulin had come to the fore once again to settle a point in biological chemistry. Few scientists now doubt that multichain proteins arise from single-chain precursors. However, this is really only a small part of the puzzle which protein chemists are trying to fit together, because accepting that the overall structure of a molecule determines its activity does not explain why it acts.

At times, knowing the exact three-dimensional structure of a protein molecule can give clues to how it works—this has been the case with some of the enzymes. All exact three-dimensional structures are obtained by x-ray diffraction studies. Use of this technique in biological studies began in the 1930s in England under the direction of J. D. Bernal. Working with him was Dorothy Hodgkin, who began work on insulin crystals in 1935.

Together with a team of helpers, she published a three-dimensional structure for insulin 34 years later, in 1969. (She had also done much other work during this time, including the structure determination of vitamin B which won her a Nobel prize in 1964.) Unfortunately, there was nothing in the structure that hinted at the mode of action.

Building Proteins in the Lab

Another way in which clues to the mode of action of a protein can be determined is to modify it chemically. Doing this on a systematic basis means synthesizing the real substance first, after which one can perform allied but slightly different syntheses. Synthesizing a protein is no easy task. To synthesize a single dipeptide (a molecule composed of only 2 amino acid residues) requires between 3 and 6 distinct chemical operations. Syntheses of small peptides with biological activity were undertaken extensively during the 1950s and 1960s—oxytocin and vasopressin, 2 octapeptides (8 amino acid residues) from the posterior pituitary gland were the first, synthesized in 1955 by American chemist Vincent du Vigneaud, who received a Nobel prize in chemistry for his achievement. This work not only established the methods of chemical synthesis of protein material, but also made clear that the first person (or group) to complete an actual protein synthesis would have to put in a tremendous effort, much of it in performing repetitious reactions. Three groups seemed, in the early 1960s, the only real contenders for the title, and all 3 were trying to synthesize insulin, because of its smallness.

A German group working at Aachen under H. Zahn synthesized 1 of the 2 chains of sheep insulin in 1963; the same chain was synthesized in Pittsburgh in the same year by P. Katsoyannis and his coworkers. In the following year, a third group, from

China, synthesized the same chain, but from bovine insulin, which has a slightly different structure (the ninth amino acid in the 21-link chain is different in the 2 species). The other chain, with 30 links, was synthesized by all 3 groups in 1964 (cows and sheep have identical structures for these chains). After that, it was a matter of joining the disulphide bonds together in the right way, and in November 1965 the Chinese group, composed of more than a score of scientists from the Academia Sinica in Shanghai and Pekin University, published results of their success. Their yield—the quantity of material actually made, as compared with the amount which can theoretically be derived from the quantities of starting material used—was only about 2 percent. Nonetheless, man had made a protein in the laboratory.

This feat has since been repeated with larger proteins, perhaps most spectacularly with the synthesis of an enzyme, ribonuclease. At the beginning of 1969, 2 American groups announced simultaneously that they had achieved synthesis of this single chain of more than 100 amino acid residues. One group, working at Merck, Sharp and Dohme and led by Drs. R. Denkewalter and R. Hirschmann, used a traditional method; the other group, headed by Bruce Merrifield of Rockefeller University, used an automated approach.

Merrifield developed his method in 1959. It does not reduce the number of chemical operations in a peptide synthesis, but it programs them so they can be automated. Peptides are synthesized in solution or liquid suspension. Merrifield's basic idea was to attach the first amino acid in his syntheses to a polymer which is available in the form of small beads. He then arranged the various chemical procedures of peptide synthesis in such a way that, at the end of each peptide bond-forming step, everything but the polymer beads was thrown away. The addition and removal of solutions was readily automated to produce the "solid phase peptide synthesis" method, with necklaces of peptide chains growing on insoluble supports.

Since the success of this method in enzyme synthesis, it has been taken up widely and improved upon by protein chemists. One disadvantage of the method is that, at any time, thousands of peptide chains are growing on the polymer support. When an amino acid is introduced to add onto these chains, not all of them may react (i.e., the yield may be less than 100 percent). When the sequence is repeated, the same thing will happen again, but it is not likely that those which did not react at the earlier stage will be unreactive again. Therefore, among the correct length protein chains—in which reaction has occurred at each step—will be a number of "sports," short chains which have stopped reacting for some reason, or chains in which 1 or more residues have been missed out. In 1969 a group led by Professor T. Wieland at the Max-Planck Institute for Medical Research, Heidelberg, developed an additional step in the process which ensures that all unreacted chains, at any stage of the synthesis, are stopped off by addition of a molecular fragment that prevents further reaction and makes these necklaces easy to separate from the required material.

Despite Merrifield's automatic procedure, the manufacture of proteins is not easy. So why do it, when supplies of needed proteins—such as insulin—can be obtained from animal sources? One reason is because it enables man to make unnatural proteins and to study the effects of changes in the composition of the biological activity of a molecule, for the delicate relationship between a molecule's shape and its activity is not shown only by the need to have disulphide bonds joined correctly.

What Will Proteins Tolerate?

In 1947 a form of anemia which still kills about 80,000 children annually was shown to be due to a fault in the hemoglobin of those who suffered from the disease. The fault was easily recognized; under the microscope their venous blood could be seen to contain deformed red cells. Because of their sickle-like shape, the disease is called sickle-cell anemia. Hemoglobin is a protein-iron complex responsible for taking oxygen from the lungs and distributing it around the body via the blood stream; sickle-cell anemia kills because the victim is incapable of supplying sufficient oxygen to his tissues.

In 1953, Vernon Ingram, working in the Laboratory of Molecular Biology at Cambridge, England, discovered the reason for this. He found that the difference between sickle-cell hemoglobin and ordinary hemoglobin is no greater than 2 amino acid residues. Since hemoglobin is made up from 4 protein chains, in 2 identical pairs, the change which kills is a single amino acid substitution (glutamic acid replaces valine) in a protein made up from more than 140 amino acid residues.

Before detailing the story of hemoglobin further—and it is mainly the story of 30 years in the life of 1 man, Max Perutz—let us turn to the more general question of protein function. The story of the sickle-cell can be misleading. Certain parts of a protein molecule are crucial, while some protein molecules can lose large chunks without losing their activity.

What became clear during the 1950s and 1960s was that, in many enzymes, the chemical substances whose reactions are catalyzed (known as substrates) come into contact with very few of the thousands of atoms in the enzyme. In 1960, one of the most prolific theoreticians of enzyme chemistry and biology, Daniel Koshland, Jr., of the University of California, Berkeley, proposed a fourfold classification for the amino acid residues in a protein: "contact" residues, those that come into contact with the substrate, with the possibility of orbital overlap and bond formation; "auxiliary" residues, which contribute to the flexibility of the "active site," as the sum of the contact residues is called; "contributing" amino acids, which maintain the structure of the enzyme in the active configuration; and "noncontributing" residues, which can be removed without loss of activity. In most cases, the contact residues are only 2 or 3 out of the hundred or more residues in an enzyme. How did the concept of such a small active site, clearly of great importance in elucidating the chemistry of life, arise? It came from the chemistry of death—in the shape of nerve gases.

The Rewards of Inactivity

Shortly before World War II, a group of organophosphorus compounds were discovered which had potent effects on living organisms; during the war, compounds in this group were manufactured as nerve gases. Fortunately, mutual fear kept both sides from unleashing chemical and biological weapons, so the gases were never used. But scientists and governments throughout the world were anxious to know how these agents worked, partly because, without an understanding of the mechanism of action, antidotes could not be designed.

It was discovered that the organophosphorus compounds attack an enzyme, acetylcholinesterase, which plays a crucial role in the functioning of the nervous system. The enzyme and the nerve gas react to form a new compound which does not have the enzyme's essential biological activity.

Acetylcholinesterase is not the only enzyme inhibited by the organophosphorus compounds; another is that well-studied digestive enzyme, chymotrypsin. When organophosphorus-treated acetylcholinesterase, chymotrypsin, and various other "inhibited" enzymes were analyzed, the phosphorus atom of the nerve gas was always found chemically bonded to the side-chain of a single residue of the amino acid serine. This reaction was quite specific. Despite the presence of up to a score of serine residues in the enzyme, only 1—and always the same residue—was phosphorylated. From this result the idea of the active site developed; for some reason, some residues in an enzyme are more active than others. In the last 15 to 20 years, scientists in many countries have designed a variety of active site inhibitors, small molecules which will inhibit enzymes and leave part of themselves attached to a single residue, labeling it as part of the active site of that enzyme.

The reason why 2 or 3 amino acid residues, not necessarily contiguous on a protein chain, form an active site becomes clear from three-dimensional studies of enzymes. These show that the active site is an actual physical site with a shape. The residues that compose it are brought close together by bends, folds, and loops in the protein, forming a cleft or cavity into which substrate molecules will just fit. Some families of enzymes have the same residues making up their active sites, but slightly different conformations alter the specificity of the enzyme, so that although the same reaction is carrried out by the whole family, individual enzymes catalyze it in different molecules.

An example is provided by the 4 major protein-digesting enzymes (proteases) in humans: elastase, trypsin, and 2 sorts of chymotrypsin. All of these catalyze the rupture of peptide bonds, but each prefers to break peptide bonds in which particular amino acid residues are involved. Recent research on their three-dimensional structures, together with sequence determinations, has led to the view that there was originally only 1 enzyme. Like all major proteins, these enzymes are synthesized by a method dependent upon hereditary information, the genetic code (see p. 175).

An evolutionary process for which there is strong evidence is "gene doubling," in which a gene suddenly doubles so that 2 genes are carrying the same code (for an enzyme protein sequence, for example). As the organism in which this gene doubling occurs evolves, the genes mutate, so that the enzymes produced are no longer identical. Close similarities among the 4 digestive enzymes are indicative of gene doubling followed by divergent evolution. Obviously, if a gene diverges too much, it may eventually code for a useless molecule without biological activity. Alternatively, a totally new biological function may appear. Before exploring this angle, convergent evolution, which does the same thing in different ways, deserves mention.

Some bacterial proteases developed separately from mammalian proteases and have totally different structures, yet perform the same function—the breaking of peptide bonds. A bacterial protease sequence worked out in 1970 in Canada showed sufficient similarities of structure to mammalian proteases to postulate evolution from a single ancestral gene, but this is not the case with better-known bacterial proteases such as subtilisin. Although both mammalian and bacterial proteases have a serine residue in the active site, no comparisons of sequence of the type needed to postulate that there was once a common gene can be made. This, as Ottawa chemist Bernard Belleau showed at the end of 1970, does not mean that the enzymes necessarily have differently shaped active sites.

Belleau synthesized an artificial substrate molecule which could be broken down by a wide range of proteases. The molecule was flexible, able to accommodate its shape to differences in shape of the different active sites. Belleau then modified the molecule so that it was no longer flexible, and had a precise shape. This did not react when placed in contact with most of the enzymes used. Only 2 of them broke it down: chymotrypsin and subtilisin. In both cases the substrate was hydrolyzed at the same rate. The conclusion is that subtilisin and chymotrypsin have identical three-dimensional spaces in their active site regions, despite the use of different building blocks in the composition of these spaces.

Now to return to divergent evolution. As more and more biologically active peptide sequences have been determined and computer comparison techniques developed, it has become clear that gene doubling, followed by complete divergence of function, has occurred on numerous occasions during evolution. As with the digestive enzymes, divergence of function is not always complete. Among the hormones involved in human alimentary operations are secretin and glucagon, responsible, respectively, for causing the pancreas to produce digestive juices, and for breaking down glycogen—a glucose polymer used by the body as an energy store—into individual glucose molecules. Despite their different effects, the 2 hormones are both about the same size (27 and 29 amino acid chains respectively) and half of the peptide sequence is the same in both molecules. Two other peptide hormones which also share parts of their structure are melanocyte-stimulating hormone (MSH) and corticotrophin, yet one is responsible for controlling skin pigmentation, while the other regulates the activity of the adrenal cortex, itself responsible for producing the steroid hormones, which play a variety of roles in the body.

Guessing the Age of Primordial Protein

When did these diversions happen? Is it possible to use the knowledge of chemical structures now available to improve our understanding of history? The answer is a qualified yes. A number of proteins are common to many species of animals, and some are found in animals, plants, and microorganisms. As more of these proteins are purified and sequence-analyzed, it is possible, with the aid of modern computing techniques, to compare the same protein from different species and to chart its evolution. For example, when the sequence of hemoglobin was compared among a few species, it was found that there was no difference between hemoglobin proteins in man and chimpanzees. Gorilla hemoglobin differed from human by 2 amino acid residues, while that of man and monkeys differed by 12. If it is assumed that, once a species splits into 2, the rate at which mutations change the structures of key molecules is roughly constant, we can draw up a scale of "closeness" between species in evolutionary history, showing how far back ancestry was common.

The respiratory protein cytochrome c has been studied extensively in different species. It is a single chain of about 100 amino acids, and several dozen species of the protein have been sequenced. Figure 18 shows a phylogenetic tree drawn from data on some of these. In order to insert an absolute time scale it is necessary to use evidence from other sources which pinpoints the divergences of groups from each other. But, accepting the linear rate of mutation, a fixed external point of reference makes it possible to use this method to go back beyond the earliest external reference.

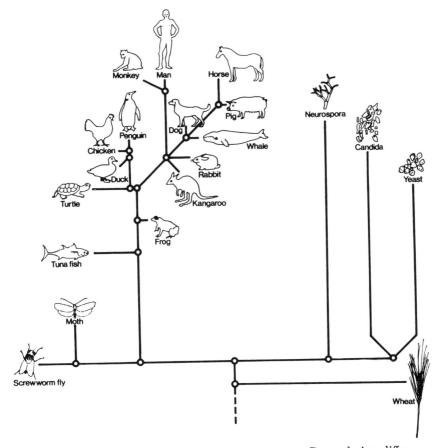

FIGURE 18. A phylogenetic tree for cytochrome c. By analyzing differences in the structures of cytochrome c—a respiratory protein—from different species, it was possible to generate this evolutionary tree, using a computer program.

However, we cannot assume that different proteins will have the same rate of change. The evidence at hand consists solely of functional proteins. Protein mutation may take place at a constant rate, but it will produce many more nonfunctional proteins than functional ones. Lethal mutations leave no evidence, so, indirectly, interspecies comparison of proteins also tells something about the structure-function relationship. In cytochrome c from all the species studied, there are 31 invariant amino acids; presumably the animals, plants, or microbes in which any of these 31 amino acids mutated found themselves with nonfunctional cytochrome c—or, rather, did not find themselves anywhere, since they were dead.

A group of proteins called histones have been partially sequenced, and it appears that 1 of them, histone IV, from cattle and peas, has undergone only 2 substitutions since these 2 groups of organisms diverged 10^9 years ago. Obviously the histone IV molecule is built to rigorous specifications and will not work if many changes are made.

Another ambiguity in this type of evolutionary dating is the possibility of back mutations. One amino acid may be substituted for by another but, given a further mutation, the original sequence may recur. Similarly, once 2 species have diverged, a protein common to them may undergo identical mutuations, so that both make the same amino acid substitution. In compiling phylogenetic trees such as that for cytochrome c, the computer program takes such possibilities into account.

On the surface, the likelihood of a back mutation seems small. There are 20 different amino acids composing protein chains, which gives a low probability of any particular substitution. However, this is only a superficial appearance, for it is not the proteins that mutate. Although proteins play a vital role in living organisms, they are not the master molecules of life. This title is taken by the nucleic acids, which carry the commands for all the living activities of a cell, and pass those commands on between generations.

The Master Molecules

The story of the unraveling of the genetic code is complex and exciting, for the science of molecular biology which arose from it has exercised some of the most fertile minds of the postwar generation in a variety of scientific disciplines. Since this book is primarily concerned with chemistry, it can only look at part of this story—the actual molecular structures and what they do. How they do it is beyond our scope.

There is a basic difference between nucleic acids and the other macromolecules mentioned in Chapter 5. Proteins are made by linking together amino acids, carbohydrates by linking together sugar molecules. The basic unit for making a nucleic acid is not, like these, a simple molecule, but a more complex entity called a nucleotide which is derived from 3 simpler molecules. According to whether the sugar part of the nucleotide is ribose or deoxyribose, the resultant nucleic acids are called ribo- or deoxyribonucleic acids, abbreviated to RNA and DNA. The fundamental parts of both DNA and RNA are the nitrogen-containing organic bases attached to the sugar residues. These fall into 2 types, the purines adenine and guanine, and the pyrimidines cytosine, thymine, and uracil, which is found in RNA in place of thymine. (A number of other bases, slight chemical modifications of these 5, occur occasionally in RNA.) In referring to nucleic acid sequences, the first letter of each base is used as an abbreviation.

It was in 1953 that James Watson and Francis Crick proposed the structure of the hereditary DNA which is now known as the double helix. In a single, elegant concept, Crick and Watson showed how heredity was possible at the molecular level.

In part their hypothesis depended on the observation by Austrian-American biochemist Erwin Chargaff that the adenine: thymine and guanine:cytosine ratios in DNA samples were always close to unity. What Crick and Watson suggested was that, in a gene, 2 long, fibrous molecules of DNA twine around each other in a complementary fashion. Purine bases (A and G) are larger than pyrimidine bases (C and T); when 2 DNA strands form a helix, the bases point inward and a large base on 1 chain forms a snug fit with a small base on the complementary chain. This "base pairing" of A with T and G with C involves substantial hydrogen bonding, which stabilizes the double helix. When the 2 complementary strands of a double helix are separated, it is possible for new DNA synthesis to reproduce the missing half of each helix. In this way the DNA forms a "code" which can be copied. This is the basis of heredity: DNA stores the information that makes us man or mouse, and ensures that our children are the same.

Through a complex and incompletely understood process, DNA strands are used in cells to synthesize RNA, and it is from the code inscribed on the RNA that cellular particles called ribosomes manufacture proteins. How does this transcription occur?

The genetic code, since it is an information source, must resemble information communication systems with which we are familiar, such as words, sentences, and books. The obvious analogy is to suggest that the 4 bases of DNA are the letters of the alphabet, and the order of these makes up "words." Although this simple idea is also correct, it does not mean that the code is solved. Achievement of this task in the late 1960s was the result of years of complex experimentation by many researchers.

The "language" of the genetic code need have only 20 words, for this is sufficient information to specify all the amino acids that make up proteins. Obviously, neither a single base nor a pair of bases are sufficient as the code words for proteins, for these provide only 4 or 16 possibilities, respectively. But a code which uses a sequence of 3 bases to specify an amino acid permits 64 possibilities. The correctness of the 3-base (triplet) code hypothesis was substantially shown by the work of Crick and his collaborators on the DNA of a bacteriophage—a virus which attacks a bacterium—known as T4. It was found possible to mutate this virus selectively, to treat its DNA in such a way that a number of different, defined effects might take place.

In a sentence written in the English language, we show where a word ends and another begins by leaving a space between them. This is a convention rather than a necessity; the Romans, for example, did not usually leave spaces between words. However, where words differ in length it is clearly advantageous to signal beginnings and endings. The words of genetic code are all the same length—3 letters—and are made up into sentences with no spaces between them; obviously the mechanism which "reads" the code knows the length of the words and behaves accordingly. That this is the case was shown by Crick's mutations which in some cases deleted or added single bases to the bacteriophage DNA; in other cases, 2 or 3 bases were deleted or added. Unlike English, nearly all the possible permutations in the genetic language make sense. Although there are only 20 amino acids, most possible triplets "code" for 1 of them (in other words, some amino acids correspond to more than 1 triplet; the genetic code contains synonyms). If, for example, we delete one letter (in this case the third) from the triplet sentence, *The man was fat and bad,* and then read off the triplets, we get nonsense: *Thm anw asf ata ndb ad.* With the synonymous genetic code, the chances are that a protein will still be formed on decoding through the RNA mechanism, but from the deletion onward it will have an amino acid sequence different from the protein produced from unmutated DNA. However, if a triplet of bases is removed or inserted, the protein produced will differ from normal protein only in having 1 amino acid less or more. Crick's experiments indicated that this did in fact happen, and clinched the triplet as the basic word length in the genetic code.

Once this had been done, everyone wanted to know what each word spelled out. Possibly the major contribution of pure chemistry to molecular biology was the work that made it possible to find out. This work could not have been accomplished without the help of biologists who developed cell-free preparations of living material capable of carrying out protein synthesis in test tubes.

Deciphering the Code

In the early 1960s Marshall Nirenberg and his collaborators at the National Heart Institute, Bethesda, Maryland, decided to check the behavior of cell-free systems when presented with some synthetic RNA. This synthetic RNA, made with the aid of an enzyme discovered by Severo Ochoa of New York University, was of several types; the sequence in the simplest contained only a single base, such as uracil. Using an all U-polymer, Nirenberg found that a cell-free system produced a polymer of just one amino acid: phenylalanine. The first of the 64 possible triplets, UUU, had been decoded.

In addition to using other single-base RNAs, Nirenberg's group also used RNA made from known mixtures of bases. If, for example, RNA is made using equal parts of U and A as the only 2 bases, statistical calculations can decipher how frequently each of the possible triplets (such as AAA, AUA, UUA) will occur. By checking these probabilities against the actual incorporation of amino acids, it was possible to assign a number of other triplets to specific amino acids.

While this work was in progress, Professor H. G. Khorana of the Institute of Enzyme Research, Madison, Wisconsin, an Indian-born chemist who had studied at Cambridge, England, under Nobel prizewinner Lord Todd, was perfecting methods for the chemical synthesis of short strands of DNA with completely specific structures. Using the appropriate starting materials, Khorana made the dinucleotide AC; he then polymerized this to a 12-base chain ACACACACACAC. By the same technique he synthesized the complementary sequence TGTGTGTGTGTG, and the 2 combined to make a small strand of double helix. With the aid of an enzyme called DNA polymerase, Khorana found that this small sequence could be polymerized into a double helix containing about 3,000 bases in which the order of the initial dinucleotide was maintained.

Khorana extended the method by making his initial synthesis more complex and producing tri- and tetranucleotides of known sequence. In all he produced 8 "artificial" DNAs. When these were presented to cell-free synthesizing systems, they produced RNA, which produced protein, which unambiguously confirmed the triplet nature of the code, and its translation. For example, take a dinucleotide based polymer, AC/TG. When this is converted to RNA by transcription, it produces a repeating sequence of either UG or AC. Either of these polymers, UGUGUGU . . . and ACACACAC . . . , can be read in 2 ways as triplets (UGU/GUG, ACA/CAC), and both were found to produce proteins made up of 2 alternating amino acids: threonine and histidine for ACACA . . . and valine and cysteine from UGUGUG. . . .

There are 2 other ways in which the code resembles language with which we are familiar. When we end a sentence, we mark the fact with a period. Two of the triplets of bases, rather than coding for amino acids, are periods. When the protein-synthesizing machinery reaches this part of an RNA molecule, it ceases to manufacture the protein and instead releases it.

The other important task that must be faced is beginning a sentence—or a protein. In the genetic code this is most important for, unless the synthetic machinery knows exactly where to begin, it may start reading from the wrong base and produce a completely nonsensical (nonfunctioning) protein. At the moment it seems that the code word for the amino acid methionine (AUG) also acts as a chain-starter. Where this is so, formylmethionine is coded for; its amino group is blocked, so that the protein can only be made in 1 direction. If amino acids are joined together in sequence, even if the addition of amino acids is given in a fixed order there are still 2 possible sequences, according to whether the second and subsequent amino acids link onto the chain through their amino or their acid groups. By blocking the amino group of methionine with a formyl group, this ambiguity is removed.

It is believed that all protein syntheses start with methionine, although in many cases this residue, and perhaps a bit more, is lopped off at some stage before the protein reaches its final form. The genetic code sequences are shown in Table 3.

TABLE 3

The Genetic Code

FIRST LETTER	SECOND LETTER				THIRD LETTER
	U	C	A	G	
U	phe	ser	tyr	cys	U
	phe	ser	tyr	cys	C
	leu	ser	end here	nonsense triplet	A
	leu	ser	end here	try	G
C	leu	pro	his	arg	U
	leu	pro	his	arg	C
	leu	pro	gln	arg	A
	leu	pro	gln	arg	G
A	ileu	thr	asn	ser	U
	ileu	thr	asn	ser	C
	ileu	thr	lys	arg	A
	met (begin here)	thr	lys	arg	G
G	val	ala	asp	gly	U
	val	ala	asp	gly	C
	val	ala	glu	gly	A
	val	ala	glu	gly	G

From this it can be seen exactly how a "point" mutation—that of a single base—can be deleterious. To take a realistic example, consider a short segment of double helix with the sequence

... TGA CTC AGG TAA ...
... ACT GAG TCC ATT ...

The simple molecule nitrous acid (HNO_2) is a powerful muta-
gen because it reacts with amino groups, and adenine, guanine,
and cytosine all have free amino groups. They are not all equally
reactive toward nitrous acid, and reactivity of individual residues in a DNA molecule differs from reactivity of the isolated
base, for the shape of the macromolecule protects some
amino groups while tending to expose others. Adenine and guanine are deaminated by HNO_2 to 2 other purine bases,
hypoxanthine and xanthine (X), while cytosine is deaminated to
the base common in RNA, uracil. Let us assume that, in the
sequence above, HNO_2 attacks all the guanine and cytosine
residues. Then, the sequence is changed chemically to:

... TXA UTU AXX TAA ...
... AUT XAX TUU ATT ...

If, in both cases, we assume it is the top strand which acts as a
template for RNA, the transcription sequences will be:

... TGA CTC AGG TAA ... ... TXA UTU AXX TAA ...
... ACU GAG UCC AUU ... ... ACU AAA UCC AUU ...

In the second case, the "wrong" RNA is produced because the
mutated bases X and U are not complementary to C and G, as
was the case originally. When the new RNA is translated into
protein, it produces the sequence Thr.Lys.Ser.Ile, rather than
the required Thr.Glu.Ser.Ile. Only 1 amino acid has changed,
admittedly, but the change could have far-reaching effects, for
while glutamic acid has an acidic side-chain, that of lysine is
basic—possibly sufficient to change the conformation of the
whole protein and make it nonfunctional.

Earlier in this chapter it was remarked that the disease sickle-
cell anemia is caused by a single amino acid substitution: glutamic acid instead of valine. The code for valine is GU(X)

(where (X) can be any of the 4 RNA bases); glutamic acid is GAA or GAG. Consequently, this lethal change can be attributed to a single change in DNA that results in the messenger RNA containing the base A at 1 position rather than U.

This is also why some of the complexities of molecular evolution are as great as they are, for a back mutation may require only a single base change. Instead of selecting from 20 possible amino acids, for mutation's sake selection is made from only 4 bases. Another reason for expressing caution about molecular genealogy is that the degeneracy of the code can lead to hidden mutations. If we find a sequence of RNA coding for an amino acid—for example, UCU (serine)—we have no way of knowing whether, at some time past, that part of the RNA did not read UCC, which also codes for serine. Nor, at present, can we tell how many of the codons of different RNAs coding for the "identical" portions of cytochrome c molecules are themselves identical. One reason for the degeneracy of the genetic code may be that it confers survival value: it can mutate within wide limits without producing dysfunctional molecules.

Two other possibilities on the chemical side of the DNA/RNA story are being explored: the sequencing of DNA/RNA molecules, and the actual synthesis of genes. With these investigations are associated names that have already appeared in this chapter: Fred Sanger and Gobind Khorana. But first meet a newcomer, Robert Holley, the first man to sequence a polynucleotide.

Analyzing a Gene

In addition to the messenger RNA, which carries the coded message from DNA to the ribosome, which reads it and converts it into protein, there is another form of RNA involved in protein synthesis. These are the relatively small molecules, known as transfer-RNAs (t-RNAs), which were mentioned in Chapter 5. They are responsible for lining up amino acids so that they are in the correct place on the assembly line when the ribosomal machinery reaches them. There are probably more than 20 different t-RNAs, although these are all that are theoretically needed for each of the 20 different amino acids to have its own.

In 1965 Holley and his collaborators at Cornell University worked out the sequences of nucleotides in the alanine t-RNA from yeast. This research—leading to a known sequence of 77 nucleotides—took 7 years, much of the time being occupied in obtaining sufficiently pure material to work with, using the technique of countercurrent distribution invented in the early 1940s by Lyman C. Craig.

Holley's method of analysis involved using an enzyme to break down the t-RNA molecule into fragments which could be separated from one another by passing them, in solution, down columns of chemically modified cellulose. In many ways the sequencing method resembled that used by Sanger on insulin a decade earlier, except that the spectroscopic and chromatographic techniques available were substantially better.

Holley's t-RNA contains several unusual bases, such as methylated guanines and dihydrouridine. The most interesting aspect of the structure, however, is its internal complementarity. Parts of the chain are able to form regions of double helix with other parts. Since Holley's success, several other t-RNAs have been sequenced, but at the moment the race is on for a bigger prize —total sequencing of a genome.[3]

At about the same time that Holley completed his sequence analysis of alanyl t-RNA, Fred Sanger took up RNA-sequencing studies. In 1968 he published the structure of a 120-sequence RNA known as 5S RNA, which can be isolated from ribosomes, but whose function is not understood. Sanger used a combination of electrophoresis and radiotracers.

Electrophoresis uses slight differences in the rates of move-

---

[3] A gene is that part of a DNA or—in some organisms—RNA molecule which codes for a single protein. The total genetic content of an organism is called its genome. It is now believed that segments of the genome may not code for proteins, but have some other, as yet not understood, function.

ment of different molecules in solution in an electric field to help separate and identify them. It is, in many respects, similar to paper chromatography, and an outgrowth from it. By using radioactive phosphorus in such a way that it is incorporated into the molecular fragments he is studying, Sanger is able to develop his electrophoretograms photographically, and from this identify substances by their position. Once simple nucleotides are identified under the experimental conditions, it is possible to use them as the basis for a grid which automatically identifies the other spots on the photographic plate. In this way small sequences are established and, using the overlap comparison method, built into bigger ones.

Following his first foray into the field, Sanger, with the help of a number of co-workers, decided to tackle the RNA from a virus called R17. This consists of a sequence of 3,300 nucleotides, and is the virus's genetic material, since some viruses use RNA in place of DNA as their information storehouse. Viruses are very simple creatures. Perhaps they are not creatures at all, but only live in the presence of life by taking over the synthetic machinery of other cells and making it translate their information rather than its own. RNA from R17 codes for 3 proteins. These are the coat protein, which in the complete virus forms a protective coat around its RNA, a replicase enzyme which participates in the reproduction of the RNA, and another protein whose function is ambiguous, as is its present name, "maturation factor."

When Sanger and his colleagues began work on this viral RNA, only the structure of the coat protein was known. Fortunately, the initial 21-base RNA fragment which they sequenced coded for a short segment of this. By May 1969, when he lectured to the Royal Society in London, Sanger was able to give the structure of a 57-base sequence that coded for nearly 20 of the coat protein amino acids; it was the first direct confirmation that the genetic code really does work in nature in the way that had been postulated from laboratory studies. (There was no real doubt about this, but it was pleasant to have the confirmation.)

Rather like Holley's t-RNA, this fragment had a structure capable of forming a helix with itself. A year after his lecture, Sanger had 2 other sequences, of 44 and 54 bases, which showed a similar property. He and his colleagues had also confirmed another small point—the genetic code is itself degenerate. In their sequences they had found all 6 possible triplets for serine. From this work came another postulate as to why the code might be degenerate. The 2 other large fragments also showed possibilities of self-helification, and if self-helification is important in the viral RNA it may be necessary for degeneracy to occur in some parts in order to form a comfortable double helix fit with other parts. R17 RNA is not the only genome that is being analyzed, nor is Sanger's group at Cambridge the only one attempting to elucidate a whole genome. In mid-1972, a group from the University of Ghent, in France, announced a 476-nucleotide sequence from the 3500-nucleotide genome of a virus called bacteriophage MS2. Like R17, the MS2 genome codes for three proteins, and the unit analyzed by the Ghent group is that for the coat protein, plus some non-coding nucleotides at either end.

Synthesizing a Gene

At the other pole from analysis is synthesis. While work goes on to sequence nucleic acids, there is an equally determined research effort to synthesize them. It is here that Khorana's name crops up again. Synthesis of a gene is a logical extension of his earlier work on nucleotide synthesis which helped unravel the language of the triplets. This does not mean that the synthesis of long nucleotides of predetermined sequence is easy.

In the summer of 1968, when he addressed the Fifth International Symposium on the Chemistry of Natural Products in London, England, Khorana said, with obvious relief, "We have synthesised an eicosanucleotide and we shall never have to make one that long again." He was able to say that this 20-base chain was the largest that needed to be synthesized by purely chemical methods because of the discovery a year before of DNA-joining enzyme. Just as Khorana had recruited an enzyme to help his earlier work on producing the controlled repeating order polymers, he commandeered DNA-joining enzyme for use in what he calls "the sticky-end technique" of DNA synthesis.

DNA-joining enzyme will link 2 nucleotide chains together, as long as a complementary strand overlapping the joining point on both sides is present. It is as if the second strand acted as an anvil on which the 2 ends can be joined together, with the enzyme acting as a hammer. Since the anvil need be only 4 or 5 base units in length, use of the sticky-end technique means that pure chemosynthesis need only extend to nucleotides about 10 units in length, as Figure 19 indicates.

This illustration shows double-stranded DNA in which the bottom strand is part of the code for the synthesis of alanyl t-RNA, the molecule sequenced by Holley in 1965. By June 1970, Khorana and his colleagues had completed manufacture of this DNA. A gene had been synthesized.

Hemoglobin: Iron in the Soul

So far, looking at life on the molecular level, we have identified the following pattern. At the heart lie the nucleic acids, which carry the coded sequences for and participate in the synthesis of proteins. The proteins, as well as providing structural materials, such as skin and horn, are responsible for the making and breaking of all the other molecules of life—the polymeric carbohydrates, the smaller lipids, and many other classes of compounds. This story is correct in outline, but it is not the whole story. The protein coding inherent in DNA only specifies amino acid sequences, and many enzymes and related substances are more than just proteins. In addition to the organic chemistry of life, there is an important area of inorganic chemistry (increasingly called bioinorganic chemistry), which perhaps

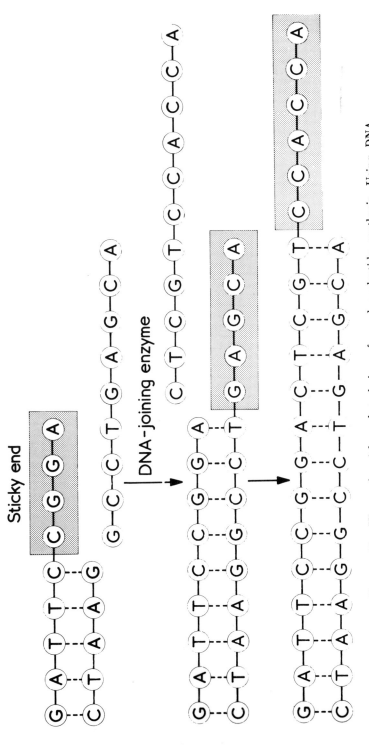

FIGURE 19. Khorana's sticky-end technique for polynucleotide synthesis. Using DNA-joining enzyme, short segments of nucleic acid can be linked together, providing a short piece of the complementary strand is available to act as an anvil for linking the chain.

cannot be better exemplified than by returning for a more detailed look at hemoglobin.

Hemoglobin is the material in the red blood cells of higher mammals which transports oxygen around the body from its pickup point in the lungs. Indirectly, it also removes the carbon dioxide formed by cellular processes to the lungs, where it is expelled. As the earlier discussion of sickle-cell anemia made clear, a large part of the hemoglobin molecule is protein.

Unraveling of the molecule's three-dimensional structure was primarily the work of 1 man, Max Perutz. In an article published in 1964, Perutz wrote: "In 1937, a year after I entered the University of Cambridge as a graduate student [he had left his native Austria as a refugee from Nazism], I chose the x-ray analysis of hemoglobin, the oxygen-bearing protein of the blood, as the subject of my research. Fortunately the examiners of my doctoral thesis did not insist on a determination of the structure, otherwise I should have had to remain a graduate student for 23 years." [4]

The major breakthrough in Perutz's work was his discovery in 1953 of the technique of "isomorphous replacement." This involves adding heavy metal atoms to a crystal without altering its structure (isomorphous means having the same form). It is then possible to relate the diffraction patterns obtained by x-ray bombardment of a complex crystalline compound with individual atoms in the molecule. The first concrete result was a low resolution map of the simpler oxygen-transport compound myoglobin, obtained in 1957 by John Kendrew, also working at Cambridge. (Perutz and Kendrew shared the 1962 Nobel prize in chemistry for their work. In the same year Crick, Watson, and Maurice Wilkins of King's College, London—who had studied the structure of DNA by x-ray crystallography—received the Nobel prize for physiology and medicine. It was a good year for molecular biologists.)

Hemoglobin is more complex than myoglobin, which is made

[4] M. F. Perutz, "The hemoglobin molecule," *Scientific American*, Vol. 211, no. 5 (1964), p. 64.

up of only 1 protein chain. It consists of 4 protein units, composed of 2 identical pairs, called alpha and beta. The 4 "globin" chains form a roughly spherical molecule, with each individual globin acting as a basket to hold the "heme" portion of the molecule, which is an iron atom and a complex, but quite small, organic structure called a porphyrin. The iron is chemically bonded to the porphyrin and to a nitrogen in a histidine residue of a globin chain (see Figure 20). This 5-coordinate arrangement changes to an octahedral complex when an oxygen molecule attaches itself to the iron through coordinate bonding.

Inorganic chemists find the 5-coordinate form of iron (as it

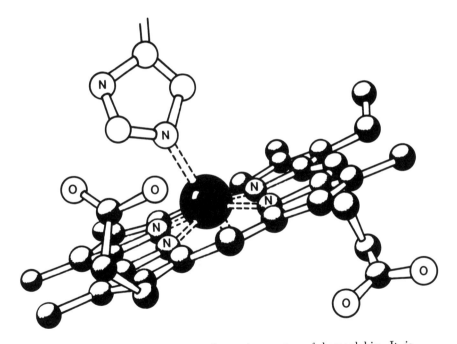

FIGURE 20. The iron atom at the active center of hemoglobin. It is joined to the porphyrin ring and to the nitrogen atom of a histidine residue in the protein (globin) chain. When an oxygen atom links to the iron atom, the iron orbitals change shape; this in turn makes the iron atom move closer to the porphyrin, tugging the globin chain into a different shape—a mechanism which facilitates the combination of oxygen atoms with the other iron atoms in the molecule.

occurs in venous blood) odd, for straightforward inorganic compounds of iron do not usually adopt such a structure. In recent years, however, it has become clear that 5-coordinate structures of this kind are involved in inorganic chemical reactions as transitional intermediates. In other words, they are the structures which occupy the top of the activation energy barrier. This may account in part for the activity of hemoglobin: it is permanently in an activated state, and has negligible activation energy to overcome before forming an addition compound with oxygen.

This is only part of the story. Evolution has led to a molecule with more than a single cunning design feature. Why, for example, should hemoglobin have evolved as a multifunctional molecule with 4 oxygen binding sites? The answer is that it can function more effectively. If a molecule of oxygen approaches 2 molecules of hemoglobin, 1 of which has already taken up 3 molecules of oxygen, the other none, the chances are 70 to 1 in favor of the triply-bound molecule grabbing yet another oxygen, while the other is still left with none. This loading mechanism also works in reverse. Once a 4-oxygen carrying hemoglobin loses 1 oxygen, the others strip off more easily. In this way efficient transport of oxygen is obtained.

The reason lies in the fine structure of the molecule. When the iron atom bonds it forms hybrid orbitals, like those described in Chapter 3, so that the 5 bonds in the 5-coordinate form come from the lone pairs on the nitrogen and are coordinate bonds. The 6 $3d$ electrons of the iron atom are in paired orbitals of their own. One of these pairs is positioned so that the iron is repelled from the plane of the porphyrin ring by neighboring porphyrin orbitals and lies slightly above it, toward the nitrogen of the histidine residue to which it is bonded. When the sixth coordinate bond is formed, the orbitals move into different positions, and the iron atom now moves into the plane of the porphyrin. The movement is through a distance of about 1 angstrom. Although this is a tiny amount, the pull on the histidine residue alters the configuration of the globin chain. This alteration changes the relationship between the different globin chains in such a way that the small constraints which otherwise slightly hinder oxygen attachment are lowered. Consequently, once primed with 1 oxygen atom, the molecule is successively more likely to gain the remainder of its complement. It was not until the summer of 1970 that Perutz put the seal to his work on hemoglobin by realizing that this was the molecule's chemical secret.

The strangely symmetrical porphyrin ring is not restricted to heme, but occurs elsewhere. Where metals are involved in biological reactions it is one of nature's favorite structures. The essential dietary substance vitamin B_{12}, for example, consists of a porphyrin ring (rather more complex than that in heme) with a cobalt atom in the middle. It was for determining the structure of vitamin B_{12} by x-ray methods that Dorothy Hodgkin, whose name has already been mentioned in connection with the structure of insulin, was awarded her Nobel prize. Porphyrins in which the metal atom is copper, manganese, and vanadium have also been found in natural systems.

Incorporation of metals into proteins with the aid of a porphyrin is not the only example of a biological molecule in which the part produced as a direct result of the genetic code —the protein—is not sufficient by itself to produce the desired effect. Vitamin B_{12} has been implicated in the activity of several enzymes, and it is now becoming apparent that many of the vitamins—substances identified, for the most part, in the early years of this century and found to be essential to healthy life— are necessary to make enzymes work properly, and are then called cofactors or coenzymes.

Other enzymes contain just a metal atom. For example, carboxypeptidase A, an enzyme which chops the end amino acid from peptide and protein chains, requires a single atom of zinc to work. Study of these complex systems is still at a very early stage, and it is not yet possible to generalize about them. However, it seems likely in some cases that the basic function performed by the biological system can be performed by the metal ion or organic cofactor alone, but only with a low efficiency. The association with protein, followed by subsequent evolution of the protein chain, has led to much enhanced efficiency and made the continuance and development of life possible. The reverse can also happen: the metal may also help the protein. Thermolysin, for example, requires one atom of zinc per molecule for its activity. It also contains several calcium atoms per molecule. Unlike most enzymes, thermolysin is stable at temperatures near the boiling point of water. X-ray analysis of the structure has shown that this stability is a result of the association with calcium ions. If the ions are removed, the enzyme is still reactive, but is no longer resistant to heat degradation.

One complex system, which involves no protein, but does involve a metal atom and the porphyrin ring and which may, more than any other, have underlain the continuance and development of life, is chlorophyll. This substance plays a key role in photosynthesis, the process which mediates the basic conversion of inorganic into organic materials—or, since these old divisions are now crumbling, the building up of carbon chains from single carbon molecules. Despite the cleverness of the genetic code, no animal can survive without the supply of some preformed carbon chains. Ultimately, it is to the plant kingdom that we owe our lives.

Let There Be Light

Although a few types of bacteria have developed life styles which allow them to survive on a diet of mineral salts and other inorganic chemicals, all higher life forms depend on the photosynthetic activities of plants. In overall terms, green plants absorb light and use its energy to convert water and carbon dioxide into carbohydrates, biochemicals composed solely of carbon, hydrogen, and oxygen (the sugar which some people use in tea and coffee is a simple carbohydrate composed of 12 carbon atoms, 22 hydrogens, and 11 oxygens per molecule).

The primary step in photosynthesis is the absorption of light energy; the key compound in this is chlorophyll a, a large part of which is a porphyrin ring with a magnesium atom in the middle. When this absorbs light, an electron is excited into a higher orbital. In view of the discussion in Chapter 3 (p. 71), it is not surprising that the basic porphyrin structure has alternating single and double bonds, making the system conducive to electron delocalization.

There are several other compounds in green plants which can absorb light: chlorophyll b has a structure similar to chlorophyll a, while beta-carotene is quite different, although a notable feature of its molecular architecture is a long chain of alternating single and double bonds. The same delocalized type of construction occurs in another series of pigments found in blue green algae, the phycobilins. (Actually these are not too different from porphyrins—it is as if one broke a carbon-carbon bond in the porphyrin ring and stretched the molecule out in a straight line.) In all cases, the really important molecule is chlorophyll a, for when the other molecules absorb light, they pass the excitation energy to an adjacent chlorophyll a molecule before it can be used further.

Before considering the next step, it is worth mentioning that we can be sure we know the correct structure of chlorophyll a, because it has been synthesized in the laboratory. Despite the sophistication of analytical methods now at their disposal, chemists still like, if possible, to make artificially the structure they have elucidated, just as a double-check on the accuracy of analysis. Chlorophyll a was synthesized in 1960 by Robert Burns Woodward of Harvard University. One of the most prolific synthetic chemists of our time, Woodward, together with large teams of research workers, has succeeded in synthesizing many biological chemicals of complex structure, including vitamin B_{12}, for which achievements he was awarded the 1965 Nobel prize in chemistry.

The energy trapped in an excited molecule of chlorophyll a

can escape again as light. Under certain conditions chlorophyll a fluoresces. Whenever a molecular electron is excited to a higher orbital, some of the excitation energy is always dissipated as heat, so that fluorescence occurs at a longer wavelength (lower energy) than that of the light initially absorbed. The other photosynthetic pigments all absorb at shorter wavelengths than chlorophyll a, so that even when some of the energy is lost, they can still excite one of the latter's electrons. It is possible that these pigments have only evolved so that plants and algae can use a broader part of the visible spectrum than would be available if there were only 1 photosynthetic pigment; however, absorption is still quite restricted, as witness the almost universal greenness of plants.

Assuming that the chlorophyll a, instead of reemitting its energy as fluorescence, disposes of it fruitfully, what happens? There is, at the moment, no completely clear answer. It is known that the overall process involves 2 light absorption steps, each of which results in the freeing of an electron (derived ultimately from the breakdown of water into gaseous oxygen and hydrogen ions). The electrons are carried down complex gradients, involving a number of other biochemicals, such as the cytochromes, in such a way that 2 crucial substances are formed. These are adenosine triphosphate (ATP) and reduced nicotinamide adenine dinucleotide phosphate (NADPH).

ATP, formed by this mechanism from adenosine diphosphate (ADP) and inorganic phosphate, is the universal energy currency of life. It plays a role, for example, in the manufacture of proteins by converting amino acids to aminoacyl phosphates, which are more reactive. It is the modern biological equivalent of the phosphates believed to have played a part in the condensation reactions on the primeval earth, but its advantage over them is that it recycles easily. When it forms an activated phosphate compound, ADP is produced as a side product, and, as in the case of photosynthesis, there are biological mechanisms which utilize energy from other sources to reconvert ADP to ATP. NADPH, on the other hand, is used for storing hydrogen atoms until they are required in biological reactions, when it gives them up to become NADP, the substance from which NADPH is made during photosynthesis.

This seems to be a very complex process for storing the energy from light but, in many ways, it is necessary. Electron excitation is a quick way of grabbing energy as it passes through a cell in the form of light. By its nature, an excited electron is in an unstable state and wants to get rid of its excess energy. An excited chlorophyll a molecule has about 10^{-9} second in which this can happen in ways other than the wasteful form of fluorescence. Consequently, a system has had to evolve which can turn transiently held energy into a more permanent form in which it can be used at leisure. Once the ATP and NADPH have formed, the remaining steps in photosynthesis, the so-called Calvin cycle, can take place in the dark.

The working out of the actual chemistry of carbon-compound synthesis in the photosynthetic scheme was the result of the bringing together of 2 at that time new techniques, and their dedicated application by a group at the University of California led by Melvin Calvin (who has also played a significant part in chemical origins of life studies).

Shortly before the beginning of World War II, Samuel Ruben and Martin Kamen began to study photosynthesis at the University of California, using newly discovered isotopes of common elements. Through the use of ^{18}O they established that the oxygen given off by photosynthesizing plants comes from water, and not from carbon dioxide. When this heavy isotope of ordinary oxygen was incorporated in the water used in their experiments, it could later be detected in evolved oxygen, whereas when they incorporated it into carbon dioxide none of the isotope appeared in the oxygen. They then extended their studies by using a radioactive isotope of carbon (^{14}C). However, the advent of war, and the subsequent death of Ruben in a laboratory accident, cut short their work. By the time the war had finished, the technology of isotope separation and purification had advanced greatly as a by-product of the development of the atomic bomb, and ^{14}C was much more readily available. In 1946 Calvin organized a group to trace the path of carbon in photosynthesis. In addition to a better supply of ^{14}C, he had another asset, the analytical method of paper chromatography, developed during the war by Martin and Synge. The basis of Calvin's tracer work was similar to that of Ruben and Kamen with ^{18}O. Feed an unusual isotope of a common element into a plant, check in which compounds that isotope gets involved, and then you can say that the biosynthetic mechanism of the plant involves the labeled atom you have used in making that compound. Where the labeled atom is carbon, analyzing mixtures of compounds obtained from the plant at different times after feeding the labeled compound to it will make it possible to establish the order in which the plant synthesizes those compounds bearing the label. The analysis consists of measuring the quantities of isotope in each compound.

One of the first points that Calvin and his colleagues discovered was that photosynthesis worked too fast to make the use of leafy plants feasible in the early experiments. Consequently, most of Calvin's work was with 2 photosynthetic single-celled organisms, the algae Chlorella pyrenoidosa and Scenedesmus obliquus. These organisms were grown in solution; at a precise time, radioactive bicarbonate ion (which can be used as a CO_2 source) was injected into the solution. After a specified period the cells were killed, and extracts made and analyzed by chromatography and autoradiography. In order to obtain a meaningful pattern of results, it was necessary in some experiments to kill the algae within a few seconds of exposure to labeled material, so quickly did they use it. Within 30 seconds, the algae had incorporated radioactivity into between 20 and 30 different compounds.

Basically, in the Calvin cycle as it is now understood, a molecule of carbon dioxide forms a carbon-carbon bond with a 5-carbon chain compound, ribulose-1,5-diphosphate; the resultant 6-carbon compound splits into 2 3-carbon molecules.

Through the action of ATP, NADPH, and various enzymes, some of these 3-carbon molecules are built up to form 6-carbon molecules, which then react with another 3-carbon molecule to form a 5-carbon and a 4-carbon molecule. The latter then gains another 3-carbon chain to form a 7-carbon compound, sedoheptulose-7-phosphate. This reacts together with another 3-carbon molecule to produce 2 5-carbon molecules which are converted into ribulose-1,5-diphosphate, and the cycle begins again.

By other biosynthetic pathways—many of which have been studied using isotope tracer techniques—the carbohydrates formed can be transformed into other carbohydrates and carbohydrate polymers such as starch, into amino acids, fatty acids (porphyrins are probably biosynthesised from the amino acid glycine and the simple analogue of the fatty acids, acetic acid), and ultimately all of the chemicals of life.

And There Is Light

Through the absorption of light, plants make all higher life forms possible, including man who, seeing what the plants do, has struggled to achieve an understanding of how they do it. Without light, of course, man would not be able to see. Perhaps more than any other of the 5, sight is the most important of the senses to man and other higher animals. What does that part of the electromagnetic spectrum which we call visible light do to enable us to see?

Such a question involves an understanding of the human brain which far transcends not only modern chemistry, but all of modern science. But, just as chlorophyll acts as a mediator between untrapped light energy and the firmly held energy of a chemical bond, so are there chemicals and chemical reactions at the interface between the photons of light that strike our eyes and the electrical impulses which pass from the optic nerve into the brain for analysis. Not surprisingly, the chemistry of that interface obeys the simple chemical rules elucidated in earlier chapters and, like much of this chapter, helps to show how the manipulation of molecular shapes can produce effects of great diversity and sophistication.

Physiologists have shown that the human brain, under carefully controlled conditions, is capable of registering a sensation of light when no more than 2 or 3 individual photons strike the eye. It has even been suggested that a single photon striking the eye and causing a reaction in 1 molecule is sufficient to be registered.

During the 1930s, Professor George Wald of Harvard University, at that time working in Berlin and Zurich, discovered that the molecule in question, the visual pigment rhodopsin (also known as visual purple), which had been found in the retinal rod cells of many types of animals before the end of the nineteenth century, consisted of 2 parts: a colorless protein (opsin) and a previously unknown carotenoid substance, now called retinal. Carotenoids, as the name implies, are a family of substances structurally similar to carotene (already mentioned in connection with light absorption during photosynthesis).

Toward the mid-1940s, R. A. Morton and his colleagues at the University of Liverpool in England showed that there was a close chemical relationship between vitamin A, an essential dietary ingredient the lack of which causes a number of bodily disturbances, including "night blindness," and retinal. He showed that retinal has 2 fewer hydrogen atoms in its molecule than vitamin A (they are removed by the conversion of NAD, a close relative of NADP, to NADH). There are also close chemical similarities between both these compounds and the carotenes widely found in plants. It is believed that vitamin A is produced in the body by splitting carotene molecules in half.

In addition to the differences between the numbers of hydrogen atoms in retinal and vitamin A, there is another important difference. Like carotene, these molecules are characterized by conjugated systems of single and double bonds. Double bonds between carbon atoms, which involve pi orbitals, can produce different compounds made up from the same ordering of atoms in the molecule, and known as geometrical isomers (see p. 70). Chemists have a convention for describing double bonds as either cis or trans, according to exactly how the remaining groups attached to a pair of doubly-bonded carbon atoms are situated in space. All the double bonds in vitamin A are trans; in retinal, 1 of them is cis. This single cis bond gives the molecule an uncomfortable shape. It is under strain which makes the molecule less stable than it would be if, like vitamin A, the double bonds were all trans. This, as workers in George Wald's laboratory at Harvard found, is the secret of vision.

In 1952, Ruth Hubbard showed that only the cis isomer of retinal would combine with the protein opsin to form the visual pigment rhodopsin. Seven years later it was discovered that the effect of light on rhodopsin is to excite an electron in retinal out of its bonding orbital. The electron excited is one of those involved in the cis double bond. Freed momentarily from the constraints of pi bonding, the retinal molecule changes shape, so that when the electron falls back into a bonding orbital reforming the pi bond, it locks the molecule into the lower energy configuration of trans retinal. This new shape does not suit the protein opsin, and the 2 molecules separate. As Ruth Hubbard wrote in 1967: "Everything else—further chemical changes, nerve excitation, perception of light, behavioral responses—are consequences of this single photochemical act." [5]

A Matter of Taste

The geometry of chemical molecules thus plays an important part in such diverse functions as oxygen transport in the blood, catalysis by enzymes, and vision. What of the other senses? Two

[5] Ruth Hubbard and Allen Kropf, "Molecular isomers in vision," *Scientific American*, Vol. 216, no. 6 (1967), p. 64.

at least, taste and smell, involve direct contact with and analysis of a wide range of chemical substances, although the analysis is in the subjective form of "pleasant," "unpleasant," "bitter," "burnt," "sweet," and "fruity," rather than in the objective chemical sense of structure analysis. To produce even a limited range of distinct sensation, it seems likely that substances must react chemically with receptors in the mouth and nose as the first step toward producing the nervous impulses that lead to our brains.

Many small carbohydrate molecules, collectively called sugars, taste sweet. One of the most effective of these is sucrose, which is what supermarkets sell as "sugar." All the sugars belong to the same family of compounds and have common structural features, but there are other substances, chemically quite unlike sugars, which also taste sweet. Saccharin is an example. To account for the diversity of chemical structure and the common sensation of sweetness, Professor R. S. Shallenberger of the New York State Agricultural Experimental Institute suggested in the mid-1960s that sweetness resulted from the formation of hydrogen bonds between the sweet molecules and receptor substances in the tongue. As part of his early work, which concentrated on the sugars themselves, Shallenberger pointed out that the simple sugars that are less sweet have more internal hydrogen bonds—that is, the bonds form between different atoms within the molecule—than those which are more sweet. Possibly, he suggested, sweetness depends on the number of hydrogen bonds which can form with receptors in the tongue.

In 1967 Shallenberger extended his theory. By this time he had found structural correlations among a wide range of different sweet-tasting chemicals. All of the compounds he investigated not only had a hydrogen atom in 1 part of the molecule available for hydrogen bonding but, at a distance of not less than 2.5 and not more than 4 angstroms from this, was another atom able to form another hydrogen bond. Shallenberger suggested that the receptor molecule must contain a similar 2-

pronged unit, enabling the sweet molecule to combine with it by forming 2 hydrogen bonds.

An interesting chemical accident in 1969 helped to support Shallenberger's theory that the sweetness and the complementary receptor portions of molecules must consist of at least 2 parts. During work on a peptide hormone (gastrin), Robert Mazur, James Shlatter, and Arthur Goldkamp, chemists working at the Chemical Research Department of the G. D. Searle Co. in Skokie, Illinois, discovered a dipeptide that was 200 times sweeter than common sugar. One amino acid, alanine, was already known to be sweet, but this is only twice as sweet as sugar, and was not a component of the dipeptide, which was made from aspartic acid and phenylalanine (which, by itself, is bitter rather than sweet).

The Searle team prepared a number of dipeptides. All the others containing phenylalanine were bitter, although several containing aspartic acid were sweet. Work at Searle has continued in this field and, in 1971, Mazur, Goldkamp, and Patricia James published a paper analyzing the criteria of peptide sweetness. The aspartic acid part is necessary, and both its amino group and the acid group in its side-chain have to be free (presumably to form hydrogen bonds), while the other end of the molecule (the second amino acid) must contain a hydrophobic group—that is, a molecular structure which has no affinity for water. The function of the second part may be to prevent interference by other molecules with the hydrogen bonding process.

At the time of the Searle chemists' original discovery, Takashi Kubota and Isao Kubo of Osaka City University in Japan had just published a paper about bitterness. They showed that a series of bitter-tasting compounds also had the 2-pin-socket arrangement found in sweet-tasting compounds, but that the optimum distance of the 2 pins was 1.5 angstroms, much less than for sweetness.

Clearly, delicate chemical geometry is involved in the determination of taste. It seems likely that the receptor molecules are proteins—a sweet-sensitive protein from cow's tongue was isolated in 1966. Before the story proceeds, it will be necessary to know more about the structure of such proteins, to see how they interact with small molecules.

Chemical Smells

Although only 4 basic taste sensations (sweet, bitter, salt, sour) are recognized by physiologists, there are about twice that number of different basic smells, all of which come down to a question of basic molecular geometry. The first person on record to have suggested that this might be so was the Greek philosopher Lucretius. Noone took him very seriously until 1949, when Scottish chemist R. W. Moncrieff proposed the existence, in the olfactory apparatus, of a few different types of receptor, each corresponding to a different primary odor. This idea was interpreted in stereochemical terms by John Amoore while he was still an undergraduate at the University of Oxford, England. During the 1950s and early 1960s, Amoore, in collaboration with James Johnston and Martin Rubin of Georgetown University School of Medicine, set out to test his theory experimentally.

Amoore searched the literature of organic chemistry, comparing the known smells of simple molecules with their general shapes. He came to the conclusion that there are 7 primary odors, and in general terms described the probable shape of the receptor site for each. A complex odor, he suggested, results from a molecule fitting more than 1 receptor shape. This hypothesis was tested by synthesizing an organic molecule which consisted of 3 chains of carbon atoms attached to a central carbon atom, to which a hydrogen atom was also attached. A fruity smell was predicted for this molecule because it fitted 3 of the theoretical receptor shapes ("floral," "pepperminty," and "ethereal"). When the single hydrogen atom attached to the central carbon was replaced with a methyl (CH_3) group, the overall shape of the molecule was changed so that it should have fitted less well into the hypothetical "floral" and "pepperminty" receptors, but just as well into the "ethereal" receptor. When tests were carried out on humans, it was found that the first compound did have a fruity odor, while in the second an ether-like tinge was clearly detectable.

Using bees, which "smell" with their antennae, as well as human subjects, Amoore, Johnston, and Rubin went on to show that molecules which fit the same single theoretical receptor site all have the same smell, while 2 molecules, each shaped to fit a single, different site, always smell different. Physiological evidence in favor of the theory came from another source when R. C. Gesteland, working at MIT, studied the stimulation by different substances of single olfactory nerve cells in the frog. He found that cells responded differently to different chemicals. Since a nerve impulse is always a yes/no situation—a cell either responds or it does not—this experiment confirmed that there are different receptors attached to the business end of the nerve cells. Gesteland estimated that there are probably 8 different types, at least 5 of which correspond to the primary odors suggested by Amoore.

A Whiff of Sex

In man, smell is an important part of life, but it is not the essence of life and death as it is to some other species. Without smell, some of these would find it difficult to survive, for the finding of mating partners is directly connected with this sense. Here the word "smell" is being stretched a little, for, as with the bee, detection of the "odorous" substances may not be through what we would call a nose.

One particular form of chemical detection is of prime importance. Some species produce a chemical which has a strong effect on other members of the same species when it is "sniffed" by them—similar in some ways to the effects of hormones.

Since 1959 such communicating chemicals have been called "pheromones."

Important pheromones—not only to the species that use them, but also of potential value to man—are the insect sex attractants. Female insects of species such as the silkworm and gypsy moth release small quantities of pheromone as an advertisement, so that males in the area can find them. It has been calculated that the average female gypsy moth carries enough sex attractant to communicate with more than 10^9 male moths. Even though the total amount is tiny, only a few molecules are needed to stimulate a male moth into looking for the source of the smell.

The smallness of the total amount of active material in any single moth is shown by details of the isolation by chemists of 2 such substances. Adolf Butenandt and his colleagues, working at the Max Planck Institute of Biochemistry, Munich, Germany, extracted material from a quarter of a million silkworm moths in order to obtain 12 thousandths of a gram of the sex attractant bombykol, while U.S. Department of Agriculture scientists Martin Jacobson, Morton Beroza, and William Jones used twice that many gypsy moths to get 20 thousandths of a gram of their sex attractant. Both compounds were identified and synthesized in the late 1950s and early 1960s, since which time it has become clear that many other insects—and higher animals —use pheromones as part of their intercommunication systems. Certain species of ants, for example, provide chemical route markers to show others in their colony the way to sources of food, and produce other pheromones to warn colleagues of any danger they have encountered.

The importance of these substances to man is primarily that they offer a way of controlling specific insect pests. Occasionally there is a secondary commercial value. In 1957 Butenandt isolated a simple substance produced by male specimens of a tropical water bug to excite females sexually. An extract of this substance, which has an odor like cinnamon to humans, has been used for many years in southeast Asia as a spice. Now the synthetic substance is sold instead. However, this use is trivial compared to the primary one mentioned above.

Insect pests cost mankind millions of dollars each year in terms of damaged crops. Yet, as is made clear in Chapter 9, man's attempts to combat these pests chemically have, until recently, met with mixed success. Synthetic pesticides have been insufficiently selective and, as a consequence, have caused serious pollution problems. In addition, insects are adept at developing strains resistant to a particular pesticide.

Combining the techniques of chemistry with an insect's own characteristic biology provides the possibility of selective attack. No insect can develop a resistance to its own sex attractant—if it did, the species would soon die out—and, because the insects have been efficient in developing attractants that attract only their own species, other species are unlikely to be affected by insect destruction methods that involve a particular pheromone. However, it was found in mid-1972 that certain Indian termites and honeybees share a common pheromone. And, early in 1973, U.S. scientists reported that cabbage looper moths and alfalfa looper moths have the same sex attractant; they do not interbreed for behavioral reasons.

When the U.S. Department of Agriculture scientists had identified gypsy moth sex attractant, they were able to synthesize it in the laboratory. They also synthesized some very similar compounds, one with 2 fewer carbon atoms (which had no effect) and one with 2 more (which was just as effective as the natural material). Since this latter product (gyplure) could be synthesized very easily from a substance that occurs naturally in castor oil, it was adopted by the nation for a program of attack on the gypsy moth. Traps were baited with gyplure and the moths flew straight into them, after which they could be easily destroyed.

Although the use of pheromones is an excellent way of attracting insects to a particular place, it does not kill them. There is one variation that goes all the way: It is possible to use some pheromonal substances to encourage females to lay eggs in unsuitable places where they are unlikely to survive. But, in general, it is necessary to kill the insect by a second method. However, the principle of using a particular species' own biological chemistry to destroy it can be extended.

Eternal Children of the Insect World

Insects have hormonal systems for communication within a single organism, and those can be turned against them. There are 2 distinct phases of the insect life cycle, a larval stage and an adult stage. Since the existence of insect hormones was established in 1934 by British biologist Sir Vincent Wigglesworth, it has become clear that 3 hormones are frequently involved in the change from larva to adult. There is a brain hormone which stimulates production of a molting hormone (ecdysone), which is responsible for inducing the shedding of the larval skin when the protoinsect inside gets too big for it. Ecdysone works in conjunction with juvenile hormone, which keeps the insect in the larval stage. The laboratory syntheses of both juvenile hormone and ecdysone were achieved in the mid-1960s, following work similar in complexity to that required for isolation and structural elucidation of sex pheromones. For example, a close relative of insect molting hormone, crustecdysone, was isolated in 1966; 2 thouandths of a gram were obtained from 1 ton of crayfish. Incidentally, it was discovered in 1972 that several species of crab use crustecdysone as a molting hormone and a sex attractant. A male crab, attracted to a female by the crustecdysone, protects her while she molts, then mates with her.

If the manufacture of juvenile hormone is not switched off at the right time, instead of metamorphosing into an adult a larval insect continues to molt—perhaps once or twice more than it usually would—and then dies. Since they are unable to take part in the reproductive process until after metamorphosis, insects that are kept "juvenile" do not produce offspring.

The potential insecticidal properties of insect hormones were realized by Carroll Williams at Harvard University in the mid-1950s, when he discovered that the Cecropia moth was a rich source of juvenile hormone. It was not until the 1960s that syntheses of the actual hormone substances were achieved by several groups using different synthetic methods. However, by chance, Williams and a collaborator, John Law, discovered that simpler, quite easily synthesized substances had juvenile hormone-like activity. This synthetic juvenile hormone was found to be useful in controlling the species of mosquito which is responsible for spreading yellow fever, and also the body louse, which can spread several human diseases, including epidemic typhus.

Czechoslovak workers led by Karel Slama manufactured similar compounds and found them to be highly active against the bug, Pyrrhocoris apterus. So effective was the material they produced that treatment of an adult male with it rendered the eggs of any female with which the male copulated sterile for the rest of her life.

In an unexpected way, the work by Williams in America and Slama in Czechoslovakia also showed the importance of international collaboration in science. In the mid-1960s, Slama sent Williams some specimens of Pyrrhocoris apterus for experimental use. However, Williams could not get them to metamorphose properly, although Slama had bred thousands of adults of the species and Williams used his breeding methods.

Williams checked all the possibilities to make sure that there was no difference between his breeding conditions and Slama's. Eventually, after eliminating all other possibilities, only 1 remained. Part of the procedure involved small strips of paper being put into the glass breeding tanks for the insects to exercise on. Williams replaced the paper he had been using with a different type. The bugs began to breed properly.

American paper is frequently made with pulp from the balsam fir, while European paper is not. The balsam fir contains a substance, juvabione, which has subsequently been identified and synthesized, that acts on P. apterus as if it were juvenile hormone.

There is a moral to this story. After some years of using nonspecific synthetic insecticides, man concluded that it might be better to look for specific defense systems against insects. This might seem to be a real bit of human ingenuity, except that certain plants have been doing it for years. In addition to balsam fir, it has been known for some time that the Australian timber tree, Podocarpus elatus, is particularly resistant to insect attack. In 1966 it was discovered that the tree is a rich source of crustecdysone, which interferes with proper insect development.

In the early 1960s it was shown that 1 of the intermediate compounds formed during the biosynthesis of ecdysone is cholesterol, a substance for which at least some insects have a dietary requirement. Cholesterol also occurs in human beings, and is structurally related to the steroid hormones, which control various aspects of sexual activity. The economy of nature is apparent: certain basic chemical structures are used over and over again, and it is by small changes in parts of the molecule, which alter its geometry and thus its reactivity, that the diverse activities of biological systems are mediated.

Underlying the superficial diversity of living nature there appears to be a unity based on a few simple chemical principles. If, for the words "living nature" we substituted "chemical industry," the sentence still reads true. Although it would be possible to fill the remainder of this book with further details of the ways in which chemists are laying bare living processes, it is now time to look at chemistry from a different angle. From Homo Sapiens, man the thinker, we pass to Homo faber, man the maker.

7 ❈ Industrious Chemists

The origin of life, or of the molecules that were necessary for formation of life, followed basic chemical laws, such as those of kinetics and thermodynamics. The time scales involved were enormous, because the processes were largely random. In the laboratory experiments that simulated the primeval production of such important building blocks as amino acids and sugars, only a few days were needed to repeat nature's long-term experiments.

One of the characteristics of laboratory chemistry is that it seeks to increase the yields of reaction and produce as much of a desired product as possible. Production of chemicals on an industrial scale might be expected to follow the same search for efficiency, but this is not so. Although industry must be efficient if it is to make a profit, the yields of many of the reactions used seem to parallel those postulated for the origin of life, rather than the practices of the laboratory chemist. Yet clearly this is a successful procedure, for chemical manufacture is one of the world's largest industries.

Chemical industry is called a service industry, for its primary function is to serve the requirements of other industries, many of them consumer industries. A consumer industry produces artifacts for sale to the general public—automobiles, television sets, clothes, and so on. Only about a quarter of the chemical industry's products are sold direct to the consumer; detergents are an example. The rest go to other industries as raw materials for textile fibers, for dyeing, or fabricating machine parts, or for use in such processes as steelmaking, which requires large quantities of strong acids.

The chemical industry has been a part of civilization since the beginning of the nineteenth century. Euthere Irenee DuPont founded the modern firm of DuPont by setting up a gunpowder mill near Wilmington, Delaware, in 1802. However, the chemical industry in the nineteenth century bore little relation to today's industry, which in the U.S. alone employs over a million workers and has a turnover of about 50×10^9 dollars a year. For its first century the chemical industry followed the pattern of laboratory chemistry, producing new compounds in the same way as they were produced in the laboratory, but on a larger scale. Nowadays this is only true of the production of such low tonnage materials as pharmaceuticals and dyestuffs. Processes used in factories were taken from the laboratory, scaled up to larger sizes, and then improved on a trial and error basis. Today a new chemical process should operate well from the start, because the scale and cost of the new plant are so enormous that there is little room for mistakes.

Many of the processes used in the chemical industry involve chemistry that has been known for a long time, and the main change in these areas in recent years has concerned scale of manufacture. But the real heart of the modern chemicals industry lies in petrochemicals, chemicals derived from oil, which lead, among other things, to the production of most of the plastics currently available. Petroleum was only viewed as a source of chemicals in the 1920s; the major growth has been since World War II.

Oil companies originally decided that they might utilize some of the materials left over from the manufacture of gasoline, which only takes a small fraction of crude oil. Consequently, the first petrochemicals works were sited near oil wells. Since 1945 oil refineries have increasingly been sited near the major points of use, large urban centers throughout the world. This change has led to the growth of a world-wide petrochemicals industry, rather than one existing almost exclusively, as was the case before the war, in the United States. The demand for chemical raw materials has become so great that at least 1 large chemical company in Europe owns its own chain of gas stations to get rid of the gasoline which is the "waste product" left over from crude oil after the chemicals needed for their manufacturing processes have been extracted.

Leo Baekeland, discoverer of 1 of the first commercially successful plastics, Bakelite, said that "the whole fabric of modern civilization becomes every day more interwoven with the endless ramifications of applied chemistry." This is certainly true today, although it is worth remembering that fewer than 1 percent of the chemical compounds known to man have ever been industrially used. The extent to which chemistry permeates every aspect of our daily lives is discussed in Chapter 8. This chapter describes the petrochemicals industry—the new chemistry of industry—and some of the aspects of how industry works. As has been intimated, industry has one constraint that the research worker does not often feel. In addition to obeying the laws of nature, it must also obey the laws of economics.

Taking Economics into Account

To combine the laws of nature and the laws of economics into a simple example may give some insight into the way in which the industrialist thinks differently from the research chemist. If we take a simple reaction in which compound A is converted into compound B, and a study of the kinetics shows that this is a simple halflife reaction (see note, p. 107), the amount of B produced depends in part on the amount of A used. In a certain amount of time—the halflife—half the amount of A present will have turned into B. After the same amount of time further, half the remaining A will have turned into B. If the halflife is 30 minutes, after an hour the reaction mix will contain a 75 percent yield of B and 25 percent unconverted A.

Imagine that this reaction is best performed in a boiling water solution. If a research chemist undertakes the reaction because he wants to study some property of compound B, he will note from early experiments that the halflife is about half an hour. Since he wants as much B as he can get, he may start the reaction before he goes to lunch and stop it after he gets back, letting it run for perhaps 2 or 2.5 hours. According to the halflife rule, he will then have a B yield of about 94 or 97 percent, which, from his point of view, is very good.

From the perspective of the industrial chemist, who perhaps wants to produce 10 tons of B to sell, this method of working is disastrous. If he lets the reaction run for 2.5 hours, the last half hour costs him as much to produce 3 percent of B as it did to produce 50 percent in the first half hour. He is paying the same amount each hour for supplying energy to the reaction to keep it boiling, for paying the workers who look after the plant, and so on. Clearly, he must take into account more factors than the laboratory chemist.

For example, in some cases it will be worth his while to spend that extra money just to get the yield of B up to 97 percent. If it is very difficult and consequently costly to separate A from B, it may even be worth letting the reaction run for 3 hours and then selling the 98+ percent pure B as it is, without removing the traces of unreacted A. On the other hand, if the customer wants 99.9 percent pure B (this is not unlikely) it may be more economical to use an expensive separation process than to keep the reaction going for 5 hours.

At the other extreme, if B separates easily from A, by filtration for example, it will probably be wiser to run the reactor for short times, separate the 2 materials, and mix the recovered A with fresh A and repeat the reaction. The modern approach to such recycling operations is to use continuous reactors in which product is continually removed and fresh material added at the same rate.

This is a simple example of the type of economic constraint felt by the industrial chemist. Another example might involve the temperature at which a reaction is carried out. The rate at which reactions occur depends on temperature, and a drop in temperature in the lab may mean that an experiment takes half an hour instead of 25 minutes. On an industrial scale, this would mean an increased running cost of over 15 percent for the production of that batch of material.

Consideration of these types of problems, and working out the best compromise, is called "optimization," a procedure that has led to a petrochemicals industry in which yields are often small by laboratory standards, and reactions usually give many products rather than 1 or 2. Optimization also includes taking into account how those different products will be used. Not only does a by-product that will not sell have no value, it frequently has negative value, such as the cost of disposing of it without polluting air, land, or water.

The approach used in the chemical industry is called "unit operations," an engineering concept which has been in use for nearly a century. A process is broken down into constituent parts or operations, each of which is looked at as a unit. Thus, a very simple process might involve only 2 unit operations, reaction in the reactor and separation after the reaction.

Reactors

To the chemist, the heart of an industrial process will always be the reactor. Early reactors developed from the type used in the laboratory—they were little more than overgrown flasks. But today many of the products of chemical industry go into reactor-building: special steels, special glasses for lining metal reactors. Today's chemical reactors are designed to withstand rigorous conditions and to keep on working without fail, for

failure of a vital part in a modern large-scale chemical plant
can cause a major disaster in both human and financial terms.

Reactors are tested before use by such nondestructive methods as ultrasonics, strain gauge tests, and gamma ray photography. A method presently under development is to listen to
metals, to hear them groaning if they are under the sort of
excess stress that will cause failure, which may mean an explosion. Although metals do not give groans audible to the
human ear, when they are bent or fractured they release energy
in a form similar to sound waves which can be detected by
microphones attached to the surface. One advantage of this
method of detecting failures in metals is that it can easily be
used on reactors while they are in service. Methods such as
ultrasonic testing can be applied to a reactor before it is put
into use, but it is difficult to utilize them later on. Since the
acoustic emission method needs only small disc microphones, it
is ideally suited to regular testing of plant in operation.

As a reaction is scaled up from lab bench to factory, an important mathematical change has to be taken into account. If
one thinks of a cylindrical reactor, it is easy to calculate how
much it will hold and what its surface area will be. With a
cylinder twice the height and twice the diameter of the first, the
surface area will be roughly 4 times as great, but the volume
increases 8 times. For a reaction which produces heat, in which
temperature has to be kept constant, heat must escape through
the walls of the larger reactor twice as fast as through the walls
of the smaller reactor. This may mean that while the first reactor loses heat from the reaction to the surrounding air, the
second will need to be designed for more effective heat transfer.

This may seem to make large reactors a bad proposition, but
possibly some other operations in a process will require heat.
If the heat given off by the reaction is used to generate steam
a reaction may be kept within the temperature limits required
and the steam piped to another part of the plant, thus turning
what is initially a nuisance into an advantage. This is an ex-

ample of optimization. To be truly economic, one must never waste one's resources—and in modern chemical industry, energy is a valuable resource.

As the chemical industry grew during the last century, the 2 commodities taken most for granted were energy and water. Energy could be obtained cheaply from fossil fuels, and water seemed to abound everywhere. Yet now there is grave concern in industrialized countries over an imminent energy and water crisis. Consequently, reuse of both these commodities by industry will become increasingly pressing as greater demands are made by domestic consumers for more baths and showers, more electric light and heating.

From our first example of scaling up it can be seen that using a large reactor can have hidden advantages. There are other, more obvious, advantages. Doubling the size of a reactor does not usually require twice the manpower to operate it, so there are savings in plant running costs. There are also disadvantages to large reactors that are just like containers. These batch reactors mean that a process cannot operate smoothly all the time. Reactors have to be emptied, cleaned, and refilled. Filling a 20,000 gallon reactor and then heating the contents to the temperature required for a reaction will take time that might be spent more profitably in making more product. This delay can be avoided with a continuous reactor, and it is to continuous reactors that large-scale chemical industry has turned increasingly since World War II.

The most common type is probably the continuous stirred tank reactor (CSTR). This is very similar to the batch reactor, except that raw materials are added continuously, the contents particularly well stirred, and a mixture of product and raw materials continually drawn off. The CSTR is ideally suited to reactions in which the products can easily be separated from the starting materials, and the latter recycled. It is not so useful for obtaining high yields or conversions of material. To obtain a 99 percent conversion of A to B requires a continuous stirred tank reactor 99 times bigger than the one required for 50 percent conversion. The reason for this lies in the kinetics of the reaction. If raw material flows into the reactor at a certain rate, the average time any molecule spends in the reactor (mean residence time) depends on the size of the reactor; the shorter the residence time, the lower the number of molecules that will react to produce product. However, in modern industry this problem has been overcome by use of multistage reactors in which the product/raw material mix from 1 reactor is passed into a second reactor, and possibly into more in sequence. If the first reactor is achieving 90 percent conversion, a second reactor of exactly the same size will achieve 90 percent conversion of the remaining raw material, giving an overall conversion of 99 percent. As a reactor giving 90 percent conversion only needs to be 9 times larger than one giving 50 percent conversion, to go from 50 percent conversion in a single step to 99 percent in 2 steps means increasing total reactor size only 18 times, 5 times smaller than the single reactor required for 99 percent conversion.

This chapter has scanned briefly some notions current in the chemical industry demanded by that industry's need to conform not only to the laws of thermodynamics and kinetics but also to the laws of economics. One area where economics must affect industrial procedure is in the cost of raw materials. In fact, the cost of raw materials may be the deciding factor between different chemical routes to the same end products. Nowhere has this been more clearly shown in recent years than in the petrochemicals industry.

Petrochemicals

The raw materials for the petrochemicals industry are natural gas, refinery gases, which come from the "cracking" of crude oil, and liquid hydrocarbons. Although some natural gas is a nearly pure chemical (methane), these raw materials are mostly mixtures from which are obtained the actual building blocks of the chemical industry, secondary raw materials such as methane, ethylene, propylene, butadiene, and higher paraffins and alkenes. At present the percentage of petroleum products used in petrochemicals production is about 5 to 7 percent of the total petroleum and natural gas production. It has been predicted that this percentage may double by the end of the century, since the major alternative use—burning the materials as a source of energy—is an appalling waste of a diversity of raw materials.

Although the percentage figures sound low, it is interesting to compare the growth of the petrochemicals industry as part of the total chemical industry. In the U.S. in 1940, just over 11 million tons of chemicals were produced, 10 percent of them from petroleum sources. By 1960 the total chemicals produced had risen to 82 million tons, 30 percent of them of petroleum origin, and by 1970, 41 percent of the 170 million tons of chemicals produced were petroleum based. Thus, in the 30 years since the start of World War II, the output of petroleum chemicals increased more than sixtyfold. About 95 percent of the organic chemicals produced in the U.S. are petroleum derived. Since there are few inorganic chemicals that can come from petroleum—sulphur, which is often found as a contaminant of natural gas and crude oil, helium, and hydrogen are the major exceptions—this shows the great extent to which petrochemicals have cornered their possible market.

When crude oils are cracked by passage through heated towers in the presence of catalysts, the molecules, which are mainly composed solely of hydrogen and carbon—the hydrocarbons—break down into smaller hydrocarbons. Refinery gas, obtained by distilling cracked crude, accounts for 15 to 20 percent by weight of the cracked material. Typically, refinery gas is made of a mixture of saturated hydrocarbons, containing from 1 to 4 carbon atoms: methane, ethane, propane, butanes, unsaturated hydrocarbons—that is, those which contain pi bonds (ethylene, propylene, butenes)—and hydrogen.

Industrially the most important of the refinery gases are the unsaturated hydrocarbons, the alkenes. These are more reactive than the saturated hydrocarbons because of the pi bonding in their structures. Probably the most important organic chemical in the world today is ethylene, not only as a source of the polymer polythene, or polyethylene as it was originally called, but also of many other chemicals formerly made from acetylene. Like ethylene, acetylene contains 2 linked carbon atoms, but has only 1 hydrogen attached to each carbon, while ethylene has 2. Although this makes acetylene even more reactive than ethylene, economics have ensured that acetylene has been replaced by ethylene as the preferred raw material for manufacturing a number of important organic chemicals.

By a process known as hydrocracking, in which thermal cracking is performed in the presence of hydrogen, it is possible to produce a refinery gas that consists mainly of saturated hydrocarbons. However, as demand for the unsaturates ethylene and propylene frequently outruns supply, it is more common to find ethane and propane converted into these 2 compounds, rather than the other way around.

Thermal cracking of ethane, for example, produces a cracker gas that contains mainly ethylene, unchanged ethane (which can be recycled through the cracker), and hydrogen, large quantities of which are needed for synthetic ammonia manufacture, together with about a dozen other substances in small quantities. Since cracking is a process which vigorously tears pieces off molecules, thermal cracking of propane is not so efficient as a source of propylene. Propane cracker gas contains about twice as much ethylene as propylene. The precise ratios of products are affected by the cracking temperature and the time the gas spends in the cracker, so some optimization of product according to need is possible.

In 1960, U.S. consumption of ethylene was about 2.5 million tons, a figure which had more than tripled by 1970. About 40 percent of the ethylene is consumed in the manufacture of polythene. The remainder is used for making products such as ethanol, acetaldehyde, ethylene dichloride, ethylene oxide, vinyl acetate, vinyl chloride, and ethyl chloride. Ethylene is now such an important raw material for heavy organic chemicals manufacture that in some places it is piped over large distances to different manufacturing sites, and it has been suggested that within a few years it may be regularly piped into chemical plants with such other services as water and electricity.

The major revolution in industrial ethylene chemistry came in the 1950s, when the price of ethylene dropped as a result of big expansion in the petrochemicals industry. Since then it has knocked the bottom out of the market for some other chemicals in manufacturing, such as acetylene.

Acetylene is manufactured in two ways. In the cracking of methane at high temperatures, 3 hydrogen atoms are torn from each methane molecule, and the CH fragments formed join up in pairs to make acetylene ($HC{\equiv}CH$). This method supplies just over half the U.S. requirements for acetylene, which totals about 400,000 tons a year. Acetylene is still obtained also by an old process, the breakdown of calcium carbide, but this is rapidly diminishing in scale.

One primary use for acetylene until the early 1960s was for vinyl chloride manufacture, the monomer from which the plastic polyvinyl chloride is made. This is a simple manufacturing process in which a molecule of hydrogen chloride joins to the acetylene molecule to give the desired product. Since vinyl chloride is itself unsaturated—it is like an ethylene molecule, except that 1 hydrogen atom has been replaced by chlorine —the triple bond of acetylene makes the addition process simple.

If hydrogen chloride is added to ethylene, the product is a saturated molecule, ethyl chloride, which will not polymerize. Consequently, a different type of process, called oxychlorination, is needed to make vinyl chloride from ethylene. Ethylene is reacted with hydrogen chloride and oxygen. Instead of the hydrogen chloride adding to the ethylene, the hydrogen part adds to the oxygen to form water, and 2 atoms of chlorine add to the ethylene to make dichloroethane, which can be cracked to produce vinyl chloride and half as much hydrogen chloride as was originally used. The latter is reused to oxychlorinate more ethylene. Once this process was worked out, it was no longer economic to make vinyl chloride from the more expensive raw material, acetylene.

One of the oldest industrial organic chemicals is ethanol, originally made by yeast fermentation. This method is still used to produce drinking alcohol—whisky, gin, and so on—and in some underdeveloped countries, lacking a petrochemicals industry, to supply industrial alcohol.

In the more developed countries nearly all ethanol, which is widely used as an industrial solvent as well as for the manufacture of large-tonnage organic chemicals such as ethyl acetate and acetaldehyde, comes from ethylene. The traditional laboratory method for converting ethylene into ethanol is to react it with sulphuric acid. This forms monoethyl and diethyl sulphates which will react with water to produce ethanol and regenerate the sulphuric acid. This process was for a time used industrially but, following the trend of the modern petrochemicals industry to look for the most uncomplicated method, the sulphuric acid step has been eliminated in the direct hydration process.

Water vapor and ethylene at 300° C and under high pressure react to form ethanol. This is an equilibrium reaction—the ethanol can break down to form ethylene and water—so the conditions of the reaction are finely balanced to find the most economical conditions, which, in this case, are a 4 to 5 percent conversion of ethylene to ethanol at each pass through the reactor. Certainly this yield would not satisfy the laboratory chemist, but when recycle is taken into account provides the best compromise between the laws of chemistry and those of economics.

This direct approach is by no means confined to ethanol production. In at least 1 case its application is a threat to ethanol producers. The traditional way to make acetaldehyde in a laboratory is by the oxidation of ethanol. Some acetaldehyde has been made industrially from acetylene, but this process has been superseded by a direct, 1-step process from ethylene. The Wacker acetaldehyde process, which has been operational for just over a decade, consists in adding an atom of oxygen derived from a molecule of water to a molecule of ethylene. Unlike the ethanol process, the Wacker process takes place in the liquid phase and involves a palladium chloride catalyst which is converted to palladium metal during the reaction, and is then regenerated. It could only have been developed successfully in recent years, for the catalyst solutions are highly corrosive, and did not become fully satisfactory until certain parts of the plant were manufactured from titanium, a metal that was not available for such large-scale usage until recently.

Soviet chemist Moiseev suggested that if the Wacker process was performed in the presence of acetic acid instead of water, vinyl acetate, another polymer raw material, could be produced. This process, which is in operation on a modest scale in both the United States and England, has been intensively developed, although corrosion problems still need to be ironed out. One way to do this is to perform the reaction in the gas phase at high temperatures, rather than in the liquid phase; this modification is now being intensively developed and could become the sole economic process for the production of vinyl acetate, since a plant could take in ethylene, convert part of it by the Wacker process to acetaldehyde (which can easily be oxidized to acetic acid), and then use ethylene and acetic acid for the manufacture of vinyl acetate.

There are 2 interesting stories behind this example of new chemistry in the industrial field. First, when Dr. J. Smidt and his colleagues at Wacker Chemicals were experimenting with passing ethylene and oxygen over palladium catalysts, they were trying to make another raw material important for the chemical industry, ethylene oxide. When they noticed that traces of acetaldehyde were formed, their investigation revealed how the palladium catalyst was operating and, in the end, developed the present process in which oxygen is supplied by water molecules. Second, the basic chemistry was not new at all. The formation of acetaldehyde from ethylene in aqueous solution containing palladium chloride was noticed in 1894, but had been forgotten. The real new chemistry of the Wacker process was in turning it into an economic process by working out the regeneration of the expensive palladium catalyst. This involved a basic scientific study of the mechanism of the reaction in order to find ways of influencing the reaction toward the desired products.

Not surprisingly, although the Wacker process did not produce ethylene oxide, a direct oxidation process to this compound has been developed. This involves reaction of ethylene and oxygen over a silver catalyst. Again, development of this process required a close study of the kinetics and mechanism of the reaction, for there is also a competitive reaction operating —complete oxidation of ethylene to water and carbon dioxide, neither of which are salable commodities. On the other hand, ethylene oxide, produced at a rate of nearly 2 million tons a year in the U.S., is needed for manufacture of ethylene glycol —used in automobile antifreeze and polyester fibers—and a number of important detergent chemicals, as well as for industrial separation processes.

The Wacker process can be applied to the next unsaturated hydrocarbon up the scale from ethylene, propylene. In this case it produces the solvent acetone, another important intermediate in the production of large-scale industrial chemicals. However, the Wacker process is in competition here with a totally different procedure, the phenol-cumene process, which converts cumene into 2 valuable products, acetone and phenol. If it comes to a fight as to which produces the cheaper acetone, a group that will benefit in any event are the propylene producers, for propylene is also a vital raw material for the manufacture of cumene.

Although propylene is not required on such a large scale as ethylene—the 1970 U.S. consumption for chemicals manufacture was 3.8 million tons—it is a fast-growing area, having increased eightfold since 1950. Much of this growth has been due to the requirement for polypropylene, an insignificant polymer before 1960 but now widely used, whose development involved important fundamental chemistry which won a Nobel prize for Italian chemist Giulio Natta.

Another new process, propylene ammoxidation, also accounts for part of propylene's fast growth. This is now the preferred route to acrylonitrile, the basic building block for such acrylic fibers as Acrilan and Courtelle. While these 2 uses each accounted for 14 percent of the 1970 consumption of propylene, the major use is still for the production of isopropanol in a manner similar to the production of ethanol from ethylene. Much of the isopropanol is used to provide yet another source of acetone.

Like ethylene oxide, propylene is also an important raw material for a wide variety of chemicals, such as the polypropoxy ethers used in manufacturing polyurethanes. A suitable catalyst for direct oxidation of propylene to its oxide is earnestly sought, but at present the closest approach is a dual process in which another organic chemical, such as ethylbenzene, is oxidized to a hydroperoxide which reacts with propylene to form propylene oxide and 1-phenylethanol. The latter can be dehydrated to styrene, required for production of polystyrene, but the success (economically) of such a process depends on the demand for styrene and the cost of alternative supplies. Other materials can be used in place of ethylbenzene (for example, isobutane, which can be converted ultimately to isobutylene or tertiary butyl alcohol), but clearly the success of the process still depends on finding a suitable market for the by-product.

One of the most successful modern processes, because of its utilization of the major by-product, must be the phenol from cumene process. Barely utilized before 1950, it now produces more than half of the world's phenol. As has been made clear, many of today's organic chemicals owe their rise to the enormous growth of the plastics industry. Phenol is no exception. About 50 percent of the phenol made is used in phenol-based resins, while a further 20 percent goes into the manufacture of caprolactam, a precursor of Nylon 6.

The cumene-phenol process had its origins during World War II when Professor H. Hock and colleagues in Germany were carrying out a basic study of the oxidation of various organic compounds by molecular oxygen. From cumene (isopropylbenzene) they isolated a hydroperoxide which, on acid treatment, split up into phenol and acetone. To Hock's group, cumene was just 1 of a number of organic chemicals they were studying, and the reaction was only mentioned in 1 of a series of research papers on the effects of molecular oxygen. However, it was noted by industrial chemists and developed simultaneously in the U.S. and Britain into an industrial process that was first used commercially at a plant in Montreal, Canada, in 1953.

Some scientists deride industry, claiming that it just makes profits from the discoveries of research workers in institutes and universities, and does not innovate itself. In the chemical industry this is untrue, for the fundamental chemical discoveries of the laboratory chemist are rarely made with any consideration for economics. Thus, the Wacker process was a piece of new industrial chemistry, for the 1894 discovery of the reaction did not include any of the work needed to overcome the cost factor of the platinium catalyst. Detailed work on the mechanism of the reaction was also carried out in industry; in 1894 the whole concept of reaction mechanism was still uncharted territory.

Similarly, without industrial research there would have been no phenol-cumene process. Not only did the reaction involve

free radicals—still a novel area of chemistry in the early 1950s
—but also it had been established only that phenol and acetone
were products, not that they were the sole products. Establishment of the complex series of reactions involved was carried
out in industry. Accurate measurements of the number and
types of products formed had to be made; the then relatively
new technique of infrared spectroscopy was used. Quantitative
measurements of the rates of various steps had to be made, and
it was in fact necessary to postulate reaction mechanisms that,
at the time, were not known to occur. Industrialization of the
process not only helped produce profits, but also added to the
sum of basic chemical knowledge.

Aromatic Petrochemicals

In the phenol-cumene process, a previously unmentioned raw
material has been discussed—benzene. Benzene is an aromatic [1]
hydrocarbon, and the aromatic hydrocarbons are also a part of
today's giant petrochemicals industry, in some ways complementing the smaller aliphatic molecules already mentioned. For
example, p-xylene, a benzene molecule with a methyl group at
each end, is the raw material for manufacturing terephthalic
acid. Together with ethylene glycol—made from ethylene oxide—this goes into the polyester fiber known as Dacron or
Terylene.

The aliphatic hydrocarbons discussed up to now are mainly
obtained from refinery gas or natural gas, the lowest boiling
fractions of cracked crude. The aromatics come in the next
boiling range, roughly from room temperature to 200° C (twice
the boiling point of water). This is the gasoline or naphtha
fraction. Commercial automobile gasoline comes out of this

[1] "Aromatic" is an historical description for those compounds based on or
containing the benzene ring structure. The name was awarded because of the
characteristic aroma of many of these compounds.

fraction, but so do other important chemical materials; to avoid confusion, it will be referred to here as naphtha.

The use of aromatic hydrocarbons in the chemical industry is long-standing, especially in the manufacture of dyes. Supplies originally came from coal distillation, hence the origin of the name "coal tar dyes" for commercial dyes in use at the end of the last century. Until recent times, coal was still a major supplier of some aromatics, notably benzene. In 1954, 165 million U.S. gallons of benzene were produced from coal, and only 92 million from oil. Since then coal has slowly declined, while oil has leaped ahead as a source of aromatics; by 1970, coal benzene production was down to 100 million gallons, while the figure from oil was 1,150 million.

A major problem faced by suppliers of petroleum aromatics was that the chemistry of the process and the demand were at variance with one another. Catalytic reforming of naphtha gives the 3 major aromatics, benzene, toluene, and mixed xylenes, in the ratio 11:55:34; demand is 58:23:19. Obviously if the demand for benzene were to be met by straightforward catalytic reforming of naphtha, there would be huge surpluses of toluene and the xylenes. To overcome this, a hydrodealkylation process was developed in which toluene and hydrogen are reacted to produce benzene.

There are 2 reasons for the growth of oil at the expense of coal as a supplier of aromatics, both depending on technologies outside the chemical field. Coal tar, the source of coal chemicals, is a by-product of coke manufacture, and the requirements for coke depend on the growth of the town gas and steelmaking industries, which have not expanded at anything like the rate of the chemical industry in recent years. Conversely, the development of jet-propelled aeroplanes has released a lot of petroleum aromatics that would otherwise have been required as aviation fuel.

Another coal-based aromatic which is increasingly produced from naphtha is naphthalene—the chemical component of old-fashioned mothballs. First produced in the U.S. from oil in 1961, this source now accounts for nearly half of U.S. naphthalene supplies. However, this is not such a growth area as the simpler aromatics, since the main product of industrial naphthalene chemistry, phthalic anhydride, can now be made from 1 of the xylene isomers.

Like the aliphatics, a major end-use area for the aromatics is in the plastics industry. In their various forms—synthetic rubbers, plastics, and fibers—the synthetic polymeric materials are the greatest growth phenomenon of modern chemistry.

The Plastics Revolution

The first synthetic plastic was a thermosetting resin called ebonite, patented in 1843. Plastics are divided into 2 broad categories, thermosets and thermoplastics. The thermosets are materials which, once heated, take on a rigid form which cannot be changed by reheating, while thermoplastics repeatedly soften on heating and harden on cooling.

Much of the early work on plastics was on thermosets, and it may have been this limitation that prevented them from becoming highly acceptable materials. Another reason is that they were looked upon as substitutes for existing materials, rather than as new materials requiring new ideas in design and usage. Part of this "substitute" outlook still survives, with people disparaging plastics as second-rate materials. However, with the major advances in formulation and use of plastics since the war, this attitude is now passing out of fashion.

Many of the early plastics were not totally synthetic, but were made from common natural polymers by chemical modification. Casein, a protein in milk, was the basis for 1 of them, while others were made by chemical modifications of cellulose. Celluloid, a form of cellulose treated with nitric acid to form cellulose nitrate, was widely used in early movie films. Because of its extraordinary inflammability, it has been replaced in nearly all applications except the manufacture of some table tennis balls; a number of movie studios have reels of old cellulose nitrate films decomposing in tubs of water to prevent their going up in flames.

The first modern synthetic plastics were discovered just before and between World Wars I and II: Bakelite, named after its discoverer, Leo Baekeland, in 1912, urea-formaldehyde resins in the 1920s, and melamine-formaldehyde in 1935. Nylon, the first of the synthetic fibers, was discovered in the 1930s by DuPont scientist Wallace Hume Carothers. Carothers set out deliberately to discover a synthetic fiber, and realized that long straight molecules would have the best chance of forming fibers if they were polymerized. Unfortunately, he died in 1937, before nylon had become a commercial article.

Carothers was undoubtedly a great chemist for, in addition to nylon, he suggested the way to make the synthetic rubber neoprene, and also worked on a group of plastics called polycarbonates which did not reach commercial production until the 1960s, but are very useful as engineering materials because they are both transparent and extremely hard. Another range of transparent plastics discovered in the 1930s are the acrylics made from polymethyl methacrylate. Used widely in World War II for aircraft canopies, acrylics have also been used for making bathtubs, advertising signs, and artificial eyes.

Undoubtedly the most successful polymer developed in the 1930s was polyethylene. Its discovery was an accident. There is a similarity between the discovery of polythene and the cumene-phenol process, for both turned up initially as integral parts of wide-ranging research programs. The difference in the case of polythene was that the basic research program was carried out in industry, and the British company where the discovery was made—ICI—followed it up.

In the late 1920s and early 1930s, very little work had been done on the effects of high pressures on chemical reactions. ICI decided to carry out a basic study of reactions at pressures above 1,000 atmospheres, to see what would happen. One of the aims put forward by Nobel laureate Sir Robert Robinson, then an adviser to the company, was to see if certain types of reaction would take place under high pressures that required catalysts at ordinary pressures. Begun in late 1931 by Dr. R. O. Gibson and E. A. Fawcett, it took a year to get the apparatus and conditions right for studying these gas reactions of pairs of compounds; in November 1932 the apparatus blew up, setting the project back for several more months.

In March 1933, Gibson and Fawcett studied the high pressure reaction between ethylene and benzaldehyde. This was expected to give either of 2 complex compounds. The experiment was started on Friday, March 24. On the following Monday Gibson and Fawcett returned to the laboratory to find that there had been a leak in the apparatus and all the benzaldehyde had escaped. When they dismantled the apparatus, Fawcett pointed out that the part of the steel gas-inlet tube which had been in the reaction zone looked as if it had been dipped into paraffin wax. In his notebook Gibson wrote: "Waxy solid found in reaction tube"—the first account of the existence of polythene. In their monthly report, they wrote: "The reaction between ethylene and benzaldehyde has been studied at 2000 atm and 170° C. A waxy solid, which appears to be a high polymer of ethylene was formed." In their July report, they wrote: "A quantity of the waxy polymer of ethylene has been prepared and work with this reaction has now ceased." [2] Polythene had been discovered, but why was it not exploited?

Describing the discovery in 1964, Gibson wrote:

In retrospect it may seem strange that work should thus have stopped on what is now claimed as an important discovery, and

[2] R. O. Gibson, *The Discovery of Polythene* (London: Royal Institute of Chemistry, 1964), pp. 17–18.

that the discovery should only have been considered of academic
interest at the time. But was it so strange?

At that time synthetic polymer science was only in its infancy,
and the immense technical and commercial developments of recent years were not even being dreamt about. The common
thermoplastics of that day were polymethyl methacrylate and
polystyrene. Both these materials were hard and transparent
and of very different physical properties to the relatively soft,
translucent ethylene polymer we had made.[3]

Another disadvantage was that increase of pressure during
the reaction led to complete decomposition to carbon and
hydrogen, instead of a waxy solid. It was not until 2.5 years
later that the reaction was studied again, this time by another
ICI worker, Michael Perrin. On December 19, 1935, he and
a colleague decided to study the behavior of ethylene at 2,000
atmospheres pressure. They added ethylene to the reaction
vessel, but could not get the pressure up. They added more
ethylene, although they suspected that the apparatus was
leaking. When they had used up all the gas, they cooled
the reaction vessel and let out what pressure there was in it.
On opening it they found it to be full of white powdery polymer. It was later found that if pressure was let out before
cooling, the polymer was of the same waxy solid appearance
as Gibson and Fawcett's original sample.

This second round of experiments produced enough polymer
to make it worthwhile for study as a material of potential
commercial interest. Commercial development required further
application of both science and technology. For example, Perrin
found that to initiate the polymerization reaction, a small
percentage of oxygen—600 parts per million—was necessary.
Technological developments were required to purify ethylene
on a large scale to the 99.9 percent purity required for polymer
production. The first commercial polythene plant came into
operation the day that World War II was declared.

[3] *Ibid.* pp. 20–21.

This is not the end of the polythene story, for the material produced on the basis of the ICI work, called low-density polythene, is made either by compressing the gas to 1,500–2,500 atmosphere pressure at 100–300° C, or by polymerizing it in an aromatic hydrocarbon solution at 1,000 atmospheres pressure. In the 1950s a new type of polythene, high-density, came on the market as a result of work on catalysts called Ziegler catalysts after their pioneer, German chemist Karl Ziegler, who shared the 1963 Nobel chemistry prize with Giulio Natta.

Low-density polythene has a molecular weight of between 50,000 and 300,000, while the high-density material can have a molecular weight of up to 3,000,000. The high density material has greater rigidity and a higher softening temperature; it is made at 6–7 atmospheres pressure in a hydrocarbon solvent at 100–170° C. In a sense, the wheel has turned full circle. Originally discovered as a by-product of research aimed at replacing catalyzed reactions by high-pressure reactions, the high-pressure process has now been matched by a catalyzed process.

However, high-density polythene has by no means replaced the low-density material. Although they are both polymers of ethylene, their characteristics are sufficiently different for them both to retain a market, and of the 2.5 million or so tons a year of polythene produced in the U.S., almost three-quarters is still the low-density type. The differences between them are perhaps best exemplified by their uses. Nearly 50 percent of the low-density material is used for producing polythene film and sheet, while half the high-density material is used for blow molding, in which air is blown into a mold containing the hot, soft plastic to produce semirigid artifacts, such as bottles. By comparison, only about 10 percent of low-density polythene is blow-molded.

A close relative of polythene is polypropylene, first produced in 1954 and insignificant in the plastics market until

1960. From a figure of less than 20,000 tons in that year, U.S. production has now increased about 25-fold. Nearly half the polypropylene produced is used for moldings, although fibers are also an important end use. A recent unusual use for polypropylene has been as a synthetic seaweed. Lengths of slit film or filamentous polypropylene have been attached to the seabed around coasts to prevent coastal erosion. As it is lighter than water, the lengths of polymer float upward like ordinary seaweed. Although still at an experimental stage, the synthetic seaweed appears to fulfill the required purpose.

From the end of the 1930s to the mid-1950s seems a long time between the birth of polythene and its sister, polypropylene. The apparent simplicity of extending polymerization from the 2-carbon ethylene to the 3-carbon propylene is deceptive; it had to await Dr. Ziegler and his catalysts, and the dedicated application of these by Italian chemist Giulio Natta.

In ethylene, 2 carbons are joined together by an unsaturated linkage; each carbon has 2 hydrogen atoms attached to it. When ethylene polymerizes to polyethylene, a very long chain of carbon atoms is formed, still with 2 hydrogen atoms on each carbon atom (see Figure 21). Propylene can be looked upon as an ethylene molecule in which 1 of the hydrogen atoms on 1 carbon has been replaced with a methyl ($-CH_3$) group. When attempts were first made to polymerize propylene, the result was a polymer without useful commercial properties—it was rubbery and had little strength. Natta, a chemist who had concerned himself with determination of the structures of molecules by x-ray crystallography, showed that these properties were a result of the random way in which the propylene units joined together: there was no order about the positioning of the methyl groups sticking out of the chain. When propylene polymerizes it forms the same basic chain as polythene, but the methyl groups that replace half of the hydrogens are not part of the chain, but branch off it. Natta

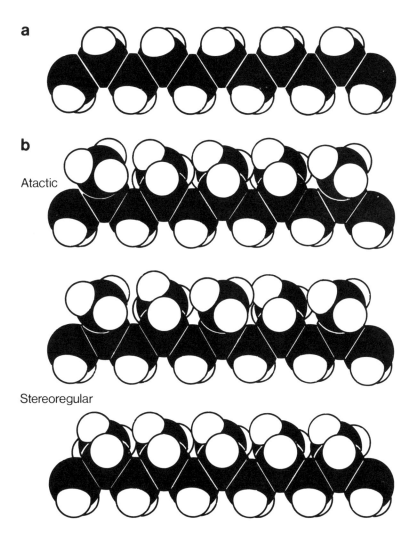

a

b

Atactic

Stereoregular

FIGURE 21. Representations of the three-dimensional structures of poly-thylene (a), and various polypropylenes (b). Until the discovery of Ziegler catalysts, it was possible to produce only the disordered atactic polypropylene; use of these catalysts by Giulio Natta led to the production of the stereoregular polypropylenes, in which the side-chains are not randomly oriented, and which have much better commercial properties than the atactic material.

thought that a better polymer could be produced if the position of the methyl branches could be controlled as the polymer formed. To achieve this, he applied the work of Karl Ziegler.

As a research chemist at Marburg University before the war, Ziegler had discovered that adding metals to the free radical compounds which he was studying made it possible to form organometallic substances—molecules in which metal atoms are chemically bonded to carbon atoms. He further found that these organometallics caused some small alkenes to polymerize.

In 1943 Ziegler became head of the Max Planck Institute at Mulheim. Here he tried to polymerize ethylene using his organometallics, but it was not until 1953 that he succeeded in devising a suitable catalytic system to produce polythene. This was the basis of the processes for high-density polythene now in use, and the reason why this material has a higher density than the original polythene is because the Ziegler catalysts help to keep the growing polyethylene chain straight. In the high-pressure process, the chain occasionally branches to give a 2-pronged growing end. This increases the three-dimensional complexity of the molecule, and, unlike the straight chains, the chains with branches are not able to pack together tightly, thus giving a lower density material.

When a similar type of catalyst was applied by Natta to the polymerization of propylene, it produced an ordered structure in which all the methyl groups were aligned on 1 side of the chain. This greater regularity produced a strong polymer similar to, but in some respects better than, polythene. Low-density polythene softens in boiling water; articles made of high-density polythene or polypropylene are resistant to boiling water. Further work showed that it was also possible to produce a polypropylene in which the methyl side-chains alternated from 1 side to the other of the backbone carbon chain.

Ziegler catalysts have been widely used by industry to produce stereospecific polymers—those with a finely ordered structure. Nearly all natural polymeric materials are stereospecific and, with the aid of Ziegler catalysts, it has been possible to make a synthetic rubber identical in structure to natural rubber.

How do Ziegler catalysts work? Organoaluminum compounds, in which there is a carbon-aluminum bond, are reactive because this bond is not very strong. If a compound such as triethyl aluminum (an aluminum atom with 3 ethyl groups attached) is heated with a 1-alkene, that is, an unsaturated carbon-chain molecule in which the double bond is at 1 end of the chain, an insertion reaction takes place. One aluminum-carbon bond is broken, the end carbon of the alkene forms a bond with the aluminum, and the carbon fragment originally attached to the aluminum joins on to the second carbon of the unsaturated molecule. If 1 molecule of triethyl aluminum reacts with 1 molecule of ethylene, diethyl butyl aluminum is formed—1 of the ethyl groups has grown into a 4-carbon chain. If there are many molecules of ethylene, each of the 3 ethyl groups originally attached to the aluminum will undergo the insertion reaction. Once an insertion reaction is complete, it can be repeated, so that the aluminum atom will eventually have 3 long, straight chains attached to it. However, as the chains lengthen, they tend to break off, so the aluminum trialkyls by themselves are unsuitable as polymerization catalysts.

By using a complex of aluminum alkyl and titanium tetrachloride, stereoregular polymerization to longer chains is possible. The stereospecificity is probably a result of using the transition metal titanium. Alkene pi electrons can coordinate to the titanium—that is, occupy its unoccupied orbitals, forming a geometrically defined complex. Held in position in this way, the alkene then inserts into the alkyl part of the catalyst complex. Since its approach route has been determined by its coordination to the titanium atom, it joins in a specific way, as all previous and following alkene molecules have done or will do, thus giving a stereoregular product.

The range of synthetic polymers which are called plastics, as distinct from rubbers and fibers, is now enormous. Two other materials with a basic skeleton similar to polythene, but with different atoms branching out of the backbone, are polyvinyl chloride (pvc) and polytetrafluoroethane (Teflon). The latter, discovered in 1938, has all the hydrogen atoms replaced by fluorine atoms. Although not commercially fabricated until 1948, it was used in World War II as a coating on reaction vessels to prevent corrosion during the process for the separation of uranium-235 from the more common isotope uranium-238 in manufacture of the atomic bomb. Its main domestic use now is in nonstick cooking utensils, where its high heat resistance and low coefficient of friction combine to ease washing-up problems.

Polyvinyl chloride was discovered much earlier—more than a century ago—but was not commercialized until the 1930s owing to the lack of a suitable plasticizer. Plasticizers are chemicals added to plastics to increase their flexibility so that they can be easily molded or formed into the required shape. Now pvc is used for a wide range of articles—curtain rails, rigid pipes, bottles, flooring compositions, and, in recent years, clothing for the more adventurous citizen.

A recent development which has expanded the range of applications of plastics—notably into the construction industry —is the foam plastics. These are ordinary plastic materials which are made to foam during manufacture, so that they set into honeycombs of tiny bubbles. Polystyrene is an example. Discovered in 1839, a good commercial polystyrene was not achieved until 1937. In its solid form it has been used for the manufacture of toys, slide viewers, vacuum flasks, refrigerator components, and so on. It was not until the 1950s that expanded polystyrene was introduced, following development work by BASF in Germany. To make the expanded material, polystyrene beads or granules are impregnated with the liquid hydrocarbon pentane, then steam heated. This causes them to expand as the pentane volatilizes and escapes. The ex-expanded material then has to be matured so that air can find its way into all the tiny crevices formed in the polymeric mass. If a molded article is required, the expanded beads can be further heated in a mold so that they expand and fuse together to give a lightweight "solid" object. The entrapped air makes expanded polystyrene a good insulator, and it can be applied as a sheet to walls or as tiles to ceilings, although its flammability has to be borne in mind. It is also widely used as a packaging material for glassware, cameras, microscopes, and similarly fragile objects, which can be packed in boxes filled with expanded polystyrene into which shapes have been cut for the objects to fit snugly.

The other major foamed plastic is polyurethane. This is a complex polymer made by reacting 2 different molecular building blocks. It is possible to choose the building blocks in such a way that the reaction between them releases carbon dioxide gas, which then foams the polymer as it forms. This property has been used for *in situ* polymerization to provide insulating foams; the ingredients are poured into the cavity between an inner and an outer wall, and the polymer immediately forms and fills the gap with a foamed mass which rapidly sets solid. The advantage over the application of foamed sheet is that the plastic gets into all the nooks or crannies in the walls. Similarly, by fixing a temporary mold around pipework and filling the intervening space with polyurethane, it is possible to insulate pipework without having to dismantle it. Polyurethane can also be made in such a way that flexible foams are produced; these are used widely for seats in automobiles and for domestic furniture.

Perhaps the most dramatic use of an expanded polymer was in the refloating of a sunken ship. A few years ago the *al Kuwait* sank in Kuwait harbor with a cargo of 5,000 sheep.

Since it sank near the inlet for the distillation plant which supplied Kuwait's fresh water, it represented a considerable health hazard. Traditional salvage methods would have taken too long to raise the wreck, so 70 tons of expanded polystyrene beads were pumped into it, and the air entrapped in these was sufficient to raise the ship. Several other sunken ships have since been brought to the surface with expanded polystyrene.

A Synthetic Yarn

Polyurethanes can also be made into stretch fibers. The fiber industry is an important consumer of synthetic polymers. The best-known synthetic, nylon, has already been mentioned, but, in fact, there is no single "nylon," but a whole family of them. The nylon discovered by Carothers is called nylon 6,6 because it is made from 2 starting materials (monomers), each of which has 6 carbon atoms in its molecule. One of the monomers has a carboxylic acid group at each end, the other an amino group at each end. These react together to form an amide bond of the type found in natural proteins, so that the resultant polymer is a long chain of carbon atoms with an amide linkage after every sixth carbon atom.

A number of different nylons have been tried, such as nylon 10,10, which, as its name implies, is made from 2 components each having 10 carbons in its chain. But the most successful postwar nylon is nylon 6. This is made from a single monomer, having a 6-carbon chain with a carboxylic acid group at 1 end and an amine group at the other. In this case, the polymer forms by monomer units linking up head to tail to form amide bonds.

Although the textile uses of nylon have been widespread— one of its major outlets during World War II was as material for parachutes—it is now used also as a solid for making plastic gear wheels and similar machine components.

In 1970 the world production of synthetic fibers was over 34.5 million tons, an increase of more than 150-fold since 1946. Immediately after the war nylon was virtually the only synthetic; by 1970 its share of the market had dropped to just under 40 percent, the 2 major competitors being polyesters (about 34 percent of the total) and acrylics (19 percent). Synthetics, as their phenomenal growth rate indicates, are rapidly taking over large areas of the clothing market, and it is estimated that by the mid-1970s over 30 percent of the total world fiber clothes market will be met by synthetics. Since many of the developing nations will still rely almost totally on natural fibers for clothes manufacture, this means that in the developed countries a high percentage of clothing will come, ultimately, from oil.

Carothers' research program, which led to the discovery of nylon, also included the synthesis of polyesters. In these the amide linkages of polyamides such as nylon are replaced by the ester linkages formed from the condensation of an acid with an alcohol. Carothers himself had no success in producing polymers that could be converted into fibers; it was not until 1941 in Britain, when J. R. Whinfield and J. T. Dickson condensed terephthalic acid and ethylene glycol (an important component of auto antifreeze) to form a material now known in Britain as Terylene and in the U.S. as Dacron, that success came. Dacron does not really compete with nylon; they have sufficiently different properties that, if used to their full advantage, they appear in different types of garments. Dacron can be processed so that it has a texture more like wool than nylon does, so is better when used in suits, but since it is not so elastic as nylon, this earlier material is still used in stockings and tights.

The acrylic fibers were developed after the war; these are polymers of acrylonitrile, a compound now made mainly from propylene by the ammoxidation process which is making obsolete earlier routes from acetylene and ethylene. About half a million tons a year of acrylonitrile are made in the U.S., and more than 50 percent of this goes into fibers, the remainder being used for copolymer resins such as ABS and for nitrile rubber. Acrylonitrile polymers, known as Orlon, Courtelle, and Acrilan, resemble good quality wool. A newer development is Teklan, a copolymer of acrylonitrile and vinylidene chloride which is more like silk, and which has flame-resistant properties. The acrylics are used widely for rugs and carpets as well as for clothing fibers.

Fiber uses for polyethylene and polypropylene are also being developed. Again, because of the different properties, the uses are different. Their fiber forms are found in such products as ropes, deck chair covers, and protective clothing for workers in industry.

Chemistry with a Bit of Bounce

Many of the advances in plastics, both the fibers and the bulk plastics, occurred during World War II when the shortages of natural materials required that substitutes be found. Nowhere was this more true than in the case of rubber, since most of the plantations which had supplied natural rubber fell into Japanese hands. Synthetics had been discovered before this but had not been seriously developed because, as is often the case, a new invention has to wait until it is needed before it is properly exploited.

Carothers' early work on synthetic fibers led to the discovery of neoprene in the early 1930s. This is the condensation product of an organic molecule called chloroprene, orginally made from acetylene, but increasingly now from butadiene. Synthetic rubbers are perhaps different from other polymers in 1 significant respect: they are more closely allied to natural materials. Natural rubber is made, by the rubber plant, from isoprene, a molecule composed of 5 carbon and 8 hydrogen atoms. Four of the carbon atoms are linked in a chain, while the fifth is attached as a branch to the second carbon from the end in the chain. Between the first and second and third and fourth carbons are double bonds, which give the molecule its polymerizing capability. Chloroprene has the same basic carbon chain, but the methyl group side-chain is replaced by an atom of chlorine. If the methyl group of isoprene is replaced by a hydrogen atom, the resultant compound is butadiene, which can also be polymerized into a synthetic rubber.

Isoprene can polymerize, in more than 1 way. Instead of forming a fully saturated chain like polyethylene, electrons from the 2 double bonds shift and form a double bond between the second and third carbon of the isoprene unit in the polymer chain. This means that each isoprene subunit is subject to the laws of geometrical isomerism. Early attempts to polymerize isoprene led to a random polymer that was like neither natural rubber nor another natural isoprene polymer, gutta percha. This is because both the natural products are almost stereoregular, natural rubber being a *cis* polymer, and gutta percha, which is not elastic, the *trans* polymer. The same question of stereospecificity applied to the polymerization of butadiene; it was not until the development of Ziegler catalysts that a useful butadiene rubber could be produced.

After the war, during which commercial uses and production of synthetic rubbers were developed, it became clear that natural rubber would never again be able to meet the world demand for rubber. As a further development of the uses of Ziegler catalysts, it is now possible to manufacture "natural" rubber by the controlled polymerization of isoprene. This has been done on only a small scale so far, despite the fact that the rubber is a little superior to the truly natural material. The Ziegler catalysts are even more stereospecific than the natural catalysts in the rubber plant, and produce a polymer more stereoregular than the approximately 90 percent regular plant rubber.

The greatest interest in synthetic rubbers has not been to find ways to beat nature at her own synthetic work, but to produce rubbers that are better suited than the natural material to man's needs. By 1970, the non-Communist world production of rubber amounted to about 7.5 million tons, of which 66 percent was synthetic; by 1985 synthetics should account for 75 percent of the market.

The major user in the U.S. is the automotive industry, tires and tire products consuming more than 60 percent of the rubber used. One of the major rubbers in the tire field is butyl rubber, a copolymer of isobutylene with a small percentage of isporene needed for "vulcanizing" the rubber. Ordinary natural rubber is not much use as an article of commerce because it tends to lose its elasticity in the cold and go sticky when hot. This problem was overcome in the 1830s by Charles Goodyear, who found that a much less changeable material could be produced by heating rubber with sulphur, a process he called vulcanization. The sulphur reacts with the double bonds in the polymer chain to form bridges between parts of the chain (somewhat analogous to disulphide bridges in proteins). Isobutylene has only 1 double bond, so that when the molecule polymerizes, it is fully saturated and is not susceptible to vulcanization unless a small amount of isoprene is added to keep some double bonds in the final polymer.

The original market for butyl rubber, tire inner tubes, disappeared with the invention of the tubeless tire; however, it is now used extensively as liner material for tubeless tires, where its low air permeability and resistance to oxidation make it particularly suitable. The major component of tires is styrene-butadiene rubber, a 1:3 copolymer of styrene and butadiene. About two-thirds of U.S. consumption, well in excess of a million tons a year, goes into tires. It is also used for foam rubbers and in shoes, although its growth potential has been sapped by development of the stereospecific rubbers.

One of the toughest rubbers around is nitrile, made from acrylonitrile and butadiene. This became important during the last war for manufacturing self-sealing gas tanks. It is very resistant to organic fluids, such as gasoline, and is now used for applications such as gas station hosepipes.

The plastics story does not end here; in a sense it is now unending, with new plastics coming up every few years. The thermosetting plastics, the original of which was Bakelite, have not been mentioned. Most of these were discovered in the 1920s and 1930s and have not shown the great rise experienced by the thermoplastics, fibers, and rubbers. They are, nonetheless, an important part of modern life, and the raw materials are petroleum-based. The silicones, a range of plastics in which alternating silicon and oxygen atoms rather than carbon form the backbone of the polymer chain, are new, but they have not been discussed in this chapter because they are not part of the petrochemicals industry.

This chapter has tried to follow a thread which joins the basic laws of chemistry to those of the marketplace. The new chemistry of industry may be old chemistry to the academic researchers. But even if he uses old chemical knowledge, the unique criteria which he must apply make the industrial chemist change this chemistry to suit the needs of his company. One of the keynotes of chemical industry, which has been obscured by the approach adopted here, is its ubiquity. Chemical products find themselves everywhere, pressed into service not only in the home but in dozens of industries. Some of the ubiquity of modern industrial chemistry is described in the next chapter.

8 ⬡ Chemistry Is Ubiquity

Wherever we look we see the effects of modern chemistry. This is not surprising for, insofar as every material thing is made of molecules, it is "chemical," and all modern artifacts are, in a sense, the product of chemistry. However, it is misleading and unjust to other branches of science to claim many modern inventions as triumphs of chemistry.

Take, for example, the transistor, which may appear in future histories as the most significant single invention of the twentieth century. The first transistor was demonstrated on June 30, 1948, by 3 scientists from Bell Telephone Laboratories, William Shockley, John Bardeen, and Walter Brattain. For their discovery they won the 1956 Nobel prize for physics. This was appropriate, for the transistor as an invention sprang from physics rather than chemistry, although what has been described as "the breakthrough that was to take transistors out of the laboratory and put them in every home," [1] zone refining, discovered in 1952 by William G. Pfann, is often considered a chemical separation process, and is probably more widely used in chemical laboratories than anywhere else.

Similarly, advances on the transistor principle, which have led to integrated circuits and microminiaturization, without which the present and predicted future ranges of computers would be impossible, are all basically physical. The contribution of chemistry has been to select the materials which fit the

[1] David Fishlock, *The New Materials* (N.Y.: Basic Books, 1967), p. 148.

244

theoretical background worked out by the physicists, and for physicists, chemists, and engineers working in collaboration to develop this new technology.

There are other areas in which it is clearly the contribution of the chemist that has led to modern advances. Four out of every 5 drugs now in use were unknown 30 years ago, and many of the most successful modern drugs—and other medical aids, such as surgical spare parts—are the result of chemical research. Here the chemistry always has to be coupled with cooperation from doctors and, in the case of drugs that have been isolated initially from plants or microorganisms, with microbiologists. The future progress of man depends on breaking down the old subject divisions of science and the creation of interdisciplinary research and development. Consequently, it is difficult to provide a coherent picture of the limits of chemistry in modern life. As we move away from the clearly defined center, exemplified by the petrochemicals operations described in Chapter 7, distinctions between chemistry and other sciences blur to an ever greater extent.

Take the field of materials science. Until the 1930s there had been very few new materials developed by science for mankind's use. Building bricks were still made on the same principles used by the ancient Egyptians, clothing came almost wholly from natural fibers processed in ways that showed clear kinship with prehistoric methods. Various changes in economic and social structures, such as the war-induced shortage of natural rubber, led to the development of embryonic new polymers. Development of the jet engine led to a need for new, high-temperature alloys.

Since the end of the war, materials science as a subject in its own right has grown phenomenally. At first, new materials such as plastics were misapplied as substitutes for natural materials—for example, plastic imitations of bone handles for knives. The true development of materials science came when engineers, physicists, and chemists merged their talents to produce synthetic materials for specific purposes which could not be met satisfactorily by natural materials. This "molecular engineering" has led to a whole new range of compounds and of composites, specially designed mixtures of compounds which have properties that excel those of either component on its own.

Hard Designs

The hardest natural material known to man is diamond, a polymer of carbon in which each atom is tetrahedrally bonded to 4 other carbon atoms. Other forms of carbon also occur naturally, but these have different structures; graphite, for example, consists of flat sheets of interlinked carbon atoms which can slide over one another, thus giving the material a characteristic slippery feel. In 1955, General Electric scientists found that graphite could be converted into diamond by heating it to a very high temperature under a pressure 100,000 times greater than normal atmospheric pressure. Diamond, at that time, was greatly in demand in industry for grinding and cutting operations, and a synthetic diamond that could be manufactured at a substantially lower price than mined diamonds was a profitable prospect.

Once the molecular engineers looked at the characteristic property of diamond and related it to its tightly-knit molecular structure, it became clear that it should be possible to make other very hard compounds. Two years after its diamond synthesis, GE produced borazon, a polymer made from equal parts of boron and nitrogen. These 2 elements are placed on either side of carbon in the periodic table; 1 has one electron less, 1 an electron more, so that the overall result of polymerizing a 1:1 mixture is to get the same electronic configuration as carbon polymer. The GE scientists started their experiments with boron nitride that was like graphite; when they finished, they had produced boron nitride like diamond. This material was not only like diamond in its hardness, in 1 respect it was better. At high temperatures carbon reacts with oxygen in the air to form the gas carbon dioxide; borazon is less reactive and therefore better for high-temperature grinding operations.

This early demonstration of molecular engineering seems unsophisticated by comparison with some modern examples. In 1967 GE developed a new technique called metalliding for diffusing boron atoms, with the aid of an electric current, onto a molybdenum surface. The effect of this was to make the normally soft molybdenum nearly as hard as diamond by forming a surface layer of tough alloy.

Other techniques for hardening materials have also been developed; most spectacular are the composite materials which may replace metals. In manufacturing composites, very strong "whiskers" of material such as silicon nitride or carbon fiber are embedded into resilient resinous material. The whiskers or fibers provide strength, while the matrix in which they are bound provides the cushioning needed to prevent these strong but brittle materials from fracturing.

Although some composites—glass-fiber reinforced plastics, for example—have been in use for some years in building small boat hulls or auto bodies, the real advances that will come from the use of composites have not yet been achieved. Recent developments indicate that the technique may be extended to traditional materials; work is in progress on carbon-fiber reinforcement of metals and glass. However, there is still more to learn before the exact advantages and limitations of these materials are known. An example of the dangers of exploiting new technology too soon was the inclusion of a carbon-fiber strengthened material in the specification for the fan blades in the Rolls-Royce RB211 jet engine. This engine, designed for the Lockheed 1011 Tristar airbus, had to be modified when it was found that accidental entry of an object, such as a bird, into the engine when traveling at high speed could cause shearing of the fan blades. As a result, Rolls-Royce had to fall back on a metal, titanium, at much greater cost. The subsequent bankrupting of Rolls-Royce in 1971 and the repercussions on the American aero-industry, which stem at least in part from this too imaginative leap into the future, made headlines throughout the world.

The "whiskers" which have been developed in recent years are specially prepared samples of nitrides, carbides, and oxides —direct chemical combinations of nitrogen, oxygen, or carbon with another element. Oxides, embedded in a matrix, have been used for centuries to confer strength on materials, although it is only recently that it has been realized that this is the case. When the oxide of silicon, silica, is heated, it forms a glass. Although glass appears solid, it is actually a supercooled liquid. Careful measurements have shown that glass flows, albeit slowly. In some European cathedrals, individual panes in stained glass windows are thinner at the top than at the bottom because of this slow flow. Glass is also brittle; ceramics, such as porcelain, are less brittle because they are reinforced by small particles of other oxides.

Because they generally withstand high temperature, much research has gone into the design of ceramics. One which has had widespread application in the home is glass ceramic, which was discovered as the result of an accident with some photoform glass. This contains metal ions which, on exposure to ultraviolet light, cause devitrification of the glass and make it opaque. Since devitrified glass is less resistant to acid attack than ordinary glass, the photoform material can be selectively exposed to radiation and the exposed parts eaten away with acid; hence the name photoform. When a sample of photoform glass was inadvertently overheated, it was found to have developed strength more appropriate to ceramics than glass, due to the formation of small crystal nuclei in the glass matrix. Such glass, marketed under names such as Pyroceram (U.S.) and Pyrosil (U.K.), is very useful for the fabrication of ovenware which will not crack when transferred from hot to cold surfaces.

Glass that Floats

Development of glass ceramics is not the only postwar innovation in glass technology. Although glass has been known for thousands of years, it is only in recent decades that a scientific understanding of its nature has been obtained. The result of this has been the extension of molecular engineering to this old material, leading to controlled changes in glass which give it new uses.

The whole technology of glass manufacture has undergone a revolution in the last decade and a half. Most of the glass manufactured is plate or sheet glass. In order to obtain flat glass in which both sides of the sheet are parallel, it used to be necessary to grind and fire polish the rough sheets of glass produced from tanks of molten material. At the end of the 1950s an English company, Pilkington Brothers, introduced the float glass process which is now used throughout the world. Molten glass is passed from a furnace onto a bath of molten tin. As it passes across the flat tin surface, the glass forms a sheet of even thickness which gradually solidifies into perfect plate glass.

One of the advantages of this process is that it can be used for making special glasses with unusual properties. Different colored glasses, for example, are made by addition of metals to glass. In the Pilkington process an electric current is passed through the molten glass as it floats on the tin; this current can be used to draw metal ions through the glass until a desired concentration of a particular metal is reached. Because the Pilkington process operates in an atmosphere of hydrogen (to prevent oxidation of the molten tin), the metal ions are converted to free metal atoms—the form which imparts color—in the glass.

In the early 1960s a new type of glass which is reactive to light was formulated. This photochromic glass contains chemicals which react reversibly with light. When the glass is exposed to strong light it darkens, but in the dark it turns transparent again. Photochromic glass can be used for prescription spectacles that enable the wearer to do away with "clip-on" sunglasses, aircraft windshields, or computer graphic display systems, but the most important potential use is probably in data storage devices. Photochromic material can be "exposed" like a photographic plate, and microimages stored in this way (10 copies of this book could be fitted easily onto a $4 \times 6''$ plate), or erased if no longer required. The secret of photochromism lies in the light-reactive molecules which are blended into the glass or, more likely in the case of data storage, transparent plastic. Molecular structural changes such as isomerism and ionization, which result in a color/no-color transition, can be produced in particular molecules by radiation of specific wavelengths, as happens in the biological case of the visual pigment rhodopsin.

More on Polymers

The new materials which really dominate our society are the organic polymers. In Chapter 7 some idea of the range of these—fibers, hard and soft plastics, and synthetic rubbers—was given. Because of the amount of basic research already done in the development of these materials, new research into polymers needs to be sophisticated. At the moment the major areas of exploration are the development of plastics for use at high temperatures, and electrically conducting plastics. In the autumn of 1964 John Lupinski and Kenneth Kopple first described a truly conducting plastic. The race is now on to develop a semiconducting plastic material which will compete with such materials as silicon and gallium arsenide in the manufacture of advanced electronics components.

With high-temperature plastics, the molecular engineers are further ahead. For nearly a decade now we have had "ladder polymers" in which 2-stranded polymer chains are held together by cross-links, like the rungs of a ladder. The instability of ordinary polymers relative to heat is caused by the breaking of bonds in the polymer chain, which leads to much shorter molecules. When a chain in a ladder polymer breaks in 2, the rungs holding it to its sister chain still keep the parts together.

The major success story of the polymers—if one can pick out a single class—is the silicones, polymers whose backbone is based not on carbon atoms, but on alternating atoms of silicon and oxygen. If this were all there were to the molecules they would be inorganic, but silicones also have organic side-chains. Like so much of modern chemistry, the division into inorganic and organic branches has little meaning here.

In 1943 Dow Chemicals and Corning Glass formed the Dow Corning company to exploit silicones; in the same year General Electric began to market a silicone rubber. This was only 2 years after Eugene Rochow—now at Harvard University—had discovered the basic process for manufacturing methyl silicones, that is, silicone polymers in which the side-chains are methyl (CH_3) groups.

Although silicon occurs directly below carbon in the periodic table, and is therefore in the same "family," it does not have carbon's power of combining with itself. Bonds between silicon and other silicon atoms are easily broken, as are bonds with other elements such as nitrogen and sulphur. In addition, silicon bonds are too long to allow the orbital overlap necessary for pi-bonding. This means that the bonds characteristic of carbon-based living molecules are unable to form. However, a repeating chain of silicon and oxygen atoms is stable, and silicon is like its relative carbon in generally forming 4 bonds—so there are 2 side groups attached to each silicon atom in a silicone, as the polymers are called.

By varying the chemical nature of the side-chains, it has been possible to produce a range of silicone fluids for uses in hydraulic systems, skin lotions, toothpaste, car and furniture polishes, and as antifoams for large-scale pharmaceutical fermentations.

Silicone greases, combinations of liquid silicones with solid silica, are electrical insulators, as are the silicone rubbers formed by cross-linking silicone chains in which some of the organic side groups are attached to two silicon atoms on different chains (this cross-linking is similar to that produced by the vulcanization of natural rubber).

It is estimated that a modern large airplane contains about half a ton of silicone rubber. Because of its noncarbon backbone, silicone rubber is nonflammable; the U.S. and British Navies use it as the covering for all electrical wiring in ships. In the event of a fire, the silicone is converted into a nonconducting coat of silica.

Cross-linked silicones are effective water repellents, and are used for treating masonry, textiles, and paper. An advance on this technique is silylation, for making glass, masonry, and minerals water repellent. These materials contain reactive hydrogen atoms which are replaced by trimethylsilyl groups, thus giving a surface coating of strongly bound, water repellent organic material.

Possibly the most successful applications of silicones have been in medicine. Because all living organisms have evolved active defensive systems against foreign materials, it is difficult to manufacture suitable spare parts: most organic plastics cause unpleasant reactions if inserted in the body. Because silicones are so "unnatural," the body does not recognize them, and consequently does not usually react against them. This means that it is possible to implant silicone materials without the danger of unpleasant side effects.

Silicones have been used for replacing defective heart valves and for enlarging the female bust, but the most important medical application is probably the Holter ventriculo-canal shunt. This is used for draining excess water from the brains of babies suffering from hydrocephalus. This condition, which consists of a build-up of water pressure in the brain, causes babies to develop overly large, distorted skulls. The Holter shunt prevents this by providing a drain for the excess water. It passes through brain, muscle, skin, and bone, and parts of it are permanently bathed in blood, yet its undoubted success is testified to by the fact that more than 50,000 of these shunts have been inserted since their invention.

Getting Enough Energy

A major theme in this book has been interactions between matter and energy. These 2 cornerstones come together once more when we look at the technology of modern life, for energy supply is a fundamental aspect of civilization. Without regular supplies of energy in diverse forms, many of the new materials at our disposal would be of little use, for they have been designed to fit in with our energy utilization patterns.

Until recently, most of man's energy supply came from burning fossil fuels—coal, oil, and natural gas—and using these to generate heat, electricity, or, as in the automobile, motion. For decades warning signs have been up that this energy supply will run out—or at least run so short as to become rapidly more expensive. It has recently been calculated that, between 1970 and 2000, man will use 70 percent of the earth's known oil reserves and 25 percent of the natural gas.

This has led, in the field of power supply, to the development of nuclear reactors which use the energy of decomposition of radioactive elements for generating electricity. Nuclear engineering, like so much of modern technology, is a multidisciplinary exercise calling on the talents of chemists, physicists, metallurgists, and engineers. In outline, a nuclear reactor contains fuel elements—often ceramic materials, carbides, or oxides of radioactive elements such as uranium and plutonium. When the radioactive atoms break down, the energy released is used to heat a liquid such as water, and the heat used to generate electricity. Water, for example, is converted into steam, which drives turbines.

This is not the only way in which to harness nuclear energy. Certain types of fuel, such as uranium carbide, which emit electrons, can be used as a cathode in a diode to produce direct current electricity in a single step. Alternatively, the heat from the nuclear processes may be used without further conversion, perhaps as a power source in flash distillation plants for water purification.

Work is currently progressing on nuclear reactors which convert uranium-based fuels into plutonium, which can itself be used as fuel. Since more usable fuel is produced than is put in, these are called breeder reactors. Commercial fast breeder reactors are expected to be in operation before 1980.

Civil nuclear energy began to develop rapidly in the mid-1960s, almost a decade after the first civil nuclear electricity generating plant had been opened in the Soviet Union. It was not until 1958, 4 years after the Soviets and 2 years after the British, that the U.S. got its first nuclear power plant for civilian electricity production at Shippingport, Pennsylvania. However, a year earlier, the U.S. Navy launched the world's first nuclear powered ship, the Nautilus.

In 1968 it was predicted that, by the end of the century, half the electricity generated in the U.S. would come from nuclear sources. Since that time, however, there has been rapidly growing concern, not restricted to the U.S., about the safety and environment aspects of nuclear power, and this "environmental lobby" may slow down—or even halt—the growth of this form of energy generation (see Chapter 9).

Cutting Down the Wastage

The demand for more energy is one of the gravest problems facing mankind, yet, in purely scientific terms, we waste far more energy than we use. When a power plant burns fossil fuels, the chemical energy locked up in the fuel is converted to thermal energy; this thermal energy is converted to mechanical energy, which is used to generate electricity. The efficiency of this 3-step process is low, and when, in the end, the consumer uses the electricity, he generally converts it back to heat or motion, again at less than 100 percent utilization, so that yet more of the precious resource is wasted.

One way in which the efficiency could be increased is to cut out the middle man. This is the basis of the fuel cell, which converts chemical energy directly to electrical energy, and may become an important energy source in developed countries in the next few years. The first fuel cell was described in 1839 by Sir William Grove, a British chemist, but it was not until 120 years later that another British scientist, Francis Bacon, developed the first modern fuel cell. This modest cell generated 5 kW from the reaction between hydrogen and oxygen.

Basically, the fuel cell generates electricity in the same way as the ordinary battery. The major differences are that fuel is continuously supplied to the electrodes, and that the power produced by the cell is a function of its size. Because they can work at very high efficiencies, fuel cells have played an important part in supplying electricity to space capsules in the U.S. space program.

In 1961 K. R. Williams and P. D. Gregory patented a microporous plastic electrode matrix on which metal and catalyst could be deposited. This enabled high currents to be drawn from fuel cells, and also permitted the use of ordinary air rather than oxygen in oxidation reactions. The second major breakthrough was the development of systems that did not require hydrogen gas, but could use alternative fuels as sources of hydrogen. Methanol is one such fuel. The methanol/air fuel cell produces carbon dioxide and water as waste products, just as combustion of methanol would; however, the efficiency of electricity generation is much higher. Hydrazine is another possible source of hydrogen ions. Hydrazine fuel cells give off nitrogen and water. Unfortunately, this substance is not only expensive, but also explosive and poisonous.

The major drawback in fuel cell utilization at the moment is that many systems have to run at high temperatures, thus making the present generation of fuel cells unsuitable for such uses as powering automobiles. However, there seems little doubt that, as technology improves, fuel cells will be used in transportation and possibly in integrated energy systems for the home —where generation of all the energy he needs is left to the consumer and his private power plant.

If enough power could be generated, direct conversion of chemical into mechanical energy might also have a bright future. Professor Aaron Katchalsky, who was a victim at the Lod Airport massacre in May 1972, worked on chemical engines for a number of years. In 1950, together with Werner Kuhn, he demonstrated that mechanical work could be obtained from polyelectrolytic compounds such as collagen—the protein found widely in man and animals as connective tissue. Polyelectrolyte fibers can be made to stretch or contract according to their environment. For example, a 10 cm long strip of collagen can lift 7,000 times its own weight through a distance of 3 cm when treated with the right chemical solution. If lithium bromide is used as the contracting agent, contraction takes only 0.1 second.

At his laboratory in Israel, Katchalsky produced chemical engines in which a belt of polyelectrolyte passes through a bath of concentrated salt solution and, later, through water. The result is to make a section of the polyelectrolyte—that in the salt solution—contract; but when a contracted portion of the belt passes through the water, so that the salt is diluted, it expands. This alternate expansion and contraction of sections of the belt can be used to make it turn around continuously, using up the energy that is normally dissipated when a strong chemical solution is diluted.

A Drop of "Oil"

For the moment, the possibility of automobiles and other engines being driven directly by chemical energy is probably far-fetched. But there is another way in which modern chemistry helps to overcome inefficiency in energy transfer processes. Wherever mechanical energy is used, part of it is wasted as thermal energy because of the friction between moving parts. To keep turning effectively, the wheels of home and industry need lubrication.

When any 2 surfaces move past one another, there is friction —resistance to the movement. The resistance depends partly on the materials involved and on their surface properties. For example, your hand slides more easily across a piece of polished or painted wood than across a brick wall. When 2 surfaces are in contact and in motion for much of the time, lubrication is necessary. In a motor, where metal parts are moving past one another all the time, a thin film of oil prevents direct contact and stops the machine seizing up.

But why should a machine seize up? The basic reason is that 2 smooth pieces of metal, such as ball bearings, are in reality very rough on a microscopic scale, with surfaces made up of myriad minute hills and valleys. When 2 such bearings come into contact, the only points that touch are a few of the hills on each bearing. If the bearings are under load, although this load may be small for the bearing as a whole, channeling it all into those few hills puts each under immense pressure which may cause them to weld together. If only small welds are formed, the energy of motion will overcome them, breaking the weld; but this exposes a fresh piece of metal, changing the contours once more.

Since the advent of the large engine during the nineteenth century, mineral oil lubricants have been used to keep wheels turning. In recent years a new concept of molecular lubrication has come into fashion. While mineral oils act by producing a thin film which coats metal parts, the new molecular lubricants react with the metals themselves, so that the chemical surface of the metals becomes lubricating.

General Electric, the largest manufacturer of rotating machinery in the world, established in 1958 a special lubrication research group to look into the whole question of lubrication. Headed by Dr. Arthur M. Bueche, now Vice President of the GE Research and Technology Center, this interdisciplinary group set out to look at the fundamental sciences underlying lubrication. One area they chose to examine was the behavior of freshly exposed metal surfaces.

Most of the metal we see around us, bright and shiny though it may appear, has a surface chemically different from its middle. Many metals react with oxygen from the air to form metal oxides, but once a coat only a few hundred thousandths of an inch thick has formed on the surface of a metal, the remainder is protected. Some metals also adsorb gases strongly, forming loosely bonded complexes with them. It was this latter property that opened a new approach to lubrication.

Using ultrahigh vacuum to prepare clean metal surfaces and keep them uncontaminated, the GE team was able to show that aluminum has a strong affinity for alkenes. When alkenes were chemisorbed on fresh aluminum, they clung tenaciously. Not even the temperature of boiling water could remove them. Since, during the friction process, clean surfaces are continually produced as miniature welds break, the GE scientists decided to compare 2 mineral oil-like long-chain hydrocarbon molecules as lubricants for aluminum. The only difference between the 2 was that 1 had a double bond in it. It was easily the superior lubricant, presumably because it was instantly adsorbed onto freshly exposed metal surfaces.

Not all the metal in a bearing is freshly exposed; part of it will already be oxidized. During the friction process, tiny particles of metal oxide can break off to form a hard grit in the lubricant which provides cutting edges that damage the bearings. By altering the molecular structure of the alkene lubricant so that it was also attracted to oxide particles, it was possible to improve its lubricating properties even more.

Many metals are very reactive when a fresh metallic surface is exposed, and some will react very quickly with iodine to form solid iodides which have a "lamellar" structure; such structures slide over one another readily. Consequently, it seemed likely that iodine would be a useful additive to conventional mineral oil lubricants, because it would mop up exposed metal surfaces and make them self-lubricating. Iodine does not dissolve in most mineral oils, but it readily forms molecular complexes with organic compounds like benzene. Consequently, such complexes —which will dissolve in mineral oil—were added to conventional lubricants. Once again the theory proved correct, and another new idea in lubrication was born.

The whole science of friction, lubrication, and wear—which has been given the name tribology—has undergone a revolution in the last few decades. Lubrication is not restricted to preventing seizure and unnecessary wear of moving parts. There are cases where it is used to promote wear. In a new automobile the freshly machined parts do not "mate" well because of the difficulties of mechanical machining. By using a highly reactive extreme-pressure lubricant, it is possible to improve the mating quickly. Lubricants of this type are organic compounds containing sulphur or chlorine. Although stable at room temperature, the molecules break up when heated to give off sulphur or chlorine. Since high spots on moving surfaces are subject to the most friction, these get hotter than the remainder of the metal. The lubricant releases sulphur or chlorine onto these hot spots, which then react to form sulphides or chlorides. Since these are softer than the metal, they break down more rapidly, thus smoothing out the roughness in the machined parts.

An important aspect of lubrication is that it should be effective over the whole range of operating conditions of the equipment it lubricates. An ordinary mineral oil, when warmed, rapidly becomes much less viscous; in an automobile it will be too stiff for satisfactory performance when the engine is cold, and too runny when the engine is hot. Consequently, modern lubricants are a complex mixture of chemical substances in a mineral oil base. In the 1950s multigrade oils were introduced, the viscosity of which changes only slightly over a large temperature range. The "magic ingredient" is a polymer, usually a polymethacrylate or polyisobutylene. When the oil is cold, the polymer molecules form random coils. As the oil heats up and its viscosity decreases, the polymers stretch out; this has a viscosity-increasing effect and thus counteracts the thinning of the oil.

Thought for Food

All of the materials and energy sources discussed so far reflect man's basic drive for pleasant shelter from a hostile environment. But his most basic need is to eat and drink. If he chooses carefully where he is to live, he may be able to do without clothing and shelter. Without food and drink, he will rapidly cease to exist. Because this addiction to eating and drinking has been around for a long time, much of the craving has been attended to by methods that involve no obvious chemistry. However, there are ways in which chemistry helps to keep us well fed, and there is a significant difference between just being fed and being well fed.

At the moment, many of us are ill fed. This is true in the developed no less than the underdeveloped countries. While those in underdeveloped countries starve for lack of food or develop deficiency diseases because their diets lack some essential ingredient, thousands of people in the developed countries shorten their lives by overeating. Chemistry can help at both ends of this spectrum.

In increasing food output, the chemical industry has been helping the farmer for years with the supply of fertilizers. Since plants contain their own mechanisms for producing the complex organic molecules which they need, fertilizers are generally mixtures of inorganic chemicals which supply the required amounts of elements such as nitrogen, phosphorus, and potassium to soils. Although this aspect of chemistry goes back to the turn of the present century, there has been continued growth in soil science. Farmers can now obtain fertilizers specially formulated to suit the soil on individual farms. In addition to N, P, and K, these contain small quantities of elements that are lacking in the soil but are essential, albeit in tiny amounts, to the optimum growth of crops.

This aspect of modern chemistry is a logical growth of the agricultural sciences that originated more than a century ago. Aspects in which new chemistry is involved are the "chemical plowing" of land to prepare it for seeding, and the preservation of crops from insect pests. The growth of pesticide usage has been rapid and, in some ways, disastrous—a subject taken up in Chapter 9. Although it is just over 3 decades since the first of the synthetic pesticides, DDT, was developed, it is already banned in many places because of environmental hazards. It seems that many of the present pesticide formulations will give way in the next few years to more cleverly designed systems, such as those mentioned near the end of Chapter 6.

One of the prime purposes of plowing land is to free it from weeds. In the last few years it has been possible to kill all plant life in a field and within days plant seed that will grow into a healthy crop. This is done with chemicals such as paraquat and diquat, simple organic molecules which interfere with the photosynthetic mechanisms of plants. The chemicals can be sprayed onto a field, where plants take them up through absorption and, depending on the weather (which affects the rate of photosynthesis), show signs of death in 1 to 3 days. The great advantage of these chemicals is their molecular structure; they are flat and electrically charged, which means that they adhere strongly to clay particles in soil, which also have flat surfaces and electrical charges. Because of this, the molecules of herbicide are inactivated and cannot harm any plants which grow subsequent to their usage. Since ingestion of paraquat is nearly always fatal, this inactivation mechanism is of prime importance to humans.

Another advantage of this system is that it leaves the surface of the soil undisturbed in a way which plowing does not. Because of the higher content of organic residues from dead plants, the surface of a soil may be less susceptible to erosion than material from below the surface which is exposed by the plow. So "no-tillage" systems of husbandry can conserve soil as well as making land in such areas as steep slopes, which cannot presently be plowed, suitable for cultivation.

These herbicides are not the whole answer. As the demand for food increases world-wide, land is being brought under cultivation which in the past was considered unsatisfactory for farming. There are many reasons why land may not be ideal for growing crops: mineral deficiencies in the soil, poor soil structure, and bad drainage are among them. Chemists are looking at all of these in an attempt to develop conditioners which will improve or stabilize soils. Both polymers and rubbers have been used to stabilize soils, in some cases too successfully; bitumen emulsions were found to make the soil waterproof.

One answer to these very complex problems is to do away with soils altogether. In a sense this is 2 answers, for doing away with soil can mean growing conventional plant foods without soil, or producing unconventional foods. The former (hydroponics) has been tried, especially in countries with large arid regions of poor soil, such as Israel. Basically, the plants are fed a carefully controlled composition of chemical solution while resting in a synthetic soil substrate, or in no substrate at all. Strange though the latter may sound, plants which grow upright can be supported in such a way that the roots hang free, gathering nutrition from pipes of chemical solution.

Algae à la Mode

The other alternative is to produce new foods—edible materials which have not been used by man before, such as yeasts, algae (although the Aztecs may have eaten this), and bacteria. One way to grow these unpleasant sounding but nutritious materials is to use partly processed petroleum oils. Following work pioneered in France by A. Champagnat and colleagues at the Sociètè Française des Pètroles B.P., a number of large oil companies have invested in projects to develop animal feedstuffs from petroleum. BP is currently building a 100,000 t/a plant at Sarroch in Sardinia; by 1980, the market for yeast proteins could reach 1 million t/a.

In 1959 the Lavera team commenced a study of the growth of yeasts on pure alkane hydrocarbons. The success of this approach soon led to the replacement of the pure chemicals with "heavy gas oils," a petroleum distillate which contains about 10 percent alkane hydrocarbons. The petroleum material is mixed with water containing mineral salts necessary for yeast growth, and air is blown into it. This keeps the immiscible liquids from separating into 2 layers, and also provides oxygen which the yeast needs to grow when its "food" is in the form of organic chemicals which do not contain oxygen.

The yeast is fastidious in its "eating" habits, with the result that the uneaten part of the gas oil can be removed after the process is over. Since the yeast consumes a commercially useless constituent, the residue is more valuable when it comes out than when it goes in.

The mass of yeast is carefully purified and dried to give a crude protein concentrate which has been found satisfactory for animal feeding. It has been suggested that it can also be used as a protein supplement to diets, such as those prevalent in underdeveloped countries, which lack protein, or else contain protein deficient in certain amino acids. However, yeast contains much larger quantities of nucleic acids than other protein sources, and it is possible that the effects of ingesting large quantities of these over a lifetime might be harmful to humans.

Natural gas is another substrate that is being used, in this case for the growth of high protein bacteria. In 1 process bacteria are grown on "refinery tail gas," a waste product from refinery operations which contains a substantial proportion of methane. Utilizing this waste product has the added advantage of cutting down pollution.

Food to Make You Not Grow

The day of the toasted yeast sandwich is probably a long way off, especially for those living in the developed countries, where personal food consumption is often greater than need be. When people are too addicted to food for their own good health, chemistry can come to their aid by producing delicious but nonnutritive food.

One of the advantages of the cow over the human being is that, with the aid of its stomach bacteria, it can digest cellulose, the structural carbohydrate of plants. For humans there is no goodness in cellulose and, in recent years, chemically modified celluloses have been used in some slimming meals. In some cases, not only is part of the content of the meal harmlessly indigestible, it also swells in the stomach through absorption of liquids, thus giving the eater a feeling of being full.

One of the most insidious of foods is common sugar. Some nutritionists claim that it not only causes obesity, but also coronary thrombosis and rotten teeth. However much of this is true —and some of it certainly is—there is a lot of money to be made from nonnutritious sugar substitutes. But it is important that the cure not be worse than the disease. The earliest sugar substitute was saccharine, which was discovered in 1879. About

550 times as sweet as sugar, saccharine has the disadvantage of a bitter aftertaste. This disadvantage does not apply to another group of compounds, the cyclamates. Following 9 years of testing in feeding trials, cyclamates were introduced as artificial sweeteners in the early 1950s. They spread rapidly to such a wide variety of foods that it became apparent that some people might consume more cyclamates than the amount which had been assumed as maximum dosage in the feeding trials. Following a number of new trials, and chemical evidence that under certain conditions the cyclamate molecule can rearrange to produce a molecule which has been linked with the induction of cancers, a wave of public feeling broke out against cyclamates in the late 1960s. In 1969, they were outlawed by the U.S. Food and Drug Administration and food processors in many parts of the world reverted to sugar and saccharine as sweetening agents.

There is no conclusive evidence of the harmfulness of cyclamates. Those who tested them clearly did not envisage the great extent to which they would catch on, and thus invalidate the tests. Since the last century, when standards of food preparation and preservation were appalling, tests for new products have become more and more stringent. This does not mean that compounds never slip through the net.

In the late 1940s a substance called agene (NCl_3) was used as a flour-maturing agent. In 1947 it was found that dogs fed large quantities of agene-treated flour developed "running fits." Although the doses were high, the evidence was sufficient to get agene banned from flour processing. It was later shown that agene reacts with the amino acid methionine to form the antimetabolite methionine sulphoximine, which has serious neurological effects on a number of animal species.

A more recent example of a food additive, the use of which has had to be restricted, is monosodium glutamate. This virtually tasteless amino acid derivative enhances the flavor of foods to which it is added, and was widely used in baby foods.

However, in late 1969 and early 1970, U.S. and U.K. food manufacturers placed a voluntary ban on its usage because of its possible action in causing brain damage. This was a wise move for, late in 1971, it was confirmed that large doses could indeed cause damage to a particular part of the brains of young rats and mice.

It is not only man-made chemicals that cause trouble in food. When something natural goes awry, the chemist may be brought in to do some detective work. Perhaps the most famous case in recent years occurred in England in 1960, when 100,000 young turkeys suddenly died from a mysterious ailment which was christened "turkey x disease." Eventually the cause was found to be the ground-nut meal on which the turkeys had been fed, which was contaminated with a microorganism called Aspergillus flavus. The active ingredient of the contamination was found to be the chemical aflatoxin; as little as 2 hundred-thousandths of a gram of this substance will kill a day-old duckling.

Water, Water Everywhere

While it is necessary to keep a watchful eye on the purity of our food, a more important problem is water supply. Water is necessary not only for animals and humans to drink, but also for all plant life. Industrialized societies use water in ever increasing quantities, yet the supplies of potable (i.e., drinkable) water are not endless. Physical science must play an expanding part in obtaining water for mankind, a task that has been left to the hydrological engineer in the past.

There is no shortage of water on the earth; most of the planet's surface is covered with it. But much of this is either salt or brackish, not suitable for human consumption or even for irrigation, since plants will not tolerate soils with a high salt content. In the hotter countries of the world, the search for new ways to obtain water has been going on for years, and a number of methods are now being tried out.

The 2 simplest processes are distillation, in which pure water is boiled off as steam from seawater or other impure water, and freezing. The ice formed in the latter process is purer than the water from which it freezes and can of course, be remelted after removal from solution. Both of the processes require large amounts of energy and complex engineering plant. Recently, simpler methods which depend on the widespread physical phenomenon of osmosis have been examined.

Many thin films of complex chemical substances are semipermeable, that is, only certain substances can pass through them. The thin lining between an eggshell and the white of the egg is a semipermeable membrane. If such a membrane is used to separate, say, a strong sugar solution from pure water, the pure water will pass through the membrane to make the sugar solution more dilute, since water molecules, being much smaller than sugar molecules, pass through the membrane with greater ease.

To prevent this from happening, it is necessary to apply pressure to the membrane. Consequently, the osmotic effect can be said to exert pressure, and is often called osmotic pressure. If a higher pressure is applied against the osmotic pressure, reverse osmosis takes place. Water from solution passes through a membrane into pure water on the other side.

Since the late 1950s, work has been going on in laboratories throughout the world to study reverse osmosis and, using films of cellulose acetate as membrane, it is now possible to construct reverse osmosis plants which will purify up to 50,000 gallons of water a day. A great advantage of this method over distillation is that it is also economical to build small plants, producing only say 1,000 gallons a day.

The mechanism of reverse osmosis is complex and is only now beginning to be sufficiently well understood for the design of alternative membrane materials. It seems likely that new membranes will be developed in the near future, although cellulose acetate films, which have been around for some years, are not difficult to make and are sufficiently sturdy for industrial usage. In Appleton, Wisconsin, Consolidated Papers, Inc., has been using a portable reverse osmosis plant for several years to clean up its effluent; 90 percent of the waste water is purified and returned to the plant, leaving behind a concentrated effluent for disposal.

At the moment, reverse osmosis has the edge over electro-dialysis, another semipermeable membrane process in which sea-water is passed into a semipermeable cell. On either side of the semipermeable membrane is an electrode, 1 positive and the other negative. When electricity is passed through the apparatus, the salts in the water ionize, and the ions pass through the semi-permeable membrane toward the electrodes. Since the amount of power required for electrodialysis is proportional to the salin-ity of the water, the method is only economical where the salt content of the water to be purified is low.

Chemistry Cures

Having fed, clothed, and sheltered himself, all man needs to enjoy himself is good health. Because of the way we choose to live, we do not often think about our health when it is good, only when it is not. The chemist has played a large part in restoring the sick to health. It would be foolish to suggest that chemistry can provide cure-alls: for example, the scourge of cancer can only infrequently be alleviated by present-day chemotherapy, although some promising drugs are currently on trial.

The most spectacular advances in the field of health care, so far as the chemist is concerned, have been associated with the discovery and development of antibiotics, substances which at-tack microorganisms and fight off their invasions of the human body. The first of these, discovered in the late 1920s, was penicillin, which is produced by a mold. Intensive study during World War II led to the large-scale production of penicillin by fermentation, as the industrial culture of microorganisms is called.

The penicillin story did not stop here. It was realized, when different fermentation methods were tried, that penicillin was not a single chemical compound, but a group of related substances. Each of these was found to have the same central core to which different "tails" are attached. In the mid-1950s, when penicillin-resistant strains of microorganisms were causing widespread infection, particularly in hospitals, Sir Ernst Chain, one of the scientists who had worked on the development of penicillin during the war and received a share in a Nobel prize as a result, advised the British company, Beecham Group Ltd., not to search for new antibiotics, but to find ways of modifying the penicillin molecule.

In 1957 a team of research workers at this company isolated the core of penicillin molecule, 6-aminopenicillanic acid (6-APA); 2 years later this compound was made synthetically by MIT chemist John C. Sheehan, but the synthetic method did not compete economically with 6-APA obtained by fermentation. By 1960 the Beecham team had not only discovered chemical methods for attaching the tail of their choice to the 6-APA core, but had found a semisynthetic penicillin that could beat the drug-resistant strains of microorganisms which had developed. They were able to produce a range of penicillins, all with slightly different properties, so that penicillin still forms a most successful group of drugs available for antibiotic therapy.

While all this was going on, other scientists had not been standing still. At Rutgers University in 1939, a student of Professor Selman Waksman, Rene Dubos, now professor of pathology at Rockefeller University, had isolated a powerful antimicrobial material, tyrothricin, from the soil-bacteria Bacillus brevis. Tyrothricin was later shown to be composed of 2 antibiotics (this word was coined in 1942 by Waksman), gramicidin and tyrocidin.

This discovery and the development of penicillin led Waksman, in collaboration with Merck and Co., to undertake a close examination of 10,000 soil cultures in search of antibiotics. In 1943 he isolated streptomycin, for which he received a Nobel prize in 1952. This substance went into production on a pilot plant scale the following year. It was followed, in the next few years, by the discoveries of chloramphenicol, chlortetracycline (aureomycin), neomycin, terramycin (Pfizer scientists screened 100,000 soil samples to find this 1), and cephaloridine (1 of about 600 modifications of a molecule called cephalosporin C). Streptomycin was among the first drugs to make a dramatic attack on tuberculosis; since its discovery a number of synthetic chemicals, such as izoniazid, p-aminosalicylic acid, and cyclo-serine, have also been introduced as antitubercular or tuber-culostatic agents.

Structurally, antibiotics are an odd assortment of molecules. The penicillin core is synthesized *in vivo* from 1 molecule each of the amino acids valine and cysteine; gramicidin and tyrocidin are made from amino acids, all of which have the opposite opti-cal configuration to natural amino acids; the tetracyclines, which include aureo-, neo-, and terramycin, are all so called because their basic core is a system made up of 4 rings of carbon atoms fused together; cephalosporin C was originally called penicillin N, because its core is similar to that of penicillin and it was ini-tially isolated from a culture containing other penicillins.

The modes of activity of antibiotics are also varied. Penicil-lin, for example, interferes with the synthesis of bacterial cell walls, and since mammals do not have similar structures, it is harmless to most humans. Some of the other antibiotics are less selective in their attack. Actinomycin D, for example, reacts with the double helix of DNA, and therefore is injurious to humans as well as bacteria and not very suitable as a thera-peutic agent. Chloramphenicol and streptomycin, on the other hand, act by joining onto bacterial ribosomes and prevent them from functioning properly, yet do not disable mammalian ribosomes.

Antibiotics are not the only therapeutic agents discovered since the war. Many new drugs have been synthesized, often on the basis of structures elucidated for drugs obtained from plant sources and known for centuries in impure form. Current theories of how drugs act are, in general, rather hazy, and drug companies find it better to mimic nature than try to design a drug solely on theoretical grounds. Cases in point are analgesic or painkilling drugs. The best known of these is morphine, obtained from the opium poppy, the therapeutic qualities of which have been known since ancient Babylonian and Egyptian times.

The constitution of the morphine molecule was first worked out in the 1920s (although the exact stereochemistry was not elucidated until later). Since then chemists have been attempting to synthesize variants which will have the analgesic properties of morphine but none of the addictive properties which make its prolonged use so dangerous. So far this work has not been greatly successful, although it has produced useful drugs. In 1964, for example, British chemist K. W. Bentley, moving in a direction opposite from previous workers in the field, decided to build a larger molecule than morphine. The result was the oripavine drugs which are many times stronger than morphine. They are too strong for human use, but have been used widely in wild game reserves for sedating large animals; one-thousandth of a gram of 1 of these drugs applied to the end of a dart is enough to quiet a 2-ton rhinoceros when the dart pierces its hide. It has been found possible with other morphine-related drugs to separate the painkilling activity from the addictive, but it has not yet been possible to produce such a drug without other undesired side effects, such as hallucinations.

Another field of synthetic drug chemistry is the production of antidotes to metal poisoning, which involves compounds known as chelates. These are multifunctional organic molecules which can surround a metal ion, forming several chemical bonds with it through the different functional groups. The behavior of the metal ion is thereby changed, often in a beneficial way. For example, an overdose of some metal may result in the ions of the metal being loosely bound to molecular structures in various organs. Administration of a chelate which can form stronger attachments to the metal will remove it from these organs and help it to pass from the body.

The first synthetic chelate to be used medically was ethylenediamine tetra-acetic acid, a hexafunctional molecule synthesized in 1935 by German chemist F. Munz. In 1951 this compound, which can wrap around metal atoms to form octahedral complexes, saved the life of a child suffering from lead poisoning. Since then many chelating structures have been designed for alleviation of poisoning by different metals. In particular, chelating agents are useful in removing the ions of various radioactive metals from the human system.

Back to Nature

As more becomes known about bodily processes, the accent in the pharmaceutical industry moves from synthetic chemicals to more natural materials, and from the cure of illness to its prevention. The latter is especially true in the case of metabolic diseases caused by genetic defects. Phenylketonuria is a genetic disease in which the ability to use the amino acid phenylalanine properly is absent. Instead, phenylalanine is converted to substances which can cause irreversible brain damage in children. Development of a chemical which reacts with these substances to produce a distinctive color change has led to a method of spot checking all babies at birth. The poison, if present, appears in the urine, and application to a wet diaper of a small stick or strip of paper impregnated with the appropriate chemical immediately checks whether or not a baby is phenylketonuronic. Those that are can be fed on special diets low in phenylalanine, thus preventing brain damage and enabling them to live healthy, normal lives.

Chemical study of the steroid hormones which control the sexual cycle led to the contraceptive pill—introduced in 1960—which replaces earlier techniques of contraception with a method which is certain, since it uses the body's own mechanism. There are possibilities of side effects, however, for although the body is not being fed "unnatural" materials, it is receiving enormous doses of material usually present only in small quantities, and this may have undesirable long-term repercussions.

The latest in the list of natural materials to be taken up by the pharmaceutical industry is the prostaglandin family. Although prostaglandin activity was detected more than 30 years ago, it was not until 1957 that Dr. Sune Bergstrom of the Karolinska Institute in Sweden, using chromatography, spectroscopy, and finance from the Upjohn Company of Kalamazoo, Michigan, isolated pure crystalline prostaglandins. It took another 5 years to elucidate the structures of the 2 20-carbon molecules he had purified. There are now 14 known prostaglandins, and the total synthesis of representatives of this group has been achieved by Professor E. J. Corey and his collaborators in the chemistry department at Harvard University.

Prostaglandins appear to be involved in the regulation of many bodily functions. In recent years the medical press has been full of accounts of abortions and terminal labor induced by prostaglandins, as well as their applications as cold decongestants and asthma relieving agents. It seems likely that the range of prostaglandin cures may not end here—treatment of high blood pressure and gastric ulcers, control of carbohydrate metabolism, and cure of infertility are just some of the other conditions where it has been predicted that prostaglandins could prove useful. However, although two prostaglandin preparations are now available in Britain, it will be some years before prostaglandins are widely marketed, since it is becoming increasingly appreciated that new drugs must be stringently tested before they can be made generally available.

No better evidence of this can be provided than the thalidomide tragedy. First made in 1953, this synthetic sleeping pill was marketed in Germany in 1957, and later in the U.K. and several other countries but not in the U.S.

Because it provided gentle sleep with no apparent side effects, thalidomide became widely prescribed for pregnant women. It was not until 1961 that some doctors began to realize that there was a suspicious coincidence of use of this drug and the appearance of hitherto rare deformities in new-born babies, characterized by lack of arms, so that the hands emerged almost directly from the shoulder blades. Thalidomide was hastily withdrawn from the market as the degree of coincidence increased and it became clear that, in some way, the "harmless" sleeping pill had been responsible for the birth of thousands of deformed babies.

Hopefully, such an incident will not recur, although, as the case of the food additive cyclamates shows, the forward movement of technology leaves us constantly exposed to new dangers. Some of these, and the way in which they can be handled, form the substance of much of Chapter 9.

The Chemistry of Art

A few pages back we made the sweeping statement that all man needs to enjoy himself are adequate food, clothing, shelter, and health. This is probably too much of a generalization: without art and culture it is unlikely that modern man would enjoy himself, however great his health and material wealth.

It has been fashionable in recent years to argue that society is divided into "2 cultures," with scientists on 1 side of the fence and everybody else on the other, both snarling at each other. Like many facile arguments, this contains some truth, but as the fruits (not all of them palatable) of science spread into every corner of society, there is an awakening of interest in what scientists are doing. This is particularly true in certain areas previously considered the exclusive province of the non-scientist, such as art and archeology. Many museums and art galleries now have laboratories attached, and the scientist can help the museum curator and archeologist as both a detective and a conservationist.

The most famous chemical breakthrough in archeology is, without doubt, radiocarbon dating, developed in the late 1940s by American chemist Willard Libby. With the increasing knowledge of nuclear transformations and the processes by which 1 element is converted into another, it became apparent in the late 1930s that nitrogen atoms in the upper atmosphere, exposed to radiation from outer space, were probably transformed into a radioactive isotope of carbon, ^{14}C.

Since carbon is continually recycled in nature, being taken into living organisms through the photosynthetic process and eventually being returned to the atmosphere, Libby proposed that all living organisms would contain a certain proportion of ^{14}C in their makeup. When an organism dies, fresh carbon is not taken in. The carbon locked up in the dead molecules gradually loses its complement of ^{14}C through radioactive disintegration. Since this disintegration occurs at a fixed rate, it should be possible to tell the age of an object by determining the ratio of radioactive to ordinary carbon in its makeup.

Libby spent several years at the University of Chicago testing his theory. The first step, to see whether carbon compounds freshly released from living organisms did contain ^{14}C, was shown to be correct through the detection of radiation in methane gas generated from sewage in Baltimore.

By developing a subtle technique which discounted radiation from external sources, Libby was able to measure the small amounts of radiation from ^{14}C in organic materials. Through Professor John Wilson of the Oriental Institute at the University of Chicago, Libby and his colleagues obtained samples of organic material of known age from early Egyptian pyramids. Using this, they were able to show that it was possible to date objects by measuring their radiocarbon contents; for this achievement Libby was awarded the 1960 Nobel prize in chemistry.

There are drawbacks to radiocarbon dating. It is based on certain assumptions which may be incorrect about the constancy of upper atmosphere bombardment by radiation. By checking radiocarbon methods against other dating methods, it has now been shown that, as one goes back in time, an increasingly large deviation occurs between dates obtained from radiocarbon studies and those from other methods. A chart of the deviations has now been plotted that goes back 7,500 years. Despite this, the method provides an invaluable asset. Since the mixing of carbon is a world-wide process, 2 objects of the same age from different parts of the world always give the same radio date. Consequently, an object of known date from 1 part of the world can be used to date objects of the same age from other parts of the world, even if no independent dating method for these other objects exists. At the moment, radiocarbon dating is causing a gigantic upheaval among scholars of early European civilizations by indicating that these developed several hundred years earlier than previously believed.

In addition to dating methods based on other radioactive transformations, different methods have been developed in recent years. The constant background radiation which reaches the earth causes damage to molecules. In an object such as an ancient pot, left lying around for thousands of years, this damage, although invisible, is substantial. It is invisible because it usually involves disruption of single atoms, causing minute changes in the material. When such materials are heated above the temperature at which they become red hot, this disruption shows up as luminosity, an effect known as theromoluminescence. The older an object, the more thermoluminescent it is. Although the accuracy of thermoluminescent dating is poor, it can be valuable in detecting fakes. The error—which can be about 10 percent—makes the method inapplicable to classical archeological dating, but such an error is insignificant when it comes to determining if an object was made 2 or 2,000 years ago. Antique objects are rare and command a high price among collectors. This fact has not escaped the notice of various entrepreneurs who have been helping to supply the demand by making "antiques"; thermoluminescent dating is an excellent way of checking whether the goods offered by these traders are the real thing.

This is but a single example of the detective work that chemists and physicists are called upon to perform in checking up on the world's art treasures. By combining chemical and physical techniques developed in recent years, such as infrared spectroscopy, gas liquid chromatography, and atomic absorption spectroscopy, it is possible to check the authenticity of many objects. For example, x-ray diffraction studies of some samples of "Roman glass" have shown that they have been artificially aged with hydrofluoric acid—a chemical not common in ancient Rome.

On the other hand, the Romans did know a few things that, until recently, we did not. In the British Museum in London is a Roman glass goblet, the Lycurgus cup, which has a rather striking property. When seen by reflected light it is a sludgy green; when seen by light transmitted through it, it is wine red. Using a minute sample of this cup (seven-thousandths of a gram), 2 British scientists found that it had a composition typical of Roman glass, except for the addition of minute percentages of gold and silver. Using this composition of raw materials and trying different methods of melting the mixture to form glass, R. H. Brill, in the 1960s, succeeded in recovering the lost technique of the Lycurgus cup's manufacturer and made glass with the same dichroic effect.

More often, the museum scientist is called upon not to mimic the products of the ancient world, but to prevent their decay. Wooden objects often keep well in water, but once removed from the water and dried out, they crumble away to nothing.

One solution to this problem is to impregnate the wood with a material that will help to preserve it. This has been done successfully with polymeric materials, the polyethylene glycol waxes, which are water soluble. They can be used to impregnate the wood as the water is removed from it, in a single step. This method has been utilized to preserve wooden objects believed to be more than 50,000 years old, and to treat a seventeenth century Swedish warship, the Wasa, salvaged from Stockholm harbor.

A modified nylon polymer which forms a matte permeable film when applied to objects in alcoholic solution has been used for consolidating flaking paint on oil paintings from Egyptian tombs, as well as for preserving illuminated manuscripts and textiles. Another technique used to restore damaged objects is consolidative reduction. Where metals have been corroded—for example, to halides or carbonates—it is sometimes possible to restore the object by electrically reducing the corroded material back to its original metallic form.

Another method of preservation which may be useful for massive ancient objects is *in situ* polymerization. In 1970, scientists at the Center for Nuclear Studies in Grenoble, France, impregnated an ancient Egyptian wooden yoke with a liquid resin, which they then irrradiated with radiation from cobalt-60. This polymerized the resin to a solid permeating the wood. (It has been suggested that such a technique could be used commercially for upgrading soft timber into hardwood.) Such *in situ* polymerization might provide an answer to the problems of crumbling stonework on such buildings as the Parthenon in Greece, where the damage of centuries of wear has been greatly accelerated in recent years by the effluent from Athenian factories. An alternative method of preservation in this case, of course, would be to eliminate air pollution. But that is a subject for Chapter 9.

9 ❦ Chemistry and Tomorrow

The last 2 chapters have indicated the ubiquity of modern chemistry, not only in the wide sense that all things at a certain level of understanding are molecular, but in the artificial sense of chemicals having been manufactured and applied in myriad ways. Since chemicals are so widespread, it is not surprising that some of them are found in the wrong place at the wrong concentration, thus resulting in pollution.

During the last decade there has been a rapid increase in public awareness of the extent to which man's power over nature can backfire and wreak havoc on his planet. The pollution of air, earth, and water are matters of wide public concern, as can be seen from the number of newspaper and magazine articles and hours of TV and radio time given over to their discussion. This examination will be restricted to forms of pollution which are clearly a part of the new chemistry.

Pesticides

About one-third of the cereal crops grown throughout the world each year are never harvested by man: disease, weeds, and insect pests destroy them. This wastage probably amounts to about 500 million tons of food each year. In some spheres of agriculture the picture is even gloomier. It has been calculated that as much sugar cane and sugar beet are lost as are harvested.

This process has been going on for a long time, and even early civilizations applied their ingenuity to overcoming the wastage. During the early years of this century, the problem of controlling insect pests was passed to the chemist. It was known by then that certain plant extracts were lethal to insects. Nicotine, from tobacco, for example, has been used as a plant spray for many years, and the flowers of pyrethrum and roots of the derris plant (ground down to "derris dust") are further examples of early, natural chemicals used in pest control. However, it seemed at the time that a simple synthetic chemical, active against a wide range of pests, would be desirable.

Paul Muller, a Swiss chemist working for the firm of Geigy, began to search for such a chemical in the mid-1930s. The search ended in September 1939 with a substance called dichlorodiphenyltrichloroethane, which, for simplicity's sake, was abbreviated to DDT. By the middle of World War II, DDT—which had been discovered in the 1870s but not put to any use—was being used by the armed forces and was also on sale to the public.

During the winter of 1943, in Allied-occupied Naples, DDT showed its power when spraying of humans with a solution of it halted an epidemic of the killer disease typhus. DDT has since been widely used throughout the world in the eradication of a variety of pests; it has been estimated that more than half a million tons of the substance have been loosed on the world in the last 30 years.

This is an enormous quantity of totally artificial chemical to release into the environment, and it has recently been noted that in some ways the use of DDT has been indiscriminate. It would be wrong to say that DDT has caused more harm than good. DDT has done and, under controlled conditions, still can do an immense amount of good, but it is possible that more thought would have allowed its deleterious side effects to be seen earlier.

Professor Barry Commoner describes a personal experience

from World War II, when he was a U.S. Navy project officer working on the development of DDT spraying by aircraft, "which proved to be of great importance in the Pacific island battles by protecting the first wave of attackers from serious insect-borne diseases." A request came to the Navy from a rocket experimental station on an island off New Jersey for help in destroying a plague of flies which was interfering with the experimental work. "We sprayed the island and, inevitably, some of the surrounding waters with DDT. Within a few hours the flies were dead, and the rocketeers went about their work with renewed vigor. But a week later they were on the telephone again. A mysterious epidemic had littered the beach with tons of decaying fish—which had attracted vast swarms of flies from the mainland. This is how we learned that DDT kills fish." [1]

Shortly after the development of DDT, a new insecticidal compound, BHC (benzene hexachloride), was discovered almost simultaneously in England and France. In the late 1940s chlordane, aldrin, and dieldrin were discovered by Julius Hyman and his colleagues, working first at the Velsicol Corporation and later in Hyman's own company. Together with heptachlor and endosulphan, these 5 are the best known of the organochlorine insecticides, so-called because they are all organic molecules (and contain at least 1 modified benzene ring), and all contain several atoms of chlorine.

It is reasonable to treat them as a group, for they tend to be long-lived substances which accumulate in living tissues. For example, the fish kill described by Commoner was trivial compared with the accident in Europe's Rhine river in June 1969. Two barrels of endosulphan, accidentally dumped in the river in Germany, are estimated to have killed 40 million fish. In addition, the Dutch, who take drinking water from the Rhine, were forced to fall back on emergency water supplies while

[1] Barry Commoner, *Science and Survival* (New York: Ballantine Books, 1970), pp. 25–26.

the "mysterious epidemic"—the cause was not discovered for several days—was rampant.

Birds have been the worst sufferers from organochlorine insecticide poisoning. DDT acts on the liver, probably interfering with body levels of the hormones concerned with reproduction; this shows up in the production of eggs with exceptionally thin shells which break before the chicks are ready to hatch.

It is not possible to say what the long-term effect on man may be. In 1969 the U.S. Food and Drug Administration condemned 700,000 coho salmon from Lake Michigan because of their DDT content. It is already an old joke to say that Americans should not become cannibals because the FDA would never pass meat for consumption with DDT levels as high as those found in human fat in some parts of America.

However, Nobel prizewinner Norman Borlaug has recently pointed out that it would be criminal to ban the use of DDT. In the underdeveloped countries of the world, cheap effective insecticides are still an urgent necessity. There is equally no excuse for the advanced countries to continue indiscriminate use of organochlorines when there are alternatives, albeit more costly ones.

Following work on organophosphorus nerve gases (see Chapter 6), a different class of insecticides, the organophosphorus compounds, was developed. These have the advantage of not being very stable chemically. They remain in soil, for example, only a few months before being degraded to harmless products, rather than the years taken by some of the organochlorines. The first world-wide success of the organophosphorus compounds was parathion, a wide spectrum insecticide. Perhaps more important from the methodological viewpoint was schradan, which proved to be the first "systemic" insecticide. It is readily taken up by plants and distributed throughout their vascular system, making the whole of the plant resistant to insect attack. When applied directly to insects, systemic insecticides are not usually effective, but once they have been absorbed by the plant, and the feeding insect swallows a mouthful of insecticide together with some plant sap, the lethal properties become apparent.

In addition, chemists have synthesized a number of other types of compounds—chemosterilants, which make the insects lay infertile eggs; antifeeding compounds, some of which are organometallic rather than straightforward organic compounds, and which work by making the insect give up eating and starve itself to death; and the sex attractants (pheromones), whose use in pest control has already been discussed.

Renewed interest has recently been shown in some of the more complex natural insecticides from plants, the structures and laboratory syntheses of which have been achieved in recent years. Pyrethrin, still obtained from plants related to the chrysanthemum and grown mainly in Kenya, is widely used in aerosol cans of flykiller, as well as larger-scale applications, because it has a potent, but short-lived, effect. Work at the Rothamsted Research Station in England has recently led to the development of 2 synthetic analogues of pyrethrin, resmethrin and bioresmethrin, which are now being manufactured in Japan, France, and the United States, and have the advantage of supplies not being dependent on a good crop of flowers.

There is no doubt that research on insecticides will continue, much of it motivated by the desire to overcome the defects of the early synthetics. The discovery of DDT in Antarctic ice and other remote regions has brought home the fact that a chemical accident can no longer be confined; it soon reaches everyone's backyard.

A Breath of Not-so-Fresh Air

The earth is a large system composed of interlocking cycles. As Libby's development of carbon-14 dating showed, there is continual and complete mixing of the planet's air. Similarly, through the water cycle, in which seawater is evaporated by solar heat, the vapor moved as clouds, and then precipitated as rain in other places, the waters of the earth are mixed—and to the seas and rivers are added substances picked up from soil as rain-water trickles through it.

Since the industrial revolution, man has poured massive quantities of chemicals into the air and water, resulting in measurable compositional changes. The industrial revolution was built on energy supplied by the burning of fossil fuels, first coal, later oil and natural gas. The products of this combustion are mainly carbon dioxide and water. It has been estimated that during the first half of the twentieth century, the concentration of carbon dioxide in the atmosphere increased by about 11 percent; according to the 1965 report of the President's Science Advisory Council's Environmental Panel, a 25 percent increase during the second half-century is anticipated. Not all, but a substantial part of this increase can be attributed to the burning of fossil fuels. Whatever the source, the increase has concerned a number of scientists who believe that the effect of this extra carbon dioxide will be to change the earth's climate.

Much of the energy which the earth receives from the sun is taken up by soil, then radiated back into space as energy of a different wavelength. Carbon dioxide can absorb this terrestrial radiation, cuting down the amount returned to space. If the carbon dioxide content increases, so may the mean temperature of the earth, and a rise of only a few degrees in world temperatures would melt sufficient of the polar ice caps to submerge many of the world's cities.

Such an effect might be countered by the emissions of grit and dust which accompany the burning of fossil fuels (but which are gradually being legislated to lower and lower emission levels). These may be increasing the turbidity of the atmosphere and cutting down the amount of radiation which reaches the earth—hence having a cooling effect, in opposition to carbon dioxide's heating effect. It is important to bear in mind that both these processes may be of only secondary importance when compared to continuing natural climatic changes. The eruption of the volcanic island Krakatoa in 1883 spewed more particulate matter into the atmosphere than man has done throughout his entire history. The earth has passed through a series of ice ages, alternating with warm spells, and the forces which dictate these long-term fluctuations may be more powerful than any of the man-made contributions. However, the problem of gaseous emissions as a result of human activity should not be ignored.

Many fossil fuels are contaminated with sulphur-containing compounds, the burning of which produces gaseous sulphur dioxide. This is an unpleasant air pollutant, but can be controlled. In general, sulphur dioxide seems to be a localized irritant, associated with the airspace over heavily industrialized areas. It has even been suggested that it may have a beneficial effect. Heavy agricultural cropping of land, made possible by widespread application of fertilizers, can lead to depletion of minerals in soil. Any sulphur deficit produced in this way may be made up at present by absorption of sulphur dioxide from the air. Cleaning up sulphurous emissions might lead to sulphur starvation in crops. However, as agricultural scientists are now more concerned with designing fertilizers individually for different areas and making up mineral deficiencies on a local basis than with selling straightforward NPK fertilizers, the worry of sulphur starvation should not be used as an excuse for not cleaning up the air.

One factor which could lead to an abrupt decline in sulphur dioxide emissions is an increase in the price of elemental sulphur. All the scientific and technological work needed to remove sulphur dioxide from smokestacks has been accomplished, but the processes, which lead to sulphur recovery, are not economically competitive with sulphur obtained from mines. If they ever become so, the laws of economics, if nothing else, will end this source of pollution.

The major increase in the burning of fossil fuels during the twentieth century is a result of the spread of the automobile. In addition to emitting carbon dioxide and its more poisonous relative, carbon monoxide, automobiles also belch out oxides of nitrogen and partly burned hydrocarbons. Under some conditions, notably those in Los Angeles, this mixture, when provided with energy from sunlight, can undergo complex photochemical and free radical reactions to produce compounds irritant to living organisms. As well as peroxyacyl nitrates, acrolein, and formaldehyde, all of which cause eye irritation, the reactions involved produce ozone, a molecule composed of 3 linked atoms of oxygen, unlike the normal diatomic oxygen molecule. Ozone is highly reactive toward substances such as rubber, and is the cause of abnormally high levels of rubber cracking in the Los Angeles area.

Morbific Metals

To make gasoline burn more efficiently in high compression engines, a number of chemicals are added to it. The most common additive is the organometallic compound, tetraethyl lead. Car exhausts emit lead and organolead compounds from combustion of fuel containing this additive, and it has recently been suggested that we may be contaminating the environment with lethal quantities of lead because of its use as an additive. This is a subject of unresolved controversy between the oil and lead processing corporations and a group of worried scientists, although the latter seem to have more right on their side than do the vested interests.

Man's usage of metals is a major cause of concern. Most metals are toxic to living organisms in all but the smallest quantities. Yet industrial activity is leading to the pollution of land and sea not only with lead, but also mercury, cadmium, copper, chromium, and zinc. It has been estimated that atmospheric transport is dumping about 200,000 tons of lead into the oceans each year, most of it derived from the tetraethyl lead in gasoline. Many of these metals are concentrated by molluscs, which thus become poisonous to whatever feeds on them.

There is no doubt that mercury in some forms can be lethal. In Japan, between 1953 and 1963, more than 100 cases of serious nervous illness leading to severe debility or death were shown to be directly attributable to consumption of oysters which had picked up methylmercury discharged by a chemical company into Minamata Bay. In late 1971, after a long legal wrangle, the company responsible had to pay out substantial compensation to victims of mercury poisoning.

In addition to metals, the most persistent pollutants of the hydrosphere are the organochlorine pesticides and other organochlorine compounds, notably the polychlorinated biphenyls (PCBs) and waste products from the manufacture of polyvinyl chloride. Since the sea is, in many respects, our last resource, not only for new supplies of minerals but also for food, pollution by materials known to concentrate in food chains should be minimized. Nevertheless, during July 1971 the tanker Stella Maris took 600 tons of chlorinated hydrocarbon waste from a Dutch factory out into the Atlantic with the intention of dumping it. Only an immediate international outcry prevented this.

Not all industrial activity is so irresponsible. In late 1970 and early 1971, Monsanto Chemicals, sole U.K. and U.S. manufacturer of PCBs, restricted sale of these products to carefully defined uses where they could not cause pollution.

Dirty Ol' Man River

The problems of marine pollution differ in many respects from those of river pollution, particularly because of the high utilization of river water for drinking. Compounds which will slowly break down to harmless materials in the sea may be dangerous in rivers, because they will be ingested by land animals before they have decomposed. Excessive applications of fertilizer—which may result in the destruction of soil structure—lead to inorganic nitrates running off into rivers. These can be converted microbiologically to nitrites, which are dangerous to human health, notably to babies, because they interfere with the respiratory process. The increase in nitrate levels can also lead to massive build-up of algae, which deoxygenate the rivers and make them uninhabitable for fish. The problem is also aggravated by the large quantities of phosphates poured into rivers as a result of household detergent usage.

Synthetic detergents are a fine example of how modern technology can go wrong. From the 1940s onward they began to replace soap as the major household cleaning agent; the basic ingredients in these detergents were branched-chain modified hydrocarbons derived from petroleum (soap is made from animal or vegetable fats). From the householder's viewpoint the major difference between the 2 is that detergents work with equal efficiency in hard or soft water, and do not form the insoluble scums characteristic of soap. To industry, reliance on a petro-chemical raw material is preferable to reliance on an animal- or plant-derived material subject to agricultural supply and price fluctuations. What was overlooked was that microorganisms, which can metabolize animal and vegetable materials, cannot break down branched chain hydrocarbons. Rivers began to foam from the waste detergent poured into them. By 1960 alone, nearly 2 million tons a year of synthetic detergents were being used and thrown away. Tapwater, culled from the rivers and purified by conventional processes which did not remove the detergents, came out of taps in some areas with a "head" on it like a glass of beer.

In 1965 detergent manufacturers voluntarily gave up the use of branched-chain hydrocarbons in their products and replaced them with straight-chain hydrocarbons, which microorganisms can break down. Since that time the spotlight has turned on the phosphates which also go into detergents (as emulsifiers and water-softening agents) because of the part they play in altering the ecology of rivers.

Detergents have also been the bête noire of another world famous incident. Part of the growing dependence of man on fossil fuels has led to a large increase in the size of oil tankers. In March 1967 the tanker *Torrey Canyon* crashed on the Seven Stones reef off the southwest coast of England. One hundred thousand tons of oil was set adrift on the sea, headed toward the beaches of England and France. The English decided to disperse the oil by massive spraying of detergents. When the exercise was studied in detail later, it was found that while the oil had been responsible for a substantial number of bird deaths, far greater havoc had been wreaked on marine life by the toxic effects of the detergents.

In January 1969, when an oilrig blowout off the Santa Barbara coast in California released 250,000 gallons of oil, at least 1 lesson had been learned: no attempt was made to use detergents on it. Since the *Torrey Canyon* disaster, a number of chemical companies have developed detergents much less toxic to marine life, and have also pioneered other methods of clearing up oil spills—for example, by soaking up the oil with a carpet of polyurethane beads or flakes. But it is small credit to cure problems when prevention would have been possible with a little foresight.

Too Energetic by Half

The pollution caused by both oil spills and the burning of fossil fuels raises an important question: Should we continue relying on these sources for our energy supply? Estimates show that coal supplies will probably hold out for only 2 or 3 centuries at the present rate of usage, while all the oil will be gone in less than a century. There are untapped reserves of fossil fuels, such as oil shales, and some recently tapped ones, such as natural gas supplies, which could increase in importance. However, in all cases, supplies are limited and, what is often overlooked, these materials can provide valuable raw materials for the manufacture of chemical products, such as polymers. To burn them is, largely, to waste them.

If we stop burning the fossil fuels, where will the world's energy come from? Overlooking the fact, for the moment, that the developed countries waste enormous amounts of energy (in the U.S., per capita energy consumption is 100 times that needed to sustain life), what are the alternatives?

In parts of the world where the geography is favorable, water power has been harnessed to generate hydroelectricity. It has been suggested that the power of sea tides could be used to generate electricity in a similar way in other parts of the globe. And, in the United States, the prospect of commercially harnessing geothermal energy is under careful scrutiny. But these methods suffer severe geographical limitations. Ideally, since there is so much of it, we could try to harness solar energy or —rather than harness it—store it, concentrate it, so that it will be there when we want it. To do this, however, a number of major technical problems must be overcome.

In the meantime, there is nuclear energy. An outline of the civil uses of this energy from decomposing atomic nuclei appeared in Chapter 8, where it was mentioned that concern about the environment could slow down, or even stop, the growth of programs in this sphere. Why should this be so? Unlike fossil fuels, fissionable nuclei decompose at a fixed rate regardless of whether or not man makes use of them. What can be harmful about harnessing the energy of this decomposition process?

The fault in this argument is that, under ordinary circumstances, the radiation given off by radioactive elements as they occur in rocks is dilute; when a nuclear fuel is made, radioactivity is concentrated. It is also probable that this concentrated radioactivity will be transported to a site near large-scale human habitation, since it is economically advantageous to have power generation facilities as close to the power user as possible. And radioactivity is extremely harmful to living matter. In addition, the new programs to develop fast breeder reactors rely on decomposition of radioactive elements into new radioactive materials that would not have been produced under "natural" conditions; man is not just using radioactivity in rocks, he is generating additional radioactivity.

The nuclear lobby argues that nuclear power stations are safe, with an extremely low likelihood of accident. When the type of accident involved may mean a nuclear explosion near a large city, the risks, some people argue, are not worth taking. One of the earliest nuclear power plants was built at Windscale in the north of England. When an accident occurred at this plant in 1957, more radiation was released than would have been given off by a small atom bomb. The question of degree of safety occurred to many people when there was a second accident at Windscale in 1970, and a third in 1973.

While their seriousness varies, there have been at least 30 accidents in nuclear power plants—an average of more than 1 a year since they were introduced. The pessimists say that it is only a matter of time before a plant explodes and, if large nuclear power plants continue to be built near large conurbations, takes much of a major city with it.

There are other worries. Even if nuclear power plants are built on uninhabited land, away from major centers of civilization (which means increased costs for transporting the energy generated), they will eventually wear out. Once a nuclear power station is obsolete, the land cannot be used for anything else because of the high radiation levels. As plants get bigger, the problem of disposing of the radioactive waste increases. In the United States alone there are at least 75 million gallons of highly radioactive waste stored in tanks, because no other satisfactory method has been found of disposing of it. A process which is effective in some ways is to seal up the radioactivity by mixing the active wastes with silicates and fusing them into glass. This localizes the radioactivity, but one still has to put the glass somewhere out of the reach of man and animals. There are already documented cases of people dying because they have found discarded radioactive materials and handled them carelessly, not knowing what they were. Death from radiation sickness is usually extremely unpleasant, and it seems clear that much hard thinking will be needed to discover a satisfactory method of ridding ourselves of nuclear waste.

At the moment everybody's ultimate garbage can, the world's oceans, are receiving their share of radioactive waste, but this may stop as concern mounts about the way we treat our massive but finite seas. It has already been shown that it is no good relying on great dilution to render noxious materials harmless, because living processes may reverse this trend. A study on water waste from the Hanford nuclear reactor, which goes into the Columbia river, has shown that the radioactivity can be concentrated 1 millionfold by river plankton.

If All the World Were Plastic

As in most social areas, the question of energy supply involves balance. If we want energy, it must come from somewhere. Apart from a few areas of the world that rely on hydroelectricity, the energy we generate pollutes either air or earth. Fossil fuels used for energy not only pollute the atmosphere, they destroy intermediates that could be of use to the petrochemical industry as future raw materials.

Yet if we save the fossil fuels for raw material use they will still, unless we are careful, become pollutants. One of the major groups of end products from petrochemicals' operations are plastics, many of which, used in packaging and similar ephemeral purposes, end up as litter. In the advanced countries we not only consume vastly more energy than we need to survive, we also consume more matter than we really use. The result, in both cases, is pollution.

In the United States the average annual per capita production of garbage is 1,000 pounds; in the United Kingdom it is 650 pounds. We are producing more garbage than ever before, and its composition is quite different from that of the garbage of our grandfathers. An investigation in London, England, showed that, between 1888 and 1967, the percentage of fine dust and cinder in household refuse fell from 82 to 19 percent. The amount of paper waste increased from none to 34 percent, while the metal and glass content increased from 0.4 percent and 1.3 percent respectively, to nearly 11 percent each.

As time goes by, the composition will change even more. Plastics are replacing paper, metal, and glass materials as containers for a variety of goods. This creates difficulties in refuse disposal; incineration of some plastics, for example, releases hydrochloric acid gas into the atmosphere. A greater problem is the disposal of such materials outside the refuse-collecting and disposal system. Paper litter left in beauty spots will disintegrate under the effects of climate, but many plastics do not degrade. They remain as unsightly messes, unpleasant to look at and dangerous to some animals, which have been known to die of starvation after eating plastic litter and getting it caught in their throats.

Work is in progress to design plastics which degrade after a few months. The principle is simple: Either an additive or integral part of the polymer molecule is made photoreactive, so that the polymer breaks down under the action of light to fine dust and, in the process, to molecular sizes amenable to biodegradation. There are problems. How do you calculate how long a container will be in use before it is thrown away? If consumers who do not consume as fast as the average find their half-full plastic containers of jam, sugar, or corn oil disintegrating in the home, they will be less than satisfied. However, photodegradable plastic carrier bags are being tried out in some

British stores. And a Dutch firm plans to produce degradable coffee cups and egg boxes.

As with the question of energy supply, many problems of pollution in the developed countries could be solved if people consumed less. To bring this about requires a revolution in society rather than in chemistry, and therefore further discussion of this topic is outside the scope of this book. But a revolution —if that is not too grand a word for it—which is of concern here, since it may have a profound effect on the next few decades of chemistry, is the scientist's changing view of his responsibility toward society.

The Role of the Scientist

Analyzing the scientist and his behavior has become a popular activity among the postwar generation of sociologists and psychologists. A major result of this has been a collection of platitudes, familiarity with which is mistaken, in some circles, for evidence of intelligence. Possibly the most basic of these platitudes is that, of all the scientists who have ever lived, 90 percent are alive today. Despite the prevalence of this statement, it is never doubted that all those alive, in some essential way, work in exactly the same manner as the 10 percent who went before them, back to the beginning of recorded time. That is, they all employ "the scientific method." Yet, as Nobel prizewinning biologist Peter Medawar pointed out in a lecture at the University of Pennsylvania in April 1968: "Most scientists receive no tuition in scientific method, but those who have been instructed perform no better as scientists than those who have not. Of what other branch of learning can it be said that it gives its proficients no advantage; that it need not be taught or, if taught, need not be learned?" [2]

---

[2] Peter Medawars, "Induction and Intuition in Scientific Thought," Memoirs of the American Philosophical Society, Vol. 75 (1969).

This might be sufficient to make us ask whether the "scientific method" has any reality other than that of an intellectual construct. Yet the common account of the scientific method has appended to it several corollaries which, until recently, all scientists have believed, or at least paid lip service to. The most important, perhaps, is that a scientific discovery is neither good nor bad; it is only the use to which it is put that can have either of these qualities. Consequently, utilization of his discoveries is not the legitimate concern of the scientist.

This ethical position was probably adequate for the early scientists, most of them amateurs, the cost of their research supported from their own pockets or from those of philanthropic patrons, and their discoveries only rarely put to use in their own lifetimes. The position of the scientist now is much different. Most scientists are paid by governments or private companies which employ them to make discoveries primarily for material gain, not for self-gratification. If a scientist works for a company whose main object is the manufacture of weapons systems, he cannot say that any discovery he makes is morally neutral. He knows perfectly well that the end to which his discoveries will be put is military, and that if his discoveries are consistently useless in this respect, the company will probably fire him.

At the time when he and his colleagues were spraying DDT during the war, Barry Commoner says they were "fat, dumb and happy." He and a growing number of other scientists are no longer prepared to stay that way. It has been suggested that, from their efforts, a new field, "critical science," is emerging. This is a slightly far-fetched claim; it seems more realistic to say that science is catching up with the world it has created. Science, like all intellectual disciplines, is organic: it grows and develops. To insist that it stick rigidly to the ground rules it obeyed in the seventeenth century is a nonsensical position.

Scientific Revolutions

One of the most stimulating theories about the growth and development of science is that put forward by Thomas S. Kuhn of the University of Chicago.[3] Kuhn suggests that sciences develop by undergoing periodic revolutions in which a major element of theory is changed. When an old theory no longer fits all the evidence, scientists struggle along with it, propping it up around the corners, until eventually somebody produces a new and better theory.

Usually there is an old guard who bitterly defend their theory against the onslaught of the new theorists. Full acceptance of the new theory often must wait until the old guard die. When a theory is put forward, it opens up new vistas of possible experimental work to verify and expand it—and eventually produce the contrary results that lead to cracks in its façade.

What may now be happening is that science itself—or our idea of it—is undergoing a Kuhnian revolution. Emergence of the youth counterculture which rejects the benefits of "progress," the growing belief among economists that there is no direct relationship between scientific discovery and greater wealth, and the increasing realization among scientists themselves that they are working in a small, virtually closed system —the earth—and are themselves a part of their experiments, are all modifying the way in which scientists look at and go about their work. This is not to say that an actual experiment is carried out according to rules of observation different from those used by Joseph Priestley, Humphry Davy, or any of the other great names of early chemistry. The changes are in the planning of which experiments are to be done and the terms in which the results are analyzed.

In many cases this means that scientists can no longer live

according to the disciplines in which they were trained. The chemist who wishes to design a new material must collaborate with biologists and microbiologists to check its effect on living systems, and with engineers to determine what design features are most needed. The work of meteorologists and hydrologists in plotting currents of air and water is of key importance to the chemist and chemical engineer concerned with the siting of new plants which will produce effluent to be disposed of.

The increased need for interactions among scientists of different disciplines may also reflect an even greater challenge: reintegration of science with the other leading concerns of society. Scientists and technologists must work together with psychologists, sociologists, urban planners, lawyers, and many others with whom they may be unfamiliar. The pressing dilemma is no longer how to achieve mastery over nature, but how to use that mastery, or, more important, how to assess whether or not it really is mastery.

A Duty to Inform

At one time, if scientific or technological innovation made it possible to make a new product, or offer a new service at a profit, then it was done. This was called "progress." Now we must learn to choose between alternative technologies. This may, for example, mean finding a basis for weighing the advantages to a select group of businessmen of time saved in supersonic air travel against the disadvantages to people on the ground who suffer excess noise nuisance as a result of this form of transportation. Scientists may argue that this is purely a social problem and that, except in his role as private citizen, the scientist has no more right to take a stand on the issue than anyone else. Others, such as Commoner, would argue that he may have no more right to take a stand, but his education and training endow him with a duty to inform his fellow citizens, so that the decisions they make are informed social choices.

Pollution is not really a scientific problem. Many of the substances which pollute our environment could be cleaned up at source if it were economically advantageous. The technical methods for controlling many forms of pollution have already been worked out; to implement them requires changes in legislation which, in the western world, spring ultimately from the people. This can only happen if the people are informed.

Rather than clean up their effluents and accept a cut in profits, some companies will mislead the public with stories of having to close factories and create unemployment if they are no longer permitted to pollute the atmosphere. Yet it is surprising how many companies have managed to survive, once legislation has forced them to act.

As Commoner has written:

> Scientific method cannot determine whether the proponents of urban superhighways or those who complain about the resultant smog are in the right, or whether the benefits of nuclear tests to the national interest outweigh the hazards of fallout. No scientific principle can tell us how to make the choice, which may sometimes be forced upon us by the insecticide problem, between the shade of the elm tree and the song of the robin.[4]

But as science is forced increasingly into the public arena, partly as a result of rapidly escalating costs of research (which mean that increasingly large subventions of public money are needed to keep it going), and partly because of the widespread and rapid effects of scientific innovation, the public has a right to call upon scientists for an explanation of what they are doing and why they are doing it. Since the obligation clearly lies with the scientist, it is up to him to keep on explaining until the public has the information it wants in a form it can grasp. It is

[4] Commoner, *Science and Survival*, p. 121.

unethical of a scientist to rely on technological jargon designed to confuse and embarrass the people into going away and leaving him to his own devices.

More than a decade ago, in its first report, the American Association for the Advancement of Science's Committee on Science in the Promotion of Human Welfare concluded:

> . . . that the scientific community on its own initiative should assume an obligation to call to public attention those issues of public policy which relate to science, and to provide for the general public facts and estimates of the effects of alternative policies which the citizen must have if he is to participate intelligently in the solution of these problems. A citizenry thus informed is, we believe, the chief assurance that science will be devoted to the promotion of human welfare.[5]

Assessing Technology

Since these words were written there have been signs of change. Perhaps most significant is the way in which governments have realized that they must justify their policies in the light of informed criticism, for this has led to a rethinking of social goals at government level. In 1969 a committee convened by the U.S. National Academy of Sciences (NAS) published its report on *Technology: Processes of Assessment and Choice.*[6] This committee, which had been convened at the request of the subcommittee on Science, Research, and Development of the U.S. House of Representatives' Committee on Science and Astronautics, recommended establishment of new federal mechanisms to look broadly at the social consequences of technological actions.

[5] "Science and Human Welfare," *Science.* Vol. 132 (1960), pp. 68–73.
[6] Report of the National Academy of Sciences, Committee on Science and Astronautics, U.S. House of Representatives, U.S. Government Printing Office, July 1969.

Panel chairman Harvey Brooks, of Harvard University, and panelist Raymond Bowers described some of the panel's conclusions and recommendations. Looking at the U.S. pesticide experience, for example, the panel argued that:

> . . . although the pesticides have undoubtedly prevented a great many deaths from starvation and disease, it is now apparent that they have also inflicted unintended but widespread losses of fish and wildlife, and it is increasingly suspected that they are causing injury to man. The experience suggests that carefully designed experiments in the early days might have influenced the technology of pesticides before the nation was so committed to certain forms of pest control as to make any significant alteration of the technology extremely difficult.[7]

In most countries, no official body has until recently looked at the growth in numbers of automobiles. The domination of land transportation systems by the private automobile is a prime example of the dangers of the refusal to plan. It would be extremely difficult to make any significant alteration in transportation technology now, although the social costs of the private automobile become clearer (smoggier?) every day.

This type of consideration led the NAS panel to lay down an important criterion for assessing technology. "The reversibility of an action should thus be counted as a major benefit, its irreversibility as a major cost." But it appreciated that "the achievement of a better system for assessing technology faces major obstacles. The society is ill-equipped to handle conflicting interests. It does not know how to value in a quantitative way such goals as a clean environment and the preservation of future choices. Analytical tools are primitive and crucial knowledge is often missing." [8]

The reorientation of science may encourage scientists to fill

[7] Harvey Brooks and Raymond Bowers, "The Assessment of Technology," *Scientific American*, Vol. 222, no. 2 (February 1970), p. 15.
[8] Ibid., p. 18.

some of those crucial gaps; certainly, technology assessment is not concerned solely with forbidding activities:

> An effective system of assessing technology would as often stimulate the development and application of desirable new technologies and underemployed ones as it would give warning of possibly harmful side effects. Many of the problems that are identified as undesirable results of technological development can also be seen as the result of failures to develop or apply technologies that would have mitigated the undesired effects. . . .
>
> The future of technology holds great promise for mankind if greater thought and effort are devoted to its development. If society persists in its present course, however, the future holds great peril, whether from the uncontrolled effects of technology itself or from an unreasoned political reaction against technological innovation—a reaction that could condemn mankind to poverty, frustration and the loss of freedom.[9]

A more recent report, which takes the problem of scientific and technological development even further, was published during the summer of 1971 by the Organization for Economic Cooperation and Development (OECD), of which the U.S., Japan, and many European countries are members. This report, prepared by a special committee also chaired by Harvey Brooks, questioned many of the economic assumptions underlying the desirability of progress, and showed how the quality of life does not necessarily improve as incomes increase:

> We must . . . recognize that increasingly man cannot live by bread alone, and that the use of the economic system to contribute to human happiness rather than merely material satisfaction presents a challenge to the imagination that the developed countries must begin to take up seriously during the coming decade. . . . Science and technology are an integral part of social and economic development, and we believe that this

[9] Ibid., p. 20.

implies a much closer relationship between policies for science and technology and all socioeconomic concerns and government responsibilities than has existed in the past.[10]

The OECD committee took a gloomy view of the failure of governments to come to terms with the new requirements to be made of science and technology.

> The world-wide culture of educated youth, which is deeply concerned with ecological perspectives and is increasingly anti-materialistic, egalitarian, anti-meritocratic, and anti-bureaucratic, could conceivably even adopt anti-rational views and could become much more influential in the next decade than our extrapolations suggest; . . . [the result of this might be] the retardation of scientific progress to the point where the world lacked the intellectual tools to cope with the complexity it has created.[11]

At the October 1971 OECD meeting of governmental officials and ministers concerned with science, the report was discussed and adopted as a blueprint for further action. Dr. Edward David, Jr., at that time science adviser to President Nixon, described it as a "good meeting." Shortly after the meeting, I talked to him and asked whether he thought the report's pessimism was justified about the extent to which the counterculture might precipitate a new dark age.

"Scientists," he replied, "must do their new thing. We've got to be responsible for what we do—I can't find anyone in the scientific community who would disagree with that. The cumulative effects of a long era of neglect have come down on us pretty hard. People are not going to stand being turned into automata. It's a question of doing things in the proper way: if we do this, I don't see the counterculture providing a threat." [12]

10 *Science, Growth, and Society* (Paris: Organization for Economic Cooperation and Development, 1971), pp. 28, 96.

11 Ibid., p. 24.

12 Martin Sherwood, "David as Goliath," *New Scientist*, Vol. 52 (1971), p. 93.

Late in 1972, the United States took a concrete step toward sorting out the modern confusion about science and its responsibilities by establishing an Office of Technology Assessment. This body has been designed to evaluate, for Congress, the likely effects of new legislation on scientific and technical matters.

Failed Forecasts

Although I have not yet made a single concrete prediction about the discoveries one can expect in years to come, I hope I have made clear the importance of growing public awareness of and, to some extent, disillusionment with scientific advance. This is what underlies the question of whether chemistry will have a future at all. Growing demands made upon scientists to show both responsibility and responsiveness will affect chemists as much as any others. One result may be to hasten the withering away of chemistry as an active science clearly different from biology or physics. In the preceding pages it has been impossible at times not to step outside the hazy borders of chemistry; without doing so, no sensible picture would have emerged. Thirty years from now those borders will be even less clearly discernible.

There is a second reason for stressing the mood of our age and its effect on science, rather than making concrete predictions. A scientific discovery is basically unpredictable. It is a venture into the unknown. This, you may say, only affects fundamental research; surely we can predict how industrial chemistry will develop? Even here the answer is only a partial yes. Had there been "futurologists" in the nineteenth century, predicting on the basis of current trends, at least 1 of them would surely have pointed with horror to the rising demand for horses as a means of transportation, and claimed that by 1950 there would be a shortage of horses so severe that civilization would grind to a halt. The invention of the automobile would have rendered any such prediction incredibly silly, just as, in our lifetimes, a sudden breakthrough in the development of controlled nuclear fusion as a source of energy could make all present predictions about energy supply look ridiculous.

Those who are not swayed by hypothetical examples may be interested in the following quotations from real people, just a few of those used to garnish a 1969 article on technological forecasting in the American Chemical Society's magazine, *Chemical & Engineering News:*

> This is the biggest fool thing we have ever done. The [atomic] bomb will never go off, and I speak as an expert in explosives —Admiral William Leahy, 1945.

> You could put in this room [his office], de Forest [inventor of the vacuum tube] and all the radiotelephone apparatus that the country will ever need—W. W. Dean, President of Dean Telephone Company, 1907.

> I have always opposed consistently high-tension and alternating systems of electric lighting . . . not only on account of danger but because of their general unreliability and unsuitability for any general system of distribution—Thomas A. Edison, 1889.[13]

These 3 examples from the past show the danger of saying what science and technology will never be able to do. But even the optimistic can be made to look foolish. Confident predictions of future developments are frequently outstripped by reality, yet people still make predictions.

In the following paragraphs I hope to identify some trends, possibilities, and likelihoods. Since the best way to avoid being proved wrong at a later date seems to be to keep this identifi-

---

[13] David M. Kiefer, "The Future Business," *Chemical & Engineering News.* Vol. 47, no. 33 (1969), pp. 62–75.

cation as general as possible, the rest of this book can in no way be called a recipe for the future; at most, it is an indication of flavor.

A Need for Theory

Underlying chemistry are a number of theories, the importance of which to the development of the subject cannot be overestimated. However, in recent years chemistry has tended to race ahead of theory in some areas, notably the synthesis of complex organic molecules. There are signs of a change here. Several new theoretical concepts of the last few years are simplifying the approach to synthetic chemistry. The Woodward-Hoffmann rules, worked out by American chemists Robert Woodward and Ronald Hoffmann, predict the stereochemistry of the products to be expected from certain reactions on the basis of orbital interactions. Similar orbital considerations occur in the concept of antiaromaticity. In conjugated double bond systems, electrons are delocalized and the compounds stabilized, which, as the discussion in Chapter 6 pointed out, is of importance in living systems. Antiaromatic systems are, in a sense, the reverse: the number of electrons involved in bonds has a destabilizing effect, which alters their reactivity dramatically. Despite these and other theories, such as the concept of "soft" and "hard" acids and bases, which covers both organic and inorganic molecules, there is a need for more theoretical rationalization of the ever-increasing mass of chemical data. Not only could new and more general theories, for example to explain the phenomenon of catalysis, have beneficial economic effects, the development of "tidying up" theories would help to restore a unity that is presently lacking from our consideration of molecules.

Ultimately, one can hope for a theory which will permit working out the physical and chemical properties of "imaginary" compounds on the basis of molecular orbital theory. Having worked out the properties, one could also hope to work out, in fine detail, how to make a compound, if such a task seemed useful, and what the reaction rates and yields of the compound and the various intermediates would be without ever having to dirty one's hands at the laboratory bench.

Perhaps someday this will be possible. The different parts of the scenario are already being worked on, thanks largely to the development of high-speed computing techniques. In the Harvard syntheses of prostaglandins, E. J. Corey and his colleagues planned their multistep synthetic routes with the aid of a computer program. They fed the computer with data on reactions and yields, likely side reactions, and all the other relevant factors they could postulate. It produced a number of possible synthetic routes of differing degrees of probability.

Similarly, physical chemists have used computer programming to simulate reaction kinetic studies and the properties of unknown molecules. Computers have also been used to generate three-dimensional images of complex molecules which can "move" in the same way as real molecules through the rotation and stretching of bonds—an advance on the static three-dimensional models usually used by chemists.

At the Argonne National Laboratory in Illinois, more fundamental work on "chemistry without chemicals" is being carried out with a computerized system called BISON. This gets right down to the theoretical bases of electron distribution in atoms and builds up chemistry from there. At the moment the system can handle small molecules, but is being extended to cope with more complex chemistry. It is still a long way from replacing the experimental worker; according to Arnold C. Wahl, who works on the BISON project: "The new computational tool is most properly viewed as a new 'instrument' for the experimental chemist." [14] However, as the developments in various spectro-

[14] Arnold Wahl, "Chemistry without Chemicals," *New Scientist*, Vol. 46 (1970), p. 221.

scopies have shown, one must never underestimate the power of a new instrument to change the face of chemistry.

New Techniques

Can one expect other new instruments, or new separation techniques that will parallel chromatography in versatility? Advances in spectroscopy occur regularly, most of them small, but some big. It is unlikely that anyone writing a book such as this 20 years ago would have predicted the way in which electron spin resonance spectroscopy would grow into an important chemical tool. Equally unexpected would have been the effects that the then new invention, the laser, would have on different forms of spectroscopy—infrared and Raman. So when we read, early in 1973 that A. D. Buckingham and his colleagues at Cambridge University have found a technique called "Raman optical activity," which may provide a method of directly probing stereochemistry in large molecules, what prediction dare we make for the future? Going on past experience, the best bet, for those inclined to gamble on some new spectroscopies, is to find out what new phenomena the physicists are turning up and see if there are any chemists can put to use.

It would be foolish to say that no revolutionary separational method will be discovered in the next few years. More likely is the further improvement and sophistication of existing techniques. A front runner at the moment is affinity chromatography —a form of chromatography for separating biologically active molecules which uses the specific reactivities of these molecules as a means of separation. As well as being a boon to the chemist who wishes to isolate, for example, a particular enzyme from a group of enzymes, this technique could be valuable in medicine, providing means of separating materials such as steroids from mixtures.

Chemical and Biological Engineering

The marriage of chemistry and biology in recent years has moved the pharmaceutical industry away from the concept of synthetic drugs, which have little relationship to any biological molecule, toward the use of natural materials, or slight modifications of them. However, as more is learned by biologists about the shape and structure of receptor sites—the target molecules with which drugs, hormones, poisons, and so on, react to produce their characteristic actions—it should become increasingly possible to design molecules with specific therapeutic effects, and thus put drug research on a more rational base than it has occupied in the past.

Among the biological substances which, according to some predictions, are likely to be available before the end of the century are drugs to increase intelligence and to treat mental illness. The study of brain chemistry is still in its infancy, and it is not yet possible to draw guidelines for future activities in this field. For the last few years there has been controversy about whether learning can be transferred from 1 animal to another through injections of brain substance. George Ungar of Baylor College of Medicine, Texas, has isolated a substance from the brains of rats which have been trained to fear the dark. When injected, this 15-amino-acid peptide, scotophobin, is claimed to transfer fear of the dark to other rats. All one can conclude at the moment is that this field will probably provide excitement in the scientific world for a few years, as work on chemical causality and cure of schizophrenia did a few years ago (without, in the end, producing any miraculous cure).

These science fiction areas of chemistry probably hold less real hope than another possibility that has been suggested: chemical stimulation of the body to produce replacement limbs and organs. Every cell in the human body contains in its gene complement all the instructions required to produce that individual. One of the key questions of molecular biology at the present is: Why and how is most of the gene content of each cell switched off? Subsidiary questions are: What is the mechanism by which a particular part of a gene is switched off at a particular time? Is this process reversible? If the cells in the stump of an amputated limb could be triggered to begin dividing and differentiating in the way they did when the limb first developed, a wide range of repairs to bodies damaged in accidents would become possible.

At the extreme of this technique is the possibility of genetic engineering—changing the molecular structure of the gene so that defects are ironed out, making it possible, for example, to cure the inborn errors of metabolism that produce sickle-cell anemia and phenylketonuria. Much of the technique of genetic engineering will be based in biology, but it seems likely that chemistry will play a part, or at least be affected by the results. It has been suggested that, in the future, agriculturists might engineer plants which can fix their own nitrogen and are pest and disease resistant, thus requiring less fertilizer and no pesticide. Of course genetic engineering, as a reality, is a double-edged sword. It need not be used for the welfare of individuals, and could be used in a variety of unpleasant ways. Consequently, it is one area of scientific possibility in which the general public must attempt to keep up with and understand the latest developments.

A less controversial area is materials science, where it seems likely that the development of new materials for a variety of purposes will continue along the molecular engineering lines described in Chapter 8. Expansion of knowledge about the behavior of different and unusual combinations of chemical bonds could lead to significant changes in the economic value of some elements. Even in the materials field, it is possible that biological chemistry will play a part. In 1970 Corning Glass patented a process for chemically bonding enzymes in glass. Such bound enzymes are more stable than the free molecules and become contenders for a place in industrial catalysis.

Resources

The balance of materials used in industrial processes may also be changed by other socioeconomic factors. It has been proposed that an economic method of disposing of large quantities of cellulose waste from discarded wrappings would be to convert it microbially into ethyl alcohol, which is at present obtained for industrial purposes petrochemically, as described in Chapter 7. However, it seems likely that there will still be a demand for many traditional materials. This may require development of new techniques for extraction from ores, for as the world's supplies of natural resources decline, it becomes necessary to utilize lower grade ores. Some metals are already being mined from heaps of slag discarded in past decades as too poor to be processed. It seems increasingly likely that the interactions between organic compounds and particular metals will be studied in order to devise more efficient metal extraction systems which rely on such properties as chelation. An outside possibility is the use of polymeric foams in minerals recovery. Early in 1970, H. J. M. Bowen of the University of Reading, England, found that gold and uranium could be extracted effectively from different solutions with a piece of polyurethane foam. Polymeric mineral extractants, since they would be lightweight solids, could be more amenable to industrial process design than organic liquids, and might offer possibilities for cheap recovery of metal wastes from factory effluent, as well as for getting metal compounds out of rocks in the first place.

Various other predictions have been made by different groups of experts. According to some of these, there is a strong likelihood that it will be possible before the end of the century to manufacture elements from subatomic particles on a commercial basis, and possible not only to make living—or at least self-replicating—chemical systems, but also to manufacture protein synthetically. Any of these prospects might have immense social effects, but I still believe that the most exciting discoveries of the next 30 years have not yet been predicted.

How many people, 30 years ago, would have predicted the invention and discovery of noble gas compounds, the transistor, the laser, holography, and gene synthesis? A few may have had inklings of 1 or 2 of these, but no more. In the late 1930s, sophisticated people no doubt laughed at the remark of W. W. Dean, quoted earlier, about the space required for radiotelephone apparatus. Had they been told then that, given another few decades which would include discovery and exploitation of the transistor, with the subsequent move into electronic microminiaturization, Dean might be proved right (albeit in a way he never intended), they would doubtless have smiled in a sophisticated fashion and moved elsewhere for "intelligent" conversation.

Envoi

To turn away from speculation, there is a remarkable phenomenon which is not chemical, but is relevant. During the last few decades, the human race has repeatedly adapted to the unpredicted inventions being sprung upon it. There are current signs that this remarkable adaptability is frayed around the edges, but there is no doubt that it still exists. I do not doubt that people will cope with the advances of chemistry in the years to come—given the single proviso that the public be informed by scientists about what they are doing. Those edges of humanity's relationship with scientific and technical knowledge that are showing the most fray are doing so because of a lack of information to lubricate them. For the future, it is the responsibility of the people to demand more information, and the duty of the scientists to supply it.

Both sides tend to throw up their hands in horror and say it is too difficult. This is a defeatist attitude based on prejudice, not fact. Whatever can be said of the chemistry of tomorrow, much of it will lie within the broad conceptual framework that this book has attempted to describe. To those who have reached this point, there remains only one thing to say: now read on.

Suggestions for Further Reading

CHAPTER 2

Baranger, Michel, and Sorensen, Raymond A. 1969. The size and shape of atomic nuclei. *Scientific American*, Vol. 221, no. 2, pp. 58–73.

Cottrell, T. L. 1970. *Chemistry*. 2nd ed. New York: Oxford University Press.

Ghiorso, Albert, and Seaborg, Glenn T. 1957. The synthetic elements —II. In *New chemistry*. New York: Simon and Schuster.

Perlman, Isadore, and Seaborg, Glenn T. 1957. The synthetic elements —I. In *New chemistry*. New York: Simon and Schuster, pp. 102–125.

Seaborg, Glenn T. 1969. Prospects for further considerable extension of the periodic table. *Journal of Chemical Education*, Vol. 46, pp. 626–634.

———, and Bloom, Justin L. 1969. The synthetic elements—IV. *Scientific American*, Vol. 220, no. 4, pp. 56–67.

———, and Frisch, Arnold R. 1963. The synthetic elements—III. *Scientific American*, Vol. 208, no. 4, pp. 68–78.

Wick, Gerald L. 1970. The island of stability. *New Scientist*, Vol. 47, pp. 30–31.

CHAPTER 3

Pimentel, George C., and Spratley, Richard D. 1969. *Chemical bonding clarified through quantum mechanics*. San Francisco: Holden-Day.

Selig, Henry; Malm, John G.; and Claassen, Howard H. 1964. Chemistry of the noble gases. *Scientific American*, Vol. 210, no. 5, pp. 66–76.

CHAPTER 4

Allen, G. 1970. Modern methods for the determination of molecular structure. In *Modern chemistry*, ed. J. G. Stark. Baltimore: Penguin Books, pp. 56–75.

Angrist, Stanley W., and Hepler, Loren G. 1967. *Order and chaos: Laws of energy and entropy.* New York: Basic Books.

Campbell, J. A. 1970. Why chemical reactions occur. In *Modern chemistry*, ed. J. G. Stark. Baltimore: Penguin Books, pp. 113–140.

Chalmers, R. A. 1968. *Aspects of analytical chemistry.* Edinburgh and London: Oliver & Boyd.

Pimentel, George C., and Spratley, Richard D. 1969. *Understanding chemical thermodynamics.* San Francisco: Holden-Day.

CHAPTER 5

Ahrens, L. H. 1966. The chemical bond and the geochemical distribution of the elements. *Chemistry in Britain*, Vol. 2, pp. 14–19.

Bassett, W. A., and Takahashi, T. 1965. The composition of the earth's interior. *Scientific American*, Vol. 212, no. 6, pp. 100–108.

Bernal, J. D. 1967. *The origin of life.* New York: Universe Books.

Cailleux, Andre. 1968. *Anatomy of the earth.* New York: Universe Books.

Calvin, Melvin. 1969. *Chemical evolution.* New York: Oxford University Press.

Eshleman, Von R. 1969. The atmospheres of Mars and Venus. *Scientific American*, Vol. 220, no. 3, pp. 78–88.

Fox, Sidney W.; Harada, Kaoru; Krampits, Gottfried; and Mueller, George. 1970. Chemical origins of life. *Chemical & Engineering News*, no. 25, pp. 80–94.

Keosian, John. 1965. *The origin of life.* New York: Reinhold.

Marquand, J. 1968. *Life: Its nature, origins and distribution.* New York: W. W. Norton.

CHAPTER 6

Brown, E. G. 1971. *An introduction to biochemistry.* London: Royal Institute of Chemistry.

Butler, J. A. V. 1970. *The life process.* New York: Basic Books.

Calvin, Melvin, and Jorgenson, Margaret J., eds. 1969. *Bio-organic chemistry*. San Francisco: Freeman. This collection of readings from *Scientific American* includes articles on insulin, hemoglobin, DNA structure, sequencing of alanyl t-RNA, pheromones, insect attractants, stereochemical theory of odor, analgesic drugs, photosynthesis, and molecular isomers in vision.

Dayhoff, Margaret O. 1969. Computer analysis of protein evolution. *Scientific American*, Vol. 221, no. 1, pp. 86–95.

Merrifield, R. B. 1968. The automatic synthesis of proteins. *Scientific American*, Vol. 218, no. 3, pp. 56–74.

Perutz, Max. 1971. Hemoglobin—the molecular lung. *New Scientist*, Vol. 50, pp. 676–679.

———. 1971. Hemoglobin: Genetic abnormalities. *New Scientist*, Vol. 50, pp. 762–765.

Sullivan, Navin. 1967. *The message of the genes*. New York: Basic Books.

CHAPTER 7

Jones, D. G., ed. 1967. *Chemistry and industry*. New York: Oxford University Press.

Lushington, Roger. 1967. *Plastics and you*. London: Pan Books.

Waddams, A. L. 1973. *Chemicals from petroleum*. 3rd ed. London: Murray.

Wynne, M. D. 1970. *Chemical processing in industry*. London: Royal Institute of Chemistry.

CHAPTER 8

Chedd, Graham. 1968. *Half-way elements: The technology of the metalloids*. New York: Doubleday.

Fishlock, David. 1967. *The new materials*. New York: Basic Books.

Libby, W. F. 1969. Radiocarbon dating. *Chemistry in Britain*, Vol. 5, pp. 548–552.

Modern chemistry in industry. 1968. London: Society of Chemical Industry.

Pyke, Magnus. 1970. *Synthetic food*. New York: St. Martin's Press.

Rowe, Geoffrey W. 1968. The chemistry of tribology (friction, lubrication, and wear). *Royal Institute of Chemistry Reviews*, Vol. 1, pp. 135–204.

Werner, A. E. 1970. Scientific methods in art and archaeology. *Chemistry in Britain*, Vol. 6, pp. 55–59.

CHAPTER 9

Brooks, Harvey, and Bowers, Raymond. 1970. The assessment of technology. *Scientific American*, Vol. 222, no. 2, pp. 13–21.

Commoner, Barry. 1970. *Science and survival.* New York: Ballantyne Books.

Forecasting the future. 1967. *Science Journal*, Vol. 3, no. 10, a single-topic issue.

Hamblin, Lynette. 1971. *Pollution: The world crisis.* New York: Barnes & Noble.

Kuhn, Thomas S. 1970. *The structure of scientific revolutions.* 2nd ed. Chicago: University of Chicago Press.

Ravetz, J. R. 1971. *Scientific knowledge and its social problems.* New York: Oxford University Press.

Science, growth, and society. 1971. Paris: Organization for Economic Cooperation and Development.

Sherwood, Martin. 1971. Compassionate Cassandra. *New Scientist*, Vol. 50, pp. 102–103. An interview with Barry Commoner.

———. David as Goliath. 1971. *New Scientist*, Vol. 52, pp. 22–23. An interview with Edward David, Jr.

This bibliography does not offer a comprehensive range of the sources consulted during the writing of this book. It includes only items which I feel may be of some benefit to readers who want to explore some aspect of chemistry further. For those who want to keep up with new advances in chemistry as they occur, the monthly *Scientific American* (415 Madison Avenue, New York, New York, 10017) and the weekly *New Scientist* (128 Long Acre, London WC2E 9QH, England) are invaluable. Both of these cover the whole range of sciences. For those interested particularly in the chemical scene, the American Chemical Society's weekly, *Chemical & Engineering News*, and the Chemical Society of London's monthly, *Chemistry in Britain*, are both recommended, as is the ACS's monthly aimed specifically at high school students, *Chemistry*.

Index

95944

QD
37
.S47

DATE DUE

APR 1 9 1993			

No Longer
the Property of
Bluffton University

Musselman Library
Bluffton College
Bluffton, Ohio 45817

DEMCO